KB054819

# 주한미군지위협정(SOFA)

# 서명 및 발효 18

---

# 주한미군지위협정(SOFA)

# 서명 및 발효 18

한국학술정보

# | 머리말

미국은 오래전부터 우리나라 외교에 있어서 가장 긴밀하고 실질적인 우호 · 협력관계를 맺어 온 나라다. 6 · 25전쟁 정전 협정이 체결된 후 북한의 재침을 막기 위한 대책으로서 1953년 11월 한미 상호방위조약이 체결되었다. 이는 미군이 한국에 주둔하는 법적 근거였고, 그렇게 주둔하게 된 미군의 시설, 구역, 사업, 용역, 출입국, 통관과 관세, 재판권 등 포괄적인 법적 지위를 규정하는 것이 바로 주한미군지위협정(SOFA)이다. 그러나 이와 관련한 협상은 계속된 난항을 겪으며 한미 상호방위조약이 체결로부터 10년이 훌쩍 넘은 1967년이 돼서야 정식 발효에 이를 수 있었다. 그럼에도 당시 미군 범죄에 대한 한국의 재판권은 심한 제약을 받았으며, 1980년대 후반 민주화 운동과 함께 미군 범죄 문제가 사회적 이슈로 떠오르자 협정을 개정해야 한다는 목소리가 커지게 되었다. 이에 1991년 2월 주한미군지위협정 1차 개정이 진행되었고, 이후에도 여러 사건이 발생하며 2001년 4월 2차 개정이 진행되어 현재에 이르고 있다.

본 총서는 외교부에서 작성하여 최근 공개한 주한미군지위협정(SOFA) 관련 자료를 담고 있다. 1953년 한미 상호방위조약 체결 이후부터 1967년 발효가 이뤄지기까지의 자료와 더불어, 이후 한미 합동위원회을 비롯해 민 · 형사재판권, 시설, 노무, 교통 등 각 분과위원회의 회의록과 운영 자료, 한국인 고용인 문제와 관련한 자료, 기타 관련 분쟁 자료 등을 포함해 총 42권으로 구성되었다. 전체 분량은 약 2만 2천여 쪽에 이른다.

2024년 3월

한국학술정보(주)

## | 일러두기

· 본 총서에 실린 자료는 2022년 4월과 2023년 4월에 각각 공개한 외교문서 4,827권, 76만여 쪽 가운데 일부를 발췌한 것이다.

· 각 권의 제목과 순서는 공개된 원본을 최대한 반영하였으나, 주제에 따라 일부는 적절히 변경하였다.

· 원본 자료는 A4 판형에 맞게 축소하거나 원본 비율을 유지한 채 A4 페이지 안에 삽입하였다. 또한 현재 시점에선 공개되지 않아 '공란'이란 표기만 있는 페이지 역시 그대로 실었다.

· 외교부가 공개한 문서 각 권의 첫 페이지에는 '정리 보존 문서 목록'이란 이름으로 기록물 종류, 일자, 명칭, 간단한 내용 등의 정보가 수록되어 있으며, 이를 기준으로 0001번부터 번호가 매겨져 있다. 이는 삭제하지 않고 총서에 그대로 수록하였다.

· 보고서 내용에 관한 더 자세한 정보가 필요하다면, 외교부가 온라인상에 제공하는 『대한민국 외교사료요약집』 1991년과 1992년 자료를 참조할 수 있다.

# | 차례

정/리/보/존/문/서/목/록

| 기록물종류 | 문서-일반공문서철 | 등록번호 | 945 9618 | 등록일자 | 2006-07-27 |
|---|---|---|---|---|---|
| 분류번호 | 741.12 | 국가코드 | US | 주제 | |

| 문서철명 | 한.미국 간의 상호방위조약 제4조에 의한 시설과 구역 및 한국에서의 미국군대의 지위에 관한 협정 (SOFA) 전59권. 1966.7.9 서울에서 서명 : 1967.2.9 발효 (조약 232호) *원본 | | | | |
|---|---|---|---|---|---|
| 생산과 | 미주과/조약과 | 생산년도 | 1952 - 1967 | 보존기간 | 영구 |
| 담당과(그룹) | 조약 | 조약 | | 서가번호 | -- |
| 참조분류 | | | | | |
| 권차명 | V.47 한.미국 양측 교섭안 | | | | |

| 내용목차 | 1. 한국측<br>2. 미국측<br><br>* 일지 :<br>1953.8.7 이승만 대통령-Dulles 미국 국무장관 공동성명<br>    - 상호방위조약 발효 후 군대지위협정 교섭 약속<br>1954.12.2 정부, 주한 UN군의 관세업무협정 체결 제의<br>1955.1월, 5월 미국, 제의 거절<br>1955.4.28 정부, 군대지위협정 제의 (한국측 초안 제시)<br>1957.9.10 Hurter 미국 국무차관 방한 시 각서 수교 (한국측 제의 수락 요구)<br>1957.11.13, 26 정부, 개별 협정의 단계적 체결 제의<br>1958.9.18 Dawling 주한미국대사, 형사재판관할권 협정 제외 조건으로 행정협정 체결 의사 전달<br>1960.3.10 정부, 토지, 시설협정의 우선적 체결 강력 요구<br>1961.4.10 장면 국무총리-McConaughy 주한미국대사 공동성명으로 교섭 개시 합의<br>1961.4.15, 4.25 제1, 2차 한.미국 교섭회의 (서울)<br>1962.3.12 정부, 교섭 재개 촉구 공한 송부<br>1962.5.14 Burger 주한미국대사, 최규하 장관 면담 시 형사재판관할권 문제 제기 않는 조건으로 교섭 재개 통고<br>1962.9.6 한.미국 간 공동성명 발표 (9월 중 교섭 재개 합의)<br>1962.9.20~ 제1-81차 실무 교섭회의 (서울)<br>  1965.6.7<br>1966.7.8 제82차 실무 교섭회의 (서울)<br>1966.7.9 서명<br>1967.2.9 발효 (조약 232호) |
|---|---|

마/이/크/로/필/름/사/항

| 촬영연도 | *롤 번호 | 화일 번호 | 후레임 번호 | 보관함 번호 |
|---|---|---|---|---|
| 2006-11-24 | I-06-0071 | 07 | 1-282 | |

0001

| 제　　　목 | 조문교환 | 토의개시 | 부분적합의 | 의견합의 |
|---|---|---|---|---|
| 1. 적용 | | | | 62.12.4. |
| 2. 노무조 정의 | | | | 63.3.13. |
| 3. 시설 및 구역 | | | | |
| 4. 항공통제 및 항행보조시설 | | | | 63.11.30. |
| 5. 합동위원회 | | | | 63.2.25. |
| 6. 출입국 관리 | | | | 63.1.7. |
| 7. 관세 업무 | | | | 1964. 7. 8 (57차) |
| 8. 선박 및 항공기 기착 | | | | 63.1.7. |
| 9. 공익물 및 용역 | | | | 64.3.6. |
| 10. 군표 | | | | 1964. 6. 19 (55차) |
| 11. 군사우편시설 및 군우행정 | | | | 64.1.2. |
| 12. 예비병의 소집 및 훈련 | | | | 63.2.25. |
| 13. 미군인, 가족 및 재산의 안전보장 | | | | |
| 14. 기상 및 기타 군번련 문제 | | | | 63.4.4. |
| 15. 차량 및 운전면허 | | | | 63.8.22. |
| 16. 의료 통제 | | | | |
| 17. 비세출기관의 활동문제 | | | | |
| 18. 접수국법의 존수문제 | | | | 63.6.12. |
| 19. 형사재판 관할권 | | | | |
| 20. 청구권 | | | | |
| 21. 조세 문제 | | | | 63.10.1. |
| 22. 편지조달 문제 | | | | 64.5.28. |
| 23. 회계절차 | | | | 64.3.13. |
| 24. 군 계약자 문제 | | | | 1964. 7. 8 (57차) |
| 25. 노무 문제 | | | | |
| 26. 협정의 비준, 발효 및 시행사항 | | | | |
| 27. 협정의 개정 및 수정 | | | | 63.12. |
| 28. 협정의 유효기간 및 반포사항 | | | | |
| 29. 보건 위생 문제 | | | | 63.7.25. |

0002

# 1. 한국측

한·미국 간의 상호방위조약 제4조에 의한 시설과 구역 및 한국에서의 미국군대의 지위에 관한 협정(SOFA)
전59권. 1966.7.9 서울에서 서명 : 1967.2.9 발효(조약 232호) (V.47 한·미국 양측 교섭안)

9

우리측이 미국측에 제의한 초안

## Preamble

Whereas the United States forces were originally disposed in and about the territory of the Republic of Korea pursuant to the resolutions of the United Nations Security Council of June 25, 1950, June 27, 1950 and July 7, 1950 to repel the Communist armed attack;

Whereas, the Article IV of the Mutual Defense Treaty between the Republic of Korea and the United States of America signed on October 1, 1953, following the conclusion of the Armistice Agreement on July 27, 1953, states that the Republic of Korea grants, and the United States of America accepts, the right to dispose United States land, air and sea forces in and about the territory of the Republic of Korea as determined by mutual agreement;

Whereas, pursuant to the aforesaid provision of the Mutual Defense Treaty, the United States of America has disposed its armed forces in and about the territory of the Republic of Korea, and;

Whereas the Republic of Korea and the United States of America are desirous of providing for practical administrative arrangements which shall govern the disposition of the United States forces in and about the territory of the Republic of Korea strengthen the close bonds of mutual interests between their two countries;

Therefore, the Governments of the Republic of Korea and of the United States of America have agreed as follows:

129

0004

<u>Article (Facilities and Areas)</u>

1. The Government of the Republic of Korea grants, under Article IV of the Mutual Defense Treaty between the Republic of Korea and the United States of America, to the United States the use of the facilities and areas in the Republic of Korea as provided for in this Agreement. Arrangements as to the specific facilities and areas shall be made by the two Governments through the Joint Committee.

2. Facilities and areas referred to in this Agreement include existing furnishings, equipment and fixtures necessary to the operation of such facilities and areas.

3. The facilities and areas of which the United States has the use at the time of entry into force of this Agreement, shall be regarded, (for the purpose of this Agreement,) as facilities and areas granted to the United States under this Agreement. For the purpose of this paragraph, all facilities and areas of which the United States has the use at the time

0005

105

of entry into force of this Agreement shall be surveyed and determined by the two Governments through the Joint Committee.

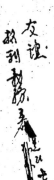

4. With regard to the private property used as facilities and areas by the United States armed forces under this Agreement, the United States shall make reasonable compensation through the Government of the Republic of Korea to the owners of such facilities and areas with a view to alleviating their losses. Detailed arrangements, including the amounts of compensation, shall be made between the two Governments through the Joint Committee.

5. The Governments of the United States bears without cost to the Republic of Korea all expenditures incident to the maintenance of the facilities and areas granted under this Agreement.

6. At the request of either Government, the Government of the Republic of Korea and the Government of the United States shall review such arrangements referred to in paragraph 1 and may agree that such

0006

106

facilities and areas shall be returned to the Republic of Korea or that additional facilities and areas may be provided.

7. The facilities and areas used by the United States shall be promptly returned to the Government of the Republic of Korea whenever they are no longer needed for the purpose of this Agreement, and the Government of the United States agrees to keep the needs for facilities and areas under continual observation with a view toward such return.

8. When facilities and areas are temporarily not being used by the United States, interim use by the authorities of the Republic of Korea or nationals may be arranged through the Joint Committee.

9. With respect to facilities and areas which are to be used by the United States for limited period s of time, the Joint Committee shall specify in the agreements covering such facilities and areas the extent to which the provisions of this Agreement shall apply.

0007

10. Within the facilities and areas, the Government of the United States may take all the measures necessary for their establishment, operation, safeguarding and control. In order to provide access for the United States forces to the facilities and areas for their support, safeguarding and control, the Government of the Republic of Korea shall, at the request of the Government of the United States and upon consultation between the two Governments through the Joint Committee, take necessary measures within the scope of applicable laws and regulations over land, territorial waters and airspace adjacent to, or in the vicinities of the facilities and areas. The Government of the United States may also take necessary measures for such purposes upon consultation between the two Governments through the Joint Committee.

11. The Government of the United States agrees not to take the measures referred to in paragraph 1 in such a manner as to interfere unnecessarily with

0008

108

navigation, aviation, communication, or land travel
to or from or within the territories of the Republic
of Korea. All questions relating to frequencies,
power and like matters used by apparatus employed by
the Government of the United States designed to emit
electric radiation shall be settled by arrangement
between the appropriate authorities of the two
Governments.

12. Operations in the facilities and areas in
use by the Government of the United States shall be
carried on with due regard to the public safety.

13. The Government of the United States is not
obliged, when it returns facilities and areas to the
Government of the Republic of Korea on the expiration
of this Agreement or at an earlier date, to restore
the facilities and areas to the conditions in
which they were at the time they became available to
the United States, or to compensate the Government
of the Republic of Korea in lieu of such restoration.

0009

109

However, in case of private property extremely demolished by the use of the United States, the Government of the United States shall, upon the request of the Government of the Republic of Korea, pay due consideration to its restoration or compensation in lieu thereof.

14. The Government of the Republic of Korea is not obliged to make any compensation to the Government of the the United States for any improvements made in the facilities and areas or for the buildings, structures, supply or any other materials left thereon on the expiration of this Agreement or the earlier return of the facilities and areas.

0010

110

ARTICLE    (Access by Aircraft and Vessel)

1.  United States and foreign vessels and aircraft
operated by, for, or under the control of the Government of the United States for the purpose of this
Agreement shall be accorded access to any port or
airport of the Republic of Korea free from toll or
landing charges.  When cargo or passengers not
accorded the exemption of this Agreement are carried
on such vessels and aircraft notification shall be
given to the appropriate Korean authorities, and
their entry into and departure from the Republic
of Korea shall be according to the laws and regulations of the Republic of Korea.

    2.  When the vessels mentioned in paragraph 1,
enter Korean ports, appropriate notification shall
be made to the appropriate Korean authorities.  Such
vessels shall have freedom from compulsory pilotage.
If, however, a pilot is taken, pilotage shall be
paid for at appropriate rates.

0011

///

<u>AGREED MINUTES TO ARTICLE</u>  (Access by Aircraft and
                                   Vessel)


I.  The vessels mentioned in paragraph 1 include
chartered vessels (bare boat charter, voyage charter
and time charter,), except space chartered vessels.

0012

112

## JOINT COMMITTEE

1. A Joint Committee shall be established as the means for consultation between the two Governments on all matters requiring mutual consultation regarding the interpretation and implementation of this Agreement.

2. The Joint Committee shall be composed of a representative of the Government of the Republic of Korea and a representative of the Government of the United States, each of whom shall have one or more deputies and a staff. The Joint Committee shall determine its own procedures, and arrange for such auxiliary organs and administrative services as may be required.
The Joint Committee shall be so organized that it may meet immediately at any time at the request of the representative of either Government.

3. If the Joint Committee is unable to resolve any matter, it shall refer that matter to the respective Governments for further consideration through diplomatic channels.

0013

/26

<u>Agreed Minute to Definition of Terms</u>

" refers to

Members of the United States armed forces
referred to in Paragraph (a) exclude the military
attaché to the Embassy of the United States of
America and those for whom status has been provided for in the Agreement between the Government
of the Republic of Korea and the Government of
the United States of January 26, 1950 regarding
the establishment of a United States Military
Advisory Group to the Republic of Korea, as amended
by the exchange of Notes between the Foreign Minister of the Republic of Korea and the Charge
D'Affairs of the Embassy of the United States
dated October 21, 1960.

127

0014

Agreed Minute to Article ___ (Definitions)


The expression "except for those for whom status has otherwise been provided" in Paragraph (a) refers only to personnel on active duty belonging to the United States land, sea or air armed services for whom status is provided in the Military Advisory Group Agreement signed on January 26, 1950, and personnel of service attache offices in the Embassy of the United States of America.

0015

## Customs Duties

1. Except as provided expressly to the contrary
in this Agreement, members of the United States forces,
the civilian component, and their dependents shall be
subject to the laws and regulations administered by
the customs authorities of the Republic of Korea.
In particular the customs authorities of the Republic
of Korea shall have the right, under the general
conditions laid down by the laws and regulations of
the Republic of Korea, to search members of the
United States forces, the civilian component and
their dependents and to examine their luggage,
and to seize articles pursuant to such laws and
regulations.

2. All materials, supplies and equipment
imported by the United States forces or by the
organizations provided for in Article _____
exclusively for the official use of the United
States forces or those organizations or for the
use of members of the United States forces, the
civilian component and their dependents shall be

0016

115

permitted entry into Korea free from customs duties and other such charges. When such materials, supplies and equipment are imported, a certificate issued by the authorities of the United States forces in the form to be determined by the Joint Committee shall be submitted to the customs authorities of the Republic of Korea.

3. Property consigned to and for the personal use of members of the United States forces, the civilian component and their dependents, shall be subject to customs duties, except that no such duties or charges shall be paid with respect to:

(a) Furniture, household goods and other personal effects for their private use imported by the members of the United States forces, the civilian component and their dependents at time of their first arrival in Korea..

(b) Reasonable quantities of clothing and household goods which are mailed into the Republic of Korea through the United States military post offices.

4. The exemption granted in paragraphs 2 and 3

0017

116

shall apply only to cases of importation of goods and shall not be interpreted as refunding customs duties and domestic excises collected by the customs authorities at the time of entry in cases of purchases of goods on which such duties and excises have already been collected.

5. Customs examination shall be exempted only in the following cases:

(a) Units of the United States forces under orders entering or leaving the Republic of Korea;

(b) Official documents under official seal;

(c) Official mail in United States military postal channels;

(d) Military cargo shipped on a United States Government bill of lading.

6. Goods imported free from customs duties and other such charges pursuant to paragraphs 2 and 3 above:

(a) May be re-exported free from customs duties and other such charges;

0018

(b) shall not be disposed of in the Republic of Korea by way of either sale o gift, to person

*117*

not entitled to import such goods free from duty,
except as such disposal may be authorized on conditions
agreed between the authorities of the Republic of
Korea and the United States.

7. (a) The authorities of the United States
forces, in cooperation with the authorities of the
Republic of Korea, shall take such steps as are
necessary to prevent abuse of the privileges granted
to the United States forces, members of such forces,
the civilian component, and their dependents in
accordance with this Article.

(b) In order to prevent offenses against
customs and fiscal laws and regulations, the
authorities of the Republic of Korea and of the
United States forces shall assist each other in the
conduct of inquiries and the collection of evidence.

(c) The authorities of the United States
forces shall render all assistance within their
power to ensure that articles liable to seizure by,
or on behalf of, the customs authorities of the
Republic of Korea are handed to those authorities.

0019

118

(d) The authorities of the United States
forces shall render all assistance within their power
to ensure the payment of duties, taxes and penalities
payable by members of the United States forces or
the civilian component, or their dependents.

(e) The authorities of the United States forces
shall provide all practicable assistance to the
customs officials dispatched to military controlled
piers and airports for the purpose of customs inspection.

0020

119

3. (c) Vehicles and parts imported by members of the U.S. armed forces or civilian component within two months after their first arrival in Korea for the private use of themselves or their dependents.

3개월

0021

120.

7.Vehicles and articles belonging to the United States armed forces seized by the customs authorities of the Government of the Republic of Korea in connection with an offense against its customs or fiscal laws or regulations shall be handed over to appropriate authorities of the force concerned.

0022

/2/

# AGREED MINUTES TO ARTICLE (Customs)

1. The quantity of goods imported under paragraph 2 by non-appropriated fund organizations of the United States armed forces for the use of the members of the United States armed forces, the civilian component, and their dependents shall be limited to the extent reasonably required for such use. Non-appropriated fund organizations referred to in paragraph 2 shall be permitted to import such materials, supplies and equipment only with non-appropriated fund.

2. Paragraph 3 (a) does not require concurrent shipment of goods with travel of owner nor does it require single loading or shipment. In this connection, members of the United States armed forces or civilian component and their dependents may import free of duty their personal and household effects during a period of three months from the date of their first arrival. The quantity of such personal and household effects shall be limited to reasonable amount.

3. The term "military cargo" as used in paragraph 5 (c) is not confined to arms and equipment but refers to all cargo consigned to the United

0023

/22

States armed forces. (deleted)

4. The United States armed forces will take
every practicable measure to ensure that goods will
not be imported into the Republic of Korea by or
for the members of the United States armed forces,
the civilian component, or their dependents, the
entry of which would be in violation of Korean
customs laws and regulations. The United States
armed forces will promptly notify the Korean
customs authorities whenever the entry of such
goods is discovered.

5. The Korean customs authorities may, if
they consider that there has been an abuse or
infringement in connection with the entry of goods
under Article     , take up the matter with the
appropriate authorities of the United States armed
forces.

6. The words "The United States armed forces
shall render all assistance within their power,"
etc., in paragraph 9 (b) and (c) refer to reasonable
and practicable measures by the United States armed
forces. (deleted)

0024

123

No-(4)

from

The Korean authorities may request the United
States military authorities whatever information
they deem necessary pertaining to all cargo consigned to the non-appropriated fund organizations
and the United States military authorities shall
promptly provide such information in the manner
as is specified by the Korean authorities.

0025

124

第54차 회의에서 제안
1968. 6. 9.

Alternative proposal to the proposed additional
sentence, agreed minute #3 of the U.S. draft:

"Pertinent information on all cargo consigned to
non-appropriated fund organizations shall routinely
be furnished to the Korean authorities and on specific
cases, additional information shall be provided to the
Korean authorities upon request through the Joint Committee.

The extent of pertinent information shall be
determined by the Joint Committee."

0026

125

ARTICLE    ( Control of Navigations and Meteorolo-
              gical Services)

I.   All civil and military air traffic control
and communications systems shall be developed in
close coordination between the two Governments and
shall be integrated to the extent necessary for
mutual security interests.  Procedures, and any
subsequent changes thereto, necessary to effect
this coordination and integration will be established by arrangements between the appropriate authorities of the two Governments.

2.  Lights and other aids to navigation of
vessels and aircraft placed or established in the
facilities and areas in use by the United States
and in territorial waters adjacent thereto or in
the vicinity thereof shall confirm to the system
in use in the Republic of Korea.  The Republic of
Korea and United States authorities which have established such navigation aids shall notify each
other of their positions and characteristics and
shall give advance notification before making any
changes in them or establishing additional navigation aids.

3.  The Governments of the Republic of Korea
and the United States shall cooperate in meteorological services through exchanges of meteorological
observations, climatological information and seismographic data in accordance with arrangements between
the appropriate authorities of the two Governments.    0027

113

Agreed Minute to Article____

The establishment and construction of aids to
navigation for vessels and aircrafts referred
to in Paragraph 2 shall be effected in accordance with arrangements between the two Governments through the Joint Committee provided for
in Article _____.

0028

114

Article ____ (Utilities and Services)

1. The United States armed forces shall have the use of all public utilities and services belonging to, or controlled or regulated by the Government of the Republic of Korea. The term "utilities and services" shall include, but not be limited to, transportation and communications facilities and systems, electricity, gas, water, steam, heat, light, power, (however produced,) and sewage disposal. In the use of such utilities and services the United States armed forces shall enjoy priorities under conditions no less favorable than ~~that~~ those that may be applicable from time to time to the ministries and agencies of the Government of the Republic of Korea.

*typological mistake erase*

*than*

*next*

2 (a). Specific arrangements as to the use of such public utilities and services by the United States armed forces and the payment therefor shall be made between the appropriate authorities of

99

the two Governments or their agencies.

(b) The existing arrangements concerning the use of such public utilities and services by the United States armed forces at the effective date of this Agreement shall be regarded as the arrangements referred to in the foregoing paragraph.

0030

/00

3. (a) The operation by the United States armed
forces of the military transportation, communication,
power, and other utilities and services shall be to
the extent which deemed necessary for the operation of
the United States armed forces and which not inconsistent
with the operation by the Republic of Korea of such
utilities and Services.

The United States armed forces may operate its
owned military transportation, communication, power,
and other utilities and services deemed necessary
for the operations of the United States armed forces.

Training of Reservists.. Agreed minute

The term 2 eligible United States citizens residing
in the Republic of Korea" includes the staff of the
United States Embassy and the civilian component of
the United States armed forces.

The Term "eligible United States citizens residing
in the Republic of Korea" includes those who are present
in Korea and obliged to comply with the alien entry,
exist and registration law of Korea"

0031

/ 0 /

## Proposed New Draft of Utilities and Services Provisions

3. (a) The United States armed forces shall have the use of all utilities and services which are owned, controlled or regulated by the Government of the Republic of Korea or local administrative subdivisions thereof. The term "utilities and services" shall include, but not be limited to, transportation and communications facilities and systems, electricity, gas, water, steam, heat, light, power, and sewage disposal. The use of utilities and services as provided herein shall not prejudice the right of the United States to operate military transportation, communication, power and such other utilities and services deemed necessary for the operations of the United States armed forces. This right shall not be exercised in a manner inconsistent with the operation by the Government of the Republic of Korea of its utilities and services.

(b) The use of such utilities and services by the United States shall be in accordance with priorities, conditions, and rates or tariffs no less favorable than those accorded any other user.

(4. Removed from this article; to be placed elsewhere in SOFA.)

/02

0032

X     1.     The Joint Committee shall be given the opportunity of discussing any changes determined by the Korean authorities of priority or rates applicable to the United States armed forces prior to their effective date.

2.     Paragraph 3 of Article _____ will not be construed as in any way abrogating the Utilities and Claims Settlement Agreement of December 18, 1958, which continues in full force and effect unless otherwise agreed by the two governments.

3.     Should the emergency operating needs of the United States armed forces so require, the Republic of Korea shall, after consultation thereon, take appropriate measures to assure provision of utilities and services necessary to meet these needs.

0033

/03

FACILITIES AND AREAS
(ARTICLE 17)

(To be presented at 61st session)

Agreed Minute #2

All removable facilities, equipment and material or portions thereof provided by the Republic of Korea under this Agreement and located within the areas and facilities referred to in this Article shall be returned to the Republic of Korea whenever they are no longer needed for the purpose of this Agreement.

0034

104

APO's Article

The United States may establish and operate,
within the facilities and areas in use by the United
States armed forces, United States military post offices
for the use of members of the United States armed forces,
the civilian component, and their dependents, for the
transmission of mail between United States military
post offices in the Republic of Korea and between such
military post offices and other United States post
offices.

0035

95

Article____(Enrollment and Training of
　　　　　Reservists)

　　The United States may enroll and train eligible
United States citizens residing in the Republic of
Korea in the reserve organizations of the United
States armed forces.

96

Article ___ (Respect for Local Law )

It is the duty of the members of the United
States armed forces, the civilian component, and their
dependents to respect the law of the Republic of
Korea, and to abstain from any activity inconsistent
with the spirit of the present Agreement, and, in
particular, from any political activity in the
Republic of Korea.

0037

97

Article____ (Meteorological Services)

The Governments of the Republic of Korea and the
United States shall cooperate in mutually furnishing
the relevant authorities of each Government with the
following meteorological services in accordance with
arrangements between the appropriate authorities of
the two Governments:

(a) Meteorological observation,

(b) Climatological information, and

(c) Seismographic data.

0038

90

## ARTICLE
## VEHICLE AND DRIVER LICENSES

1.  The Republic of Korea shall accept as valid, without a driving test or fee, the driving permit or license or military driving permit issued by the United States to a member of the United States armed forces, the civilian component, and their dependents.

2.  (a) Official vehicles of the United States armed forces and the civilian component shall carry a distinctive numbered plate or individual marking which will readily identify them.

(b) Privately owned vehicles of the members of the United States armed forces, the civilian component, and their dependents shall carry Korean number plates to be acquired under the same conditions as those applicable to the nationals of the Republic of Korea.

0039

81

Article ____ (Safety and Security Measures
for U.S. Armed Forces, Its
Members, Dependents, and
Property)


The Republic of Korea and the United States
will cooperate in taking such steps as may from
time to time be necessary to ensure the security of
the United States armed forces, the members thereof,
the civilian component, their dependents, and their
property.  The Government of the Republic of Korea
agrees to seek such legislation and to take such other
action as may be necessary to ensure the adequate
security and protection within its territory of
installations, equipment, property, records and
official information of the United States, and for
the punishment of offenders under the applicable laws
of the Republic of Korea.


0040


78

ARTICLE ____ (Taxation)

1.  The United States armed forces shall not be
subject to taxes or similar charges on property held,
used or transferred by such forces in the Republic of
Korea.

2.  Members of the United States armed forces,
the civilian component, and their dependents shall
not be liable to pay Korean taxes to the Government
of the Republic of Korea or to any other taxing agency
in the Republic of Korea on income received as a
result of their service with or employment by the
United States armed forces, or by the organizations
provided for in Article _____. The provisions of
this Article do not exempt such persons from payment
of Korean taxes on income derived from sources other
than those provided for in this paragraph.

3.  Members of the United States armed forces,
the civilian component, and their dependents shall be
exempt from taxation in the Republic of Korea on the
holding, use, transfer inter se, or transfer by death
of any movable property, the presence of which in
the Republic of Korea is due solely to the temporary

0041

presence of these persons in the Republic of Korea provided
that such exemption shall not apply to property held
for the purpose of investment or the conduct of business
in the Republic of Korea.

4.  Periods during which the persons referred
to in the preceding paragraph are in the Republic of
Korea solely by reason of being members of the United
States armed forces or of the civilian component, or
their dependents shall not be considered as periods
of residence or domicile in the Republic of Korea for
the purpose of Korean taxation.

0042

80

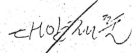

1. Persons, including corporations organized under the laws of the United States, and their employees who are ordinarily resident in the United States and whose presence in the Republic of Korea is solely for the purpose of executing contracts with the United States for the benefit of the United States armed forces, and who are designated by the Government of the United States in accordance with the provisions of the paragraph 2 below, shall, except as provided in this Article, be subject to the laws and regulations of the Republic of Korea.

2. The designation referred to in paragraph 1 above shall be made upon consultation with the Government of the Republic of Korea and shall be restricted to cases where open competitive bidding is not practicable due to security considerations, to the technical qualifications of the contracts involved, or to the unavailability of materials or services required by United States standards, or to the limitations of United States law.

0043

82

The designation shall be withdrawn by the
Government of the United States.

(a) upon completion of contracts with the
United States for the United States armed forces;

(b) upon proof that such persons are engaged
in business activities in the Republic of Korea other
than those pertaining to the United States armed
forces; or

(c) when such persons are engaged in practices
illegal in the Republic of Korea.

3. Upon certification by the appropriate authorities of the United States as to their identity,
such persons and their employees shall be accorded
the following benefits of this Agreement:

(a) Entry into the Republic of Korea in
accordance with the provisions of Article ___;

(b) The exemption from customs duties, and
other such charges provided for in Article ____,
paragraph 3 for members of the United States forces,
the civilian component, and their dependents;

(c) If authorized by the Government of the
United States, the right to use the services of the
organizations provided for in Article ___;

0044

83

(d) Those provided for in Article ___,
paragraph 2, for members of the United States armed
forces, the civilian component, and their
dependents;

(e) If authorized by the Government of the
United States, the right to use military payment
certificates, as provided for in Article ___;

(f) The use of postal facilities provided
for in Article ___;

(g) Exemption from the laws and regulations
of the Republic of Korea with respect to terms and
conditions of employment.

4. Such persons and their employees shall be
subject to the Korean passport and visa regulations
and shall possess passports with their status described
therein. Their arrival, departure and their residence
while in the Republic of Korea shall be notified by
the United States to the Government of the Republic
of Korea.

5. Upon certification by an authorized officer
of the United States armed forces, such contractors
and their employees shall be exempt from taxation

0045

84

in the Republic of Korea on the holding, use, transfer by death, or transfer to persons or agencies entitled to tax exemption under this Agreement, of any movable property, the presence of which in the Republic of Korea is due solely to the temporary presence of these persons in the Republic of Korea, provided that such exemption shall not apply to property held for the purpose of investment or the conduct of other business than those executing contracts as described in paragraph 1 of this Article in the Republic of Korea.

6. The persons and their employees referred to in paragraph 1 shall not be liable to pay income tax to the Government of the Republic of Korea or to any other taxing agency in the Republic of Korea on any income derived under a contract made in the United States with the Government of the United States in connection with the construction, maintenance or operation of any of the facilities or areas covered by this Agreement. The provisions of this paragraph do not exempt such persons from payment of income or corporation taxes on income derived from other engagement than those mentioned in this paragraph.

0046

7. The Korean authorities shall have the primary right to exercise jurisdiction over the contractors and their employees referred to in paragraph 1 of this Article in relation to offences committed in the Republic of Korea and punishable by the law of the Republic of Korea. In those cases in which the Korean authorities decide not to exercise such jurisdiction they shall notify the military authorities of the United States as soon as possible. Upon such notification the military authorities of the United States shall have the right to exercise such jurisdiction over the persons referred to as is conferred on them by the law of the United States.

0047

1. Persons, including corporations organized under the laws of the United States, and their employees, who are ordinarily resident in the United States and whose presence in the Republic of Korea is solely for the purpose of executing contracts with the United States for the benefit of the United States armed forces or other armed forces in Korea under the Unified Command receiving logistical support from the United States armed forces, who are designated by the Government of the United States in accordance with the provisions of the paragraph 2 below, shall, except as provided in this Article, be subject to the laws and regulations of the Republic of Korea.

2. The designation referred to in paragraph 1 above shall be made upon consultation with the Government of the Republic of Korea and shall be restricted to cases where open competitive bidding is not practicable due to security considerations, to the technical qualifications of the contractors involved, to the unavailability of materials or services required by United States standards, or to limitations of United States law. The designation shall be withdrawn by the Government of the United States:

0048

81

(a) Upon completion of contracts with the United States armed forces or other armed forces in Korea under the Unified Command receiving logistical support from the United States armed forces;

(b) Upon proof that such persons are engaged in business activities in Korea other than those pertaining to the United States armed forces or other armed forces in Korea under the Unified Command receiving logistical support from the United States armed forces;

(c) Upon proof that such persons are engaged in practices illegal in Korea.

3. Upon certification by appropriate United States authorities as to their identity, such persons shall be accorded the following benefits of this Agreement:

(a) Accession and movement, as provided for Article        , paragraph 2;

(b) Entry into Korea in accordance with the provisions of Article        ;

(c) The exemption from customs duties, and other such charges provided for in Article        , paragraph 3, for members of the United States armed forces, the civilian component, and their dependents;

(d) If authorized by the Government of the United States, the use of the services of the organizations provided

88

for in Article

(e) Those provided in Article        , paragraph 2,

for members of the United States armed forces, the civilian

component, and their dependents;

(f) If authorized by the Government of the United

States, the use of military payment certificates, as

provided for in Article        ;

- (g) The use of postal facilities provided for

in Article        ;

(h) The use of utilities and services in accordance

with those priorities, conditions, rates, or tariffs

accorded the United States armed forces by Article para-

graph 3, relating to utilities and services;

(i) Exemption from the laws and regulations of

Korea with respect to licensing and registration of

business and corporations.

4. The arrival, departure, and place of residence

in Korea of such persons shall from time to time be

notified by the United States armed forces to the Korean

authorities.

5. Upon certification by an authorized representative

of the United States armed forces, depreciable assets,

except houses, held, used or transferred by such persons

exclusively for the execution of contracts referred to

in paragraph 1 shall not be subject to taxes or similar

0050

charges of Korea.

6. Upon certification by an authorized representative of the United States armed forces, such persons shall be exempt from taxation in Korea on the holding, use, transfer by death, or transfer to persons or agencies entitled to tax exemption under this Agreement, of movable property, tangible or intangible, the presence of which in Korea is due solely to the temporary presence of these persons in Korea, provided that such exemption shall not apply to property held for the purpose of investment or the conduct of other business than those executing contracts as described in paragraph 1 of this Article in Korea or to any intangible property registered in Korea.

7. The persons referred to in paragraph 1 shall not be liable to pay income or corporation taxes to the Government of Korea or to any other taxing agency in Korea on any income derived under a contract with the Government of the United States in connection with the construction, maintenance or operation of any of the facilities or areas covered by this Agreement. Persons in Korea in connection with the execution of such a contract with the United States shall not be liable to pay any Korean taxes to the Government of Korea or to any taxing agency in Korea on income derived from sources

0051

outside of Korea nor shall periods during which such persons are in Korea be considered periods of residence or domicile in Korea for the purposes of Korean taxation. The provisions of this paragraph do not exempt such persons from payment of income or corporation taxes on income derived from Korean sources, other than those sources referred to in the first sentence of this paragraph, nor do they exempt such persons who claim Korean residence for United States income tax purposes from payment of Korean taxes on income.

8. The Korean authorities shall have the primary right to exercise jurisdiction over the contractors and *and the dependents of such persons* their employees, referred to in paragraph 1 of this Article in relation to offences committed in the Republic of Korea and punishable by the law of the Republic of Korea. In those cases in which the Korean authorities decide not to exercise such jurisdiction they shall notify the military authorities of the United States as soon as possible. Upon such notification the military authorities of the United States shall have the right to exercise such jurisdiction over the persons referred to as is conferred on them by the law of the United States.

0052

91

1.  This Article shall not prevent the persons referred to in paragraph 1 from employing third-country nationals who shall, except as provided in paragraph 2, and sub-paragraphs (a), (d), (e), (f), (g) of paragraph 3, be subject to the laws and regulations of the Republic of Korea.

2.  The dependents of the persons and their employees, including third-country nationals, shall, except those benefits as provided in sub-paragraphs (d), (f) and (g), be subject to the laws and regulations of the Republic of Korea.

3.  There is no obligation under this Article to grant exemption from taxes payable in respect of the use and ownership of private vehicles.

0053

92

1. (a) Navy exchanges, post exchanges, messes,
commissaries, social clubs, theaters and other non-
appropriated fund organizations authorized and
regulated by the authorities of the United States armed
forces may be established within the facilities and
areas in use by the United States armed forces for
the exclusive use of the members of such forces, the
civilian component, and their dependents. Except
as otherwise provided in this Agreement, such
organizations shall not be subject to Korean
regulations, license, fees, taxes or similar controls.

(b) When a newspaper authorized and
regulated by the authorities of the United States
armed forces is sold to the general public, it shall
be subject to Korean regulations, license, fees,
taxes or similar controls so far as such circulation
is concerned .

2. No Korean tax shall be imposed on sales of
merchandise and services by such organizations, except *except for Par.(b)*
as provided in paragraph 1 (b) but purchase within

0054

*93*

the Republic of Korea of merchandise and supplies by
such organizations shall be subject to Korean taxes
unless otherwise agreed between the two Governments.

3. Goods which are sold by such organizations
shall not be disposed of in the Republic of Korea to
persons not authorized to make purchases from such
organizations. Administrative measures shall be taken
by the authorities of the United States to prevent
such disposition.

4. The quantity of goods imported by such
organizations for use of the members of the United
States armed forces, the civilian component, and their
dependents shall be limited to the extent reasonably
required for such use.

5. The organizations referred to in this
Article shall provide such information to the auth-
orities of the Republic of Korea as is required by
Korean legislations.

0055

9¥

<u>ARTICLE</u>

1. (a) United States military payment
certificates denominated in dollars may be used
by persons authorized by the United States for
<u>internal</u> transaction within the facilities and
areas in use by the United States forces. ⌐ *maneuver tourist hotel*

(b) The United States Government will
take appropriate action to ensure that authorized
personnel are prohibited from engaging in
transactions involving military payment certificates
except as authorized by United States regulations.

(c) The Government of the Republic of
Korea will take necessary action to prohibit
unauthorized person from engaging in transactions
involving military payment certificates and with
the aid of United States authorities will undertake to apprehend and punish any person or persons
under its jurisdiction involved in the counterfeiting or uttering of counterfeit military
payment certificates.

67

0056

(d) It is agreed that the United States authorities will apprehend and punish members of the United States forces, the civilian component, or their dependents, who tender military payment certificates to unauthorized persons and that no obligation will, [after the date of coming into force of this Agreement,] be due to such unauthorized persons or to the Government of the Republic of Korea or its agencies from the United States or any of its agencies as a result of any unauthorized use of military payment certificates within the Republic of Korea.

2. (a) In order to exercise control of military payment certificates the United States may designate certain American financial institutions to maintain and operate, under United States supervision, facilities for the use of persons authorized by the United States to use military payment certificates.

68

0057

(b) Institutions authorized to maintain
military banking facilities will establish and
maintain such facilities physically separated
from their Korean commercial banking business,
with personnel whose sole duty is to maintain
and operate such facilities.   Such facilities
shall be permitted to maintain United States
currency bank accounts and to perform all
financial transactions in connection therewith
including receipt and remission of funds to the
extent provided by Article ____, paragraph 2,
of this Agreement.

(c) The United States Governmrnt shall
take proper measures necessary to ensure the
implementation of the foregoing paragraph.

*17차회의에서 철회* (handwritten)

69

## Agreed Minute to Article____

United States military payment certificates under custody of the Government of the Republic of Korea at the time of entry into force of this Agreement shall be disposed in accordance with the agreement between the two governments.

70

0059

tabled at 54th session
1964. 6. 9.

Alternative proposal to the proposed additional
sentence, agreed minute #3 of the U.S. draft:

"Pertinent information on all cargo consigned to
non-appropriated fund organizations shall routinely
be furnished to the Korean authorities and on specific
cases, additional information shall be provided to the
Korean authorities upon request through the Joint Committee.

The extent of pertinent information shall be
determined by the Joint Committee."

71                    0060

## Article _____

1. Members of the United States armed forces, the civilian component, and their dependents shall be subject to the foreign exchange controls of the Government of the Republic of Korea.

2. The preceding paragraph shall not be construed to preclude the transmission into or outside of the Republic of Korea of the United States dollars or dollar instruments representing the official funds of the United States or realized as a result of service or employment in connection with this Agreement by members of the United States armed forces and the civilian component, or realized by such persons and their dependents from sources outside of the Republic of Korea.

3. The United States authorities shall take suitable measures to preclude the abuse of the privileges stipulated in the preceding paragraph or circumvention of the Korean foreign exchange controls.

0061

72

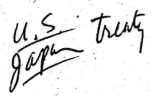

Agreed Minutes to Article ____

Payment in Korea by the United States armed
forces and by those organizations provided in Article
____ to persons other than members of the United
States armed forces, civilian component, their dependents and those persons referred to in Article ____
shall be effected in accordance with the Korean
Foreign Exchange Control Law and regulations.  In
these transactions the basic rate of exchange shall
be used.

0062

73

1.  Each Party waivers all its claims against the other Party for damage to any property owned by it and used by its armed services, if such damage –

    (a)    was caused by a member or an employee of the armed services of the other Party, in execution of his official duties; or

    (b)    arose from the use of any vehicle, vessel or aircraft owned by the other Party and used by its armed services, provided either that the vehicle, vessel or aircraft causing the damage was being used in the execution of its official duty or that the damage was caused to property being so used.

Claims for maritime salvage by one Party against the other Party shall be waived, provided that the vessel or cargo salved was owned by the other Party and being used by its armed services for official purposes.

2.  (a)    In the case of damage caused or arising as stated in paragraph 1 to other property owned by either Party and located in the Republic of Korea, the issue of liability of the other Party shall be determined and the amount of damage shall be assessed, unless the two Governments agree otherwise, by a sole arbitrator selected in accordance with subparagraph (b) of this paragraph. The arbitrator shall also decide any counter measures arising out of the same incidents.

    (b)    The arbitrator referred to in subparagraph (a) above shall be selected by agreement between the two Governments from amongst the nationals of the Republic of Korea who hold or have held high judicial office.

60

0063

(c) Any decision taken by the arbitrator shall be binding and conclusive upon the Parties.

(d) The amount of any compensation awarded by the arbitrator shall be distributed in accordance with the provisions of paragraph 5 (e) (i), (ii) and (iii) of this Article.

(e) The compensation of the arbitrator shall be fixed by agreement between the two Governments and shall, together with the necessary expenses incidental to the performance of his duties, be defrayed in equal proportions by them.

(f) Each Party waives its claim in any such case up to the amount equivalent to 800 United States dollars or 104,000 won. In the case of considerable variation in the rate of exchange between these currencies the two Governments shall agree on the appropriate adjustments of these amounts.

3. For the purpose of paragraph 1 and 2 of this Article the expression "owned by a Party" in the case of a vessel includes a vessel on bare boat charter to that Party or requisitioned by it on bare boat terms or seized by it in prize (except to the extent that the risk of loss or liability is borne by some person other than such Party).

4. Each Party waives all its claims against the other Party for injury or death suffered by any member of its armed services while such member was engaged in the performance of his official duties.

5. Claims (other than contractual claims and those to which paragraph 6 or 7 of this Article apply) arising out of acts or omissions of members or employees of the United States armed forces, including those employees

61

0064

who are nationals of or ordinarily resident in the
Republic of Korea, done in the performance of official
duty, or out of any other act, omission or occurence
for which the United States armed forces are legally
responsible, and causing damage in the Republic of
Korea to third Parties, other than the Government of
the Republic of Korea, shall be dealt with by the
Republic of Korea in accordance with the following
provisions:

(a)  Claims shall be filed, considered and
     settled or adjudicated in accordance with
     the laws and regulations of the Republic of
     Korea with respect to the claims arising
     from the activities of its own armed forces.

(b)  The Republic of Korea may settle any such
     claims, and payment of the amount agreed
     upon or determined by adjudication shall
     be made by the Republic of Korea in won.

(c)  Such payment, whether made pursuant to a
     settlement or to adjudication of the case
     by a competent tribunal of the Republic of
     Korea, or the final adjudication by such
     a tribunal denying payment, shall be binding
     and conclusive upon the Parties.

(d)  Every claim paid by the Republic of Korea
     shall be communicated to the appropriate
     United States authorities together with
     full particulars and a proposed distribution
     in conformity with subparagraph (e) (i) and
     (ii) below.

In default of a reply within two months, the proposed
distribution shall be regarded as accepted.

(e)  The coast incurred in satisfying claims

62

0065

pursuant to the preceding subparagraph and paragraph 2 of this Article shall be distributed between the Parties as follows:

(i) Where the United States alone is responsible, the amount awarded or adjudged shall be distributed in the proportion of 15 per cent chargeable to the Republic of Korea and 85 per cent chargeable to the United States.

(ii) Where the Republic of Korea and the United States are responsible for the damage, the amount awarded or adjudged shall be distributed equally between them. Where the damage was caused by the armed forces of the Republic of Korea and the United States and it is not possible to attribute it specifically to one or both of those armed services, the amount awarded or adjudged shall be distributed equally between the Republic of Korea and the United States.

(iii) Every half-year, a statement of the sums paid by the Republic of Korea in the course of the half-yearly period in respect of every case regarding which the proposed distribution on a percentage basis has been accepted, shall be sent to the appropriate authorities of the United States, together with a request for reimbursement. Such reimbursement shall be made, in won, within the shortest possible time.

(f) Members or employees of the United States armed forces, excluding those employees who are nationals of or ordinarily resident in the Republic of Korea, shall not be sub-

0066

ject tp any proceedings for the enforcement of
any judgement given against them in the Republic
of Korea in a matter arising from the performance
of their official duties.

(g) Except in so far as subparagraph (e) of this
paragraph applies to claims covered by paragraph 2 of this Article, the provisions of
this paragraph shall not apply to any claims
arising out of or in connection with the navigation or operation of a ship or the loading,
carriage, or discharge of a cargo, other than
claims for death or personal injury to which
paragraph 4 of this Article does not apply.

6. Claims against members or employees of the
United States armed forces (except employees who are
nationals of or ordinarily resident in the Republic of
Korea) arising out of tortious acts or omissions in
the Republic of Korea not done in the performance of
official duty shall be dealt with in the following
manner:

(a) The authoritoes of the Republic of Korea shall
consider the claim and access compensation to
the claimant in a fair and just manner, taking
into account all the circumstances of the
case, including the conduct of the injured
person, and shall prepare a report on the
matter.

(b) The report shall be delivered to the appropriate
United States authorities, who shall then decide
without delay whether they will offer an ex
gratia payment, and if so, of what amount.

(c) If an offer of ex gratia payment is made,
and accepted by the claimant in full satisfaction of his claim, the United States
authorities shall make the payment themselves

0067

and inform the authorities of the Republic of
Korea of their decision and of the sums paid.

(d) Nothing in this paragraph shall affect the
jurisdiction of the courts of the Republic of
Korea to entertain an action against a member
or an employee of the United States armed
forces unless and until there has been payment in full satisfaction of the claim.

7. Claims arising out of the unauthorized use of
any vehicle of the United States forces shall be dealt
with in accordance with paragraph 6 of this Article,
except in so far as the United States forces are legally
responsible.

8. If a dispute arises as to whether a tortious act
or omission of a member or an employee of the United
States armed forces was done in the performance of
official duty or as to whether the use of any vehicle of
the United States armed forces was unauthorized, the
question shall be submitted to an arbitrator appointed
in accordance with paragraph 2(b) of this Article, whose
decision on this point shall be final and conclusive.

9. (a) The United States shall not claim immunity
from the jurisdiction of the courts of the
Republic of Korea for members or employees
of the United States armed forces in respect
of the civil jurisdiction of the courts of
the Republic of Korea except to the extent
provided in paragraph 5(f) of this Article.

(b) In case any private movable property, excluding
that in use by the United States armed
forces, which is subject to compulsory
execution under the Korean law, is within
the facilities and areas in use by the United
States armed forces, the United States
authorities shall, upon the request of the

0068

courts of the Republic of Korea, possess
and turn over such property to the authorities
of the Republic of Korea

(c) The authorities of the Republic of Korea and
the United States shall cooperate in the
procurement of evidence for a fair hearing
and disposal of claims under this Article.

10. Disputes arising out of contracts concerning
the procurement of materials, supplies, equipment, services
by or for the United States armed forces, which are
not resolved by the Parties to the contract concerned,
may be submitted to the Joint Committee for conciliation,
provided that the provisions of this paragraph shall not
prejudice any right, which Parties to the contract may
have, to file a civil suit.

11. Paragraphs 2 and 5 of this Article shall apply
only to claims arising incident to non-combat activities.

66

# Criminal Jurisdiction Article

## Agreed Minute Re Paragraph 3

The authorities of the Republic of Korea, recognizing that it is the primary responsibility of the United States military authorities to maintain good order and discipline where persons subject to United States military law are concerned, will, upon the request of the military authorities of the United States pursuant to paragraph 3(c), waive their primary right to exercise jurisdiction under paragraph 3(b) except when they determine that it is of particular importance that jurisdiction be exercised by the authorities of the Republic of Korea. In case where any question arises concerning such determination as may be made by the authorities of the Republic of Korea in accordance with the foregoing provisions, the United States diplomatic mission will be afforded an opportunity to confer with the proper authorities of the Republic of Korea.

Trials of cases in which the authorities of the Republic of Korea waive the primary right to exercise jurisdiction, and trials of cases involving offenses described in paragraph 3(a) (ii) committed against the state or nationals of the Republic of Korea will be held within a reasonable distance from the place where the offenses are alleged to have taken place unless other arrangements are mutually agreed upon.

0070

36

Representatives of the Republic of Korea may be present at
such trials.

To facilitate the expeditious disposal of offenses of
minor importance, arrangements may be made between the United
States military authorities and the Competent authorities
of the Republic of Korea to dispense with notification.

0071

3/)

## Criminal Jurisdiction Article

### Agreed Minute 1 Re Paragraph 3(a) (ii)

"Where a member of the United States armed forces or civilian component is charged with an offense, a certificate issued by a staff judge advocate on behalf of his commanding officer stating that the alleged offense, if committed by him, arose out of an act or omission done in the performance of official duty shall be sufficient evidence of the fact for the purpose of determining primary jurisdiction.

In those exceptional cases where the chief district prosecutor of the Republic of Korea considers that there is proof contrary to a certificate of official duty, it shall be made the subject of review through discussions between appropriate officials of the Government of the Republic of Korea and the diplomatic mission of the United States."

### Agreed Minute 2 Re Paragraph 3(a) (ii)

"The term 'official duty' as used in Article ____ and the Agreed Minute is not meant to include all acts by members of the United States armed forces and the civilian components during periods when they are on duty, but is meant to apply only to acts which are required to be done as functions of those duties the individuals are performing. Thus, any departure from the acts a person is required to perform in a particular duty usually will indicate an act outside of his official duty.

38

0072

## Criminal Jurisdiction Article

<u>Paragraph 5</u>

5(c). The military authorities of the United States shall promptly notify the authorities of the Republic of Korea of the arrest of a member of the United States armed forces, the civilian component, or a dependent <u>in any case in which the Republic of Korea has the primary right to exercise jurisdiction</u>.

5(d). An accused member of the United States armed forces or civilian component, or of a dependent over whom the Republic of Korea is to exercise jurisdiction will, if he is in the hands of the military authorities of the United States, be in the custody of the military authorities of the United States during all judicial proceedings and until custody is requested by the authorities of the Republic of Korea.

<u>If an accused is in the hands of the Republic of Korea, he will</u>, on request, <u>be handed over to the military authorities of the United States</u>, unless the authorities of the Republic of Korea consider that there is adequate cause and necessity to retain him. <u>Such accused will be in the custody of the military authorities of the United States during all judicial proceedings and until custody is requested by the authorities of the Republic of Korea</u>.

0073

39

5(e). In respect of offenses solely against the security of the Republic of Korea provided in paragraph 2(c), <u>an accused shall be in the custody of</u> the authorities of the Republic of Korea.

5(f). <u>Where an accused has been in the custody of the military authorities of the United States under paragraph 5(d), the military authorities of the United States may transfer custody to the authorities of the Republic of Korea at any time, and shall give sympathetic consideration to any request for the transfer of custody which may be made by the authorities of the Republic of Korea in specific cases.</u>

<u>The military authorities of the United States shall promptly make any such accused available to the authorities of the Republic of Korea upon their request for purposes of investigatin and trial.</u>

<u>The authorities of the Republic of Korea will give sympathetic consideration to a request from the military authorities of the United States for assistance in maintaining custody of an accused member of the United States armed forces, the civilian component, or a dependent.</u>

0074

40

## Criminal Jurisdiction Article

### Paragraph 3 of the Agreed Minute Re Paragraph 9

No confession, admission, or other statement, obtained by torture, violence, threat, deceit, or after prolonged arrest or detention, or which has been made involuntarily, will be considered by the courts of the Republic of Korea as evidence in support of the guilt of the accused under this Article.

0075

41

Criminal Jurisdiction Article
(ROK Modifications based on U.S. draft)

Paragraph 7(b)

(b) The authorities of the Republic of Korea shall give sympathetic consideration to a request from the military authorities of the United States for assistance in carrying out a sentence of imprisonment pronounced by the military authorities of the United States under the provisions of this Article within the territory of the Republic of Korea. The authorities of the Republic of Korea shall also give sympathetic consideration to a request from the authorities of the United States for the custody of any member of the United States armed forces or civilian component or a dependent, who is serving a sentence of confinement imposed by a court of the Republic of Korea. If such custody is released to the military authorities of the United States, the United States shall be obliged to continue the confinement of the individual in an appropriate confinement facility of the United States until the sentence to confinement shall have been served in full or until release from such confinement shall be approved by competent authorities of the Republic of Korea. In such cases, the authorities of the United States shall furnish relevant information on a routine basis to

- 1 -

0076

42

the authorities of the Republic of Korea, and a representative of the Government of the Republic of Korea shall have the right to have access to a member of the United States armed forces, the civilian component, or a dependent who is serving a sentence imposed by a court of the Republic of Korea in confinement facilities of the United States.

- 2 -

0077

Additional Sentence to Paragraph 4, Agreed Minute re Paragraph 3(b)

In case where the Government of the Republic of Korea, in resolving disagreement in accordance with the foregoing provisions, determines that it is imperative that jurisdiction be exercised by the authorities of the Republic of Korea, the recall of waiver shall be final and conclusive.

- 3 -

0078

44

Agreed Minute Re Paragraph 9(a)

The right to communicate with a representative of the Government of the United States shall exist from the moment of arrest or detention, and no statement of the accused taken in the absence of such a representative shall be admissible as evidence in support of the guilt of the accused. Such representative shall be entitled to be present at all preliminary investigations, examinations, pretrial hearings, the trial itself, and subsequent proceedings, at which the accused is present, except where his presence is incompatible with the rules of the court of the Republic of Korea or with the security requirements of the Republic of Korea, which are not at the same time the security requirements of the United States.

- 4 -

0079

45

Agreed Minute Re Paragraph 10(a) and 10(b)

The United States military authorities will normally make all arrests within facilities and areas in use by the United States armed forces. This shall not preclude the authorities of the Republic of Korea from making arrests within facilities and areas in cases where the competent authorities of the United States armed forces have given consent, or in cases of pursuit of a flagrant offender who has committed a serious crime.

Where persons whose arrests is desired by the authorities of the Republic of Korea and who are not subject to the jurisdiction of the United States military authorities within facilities and areas in use by the United States armed forces, the United States military authorities shall undertake, upon request, to arrest such persons. Any such person whose custody is to be in the hands of the authorities of the Republic of Korea in accordance with paragraph 5 of this Article, or any such person who is not a member of the United States armed forces, civilian component, or a dependent shall immediately be turned over to the authorities of the Republic of Korea. The authorities of the Republic of Korea will normally not exercise the right of search, seizure, or inspection with respect to any person or

- 5 -

0080

46

property within facilities and areas in use by the
military authorities of the United States or with respect
to property of the United States wherever situated,
except in cases where the competent military authorities
of the United States consent to such search, seizure,
or inspection by the Korean authorities of such
persons or property.

Where search, seizure, or inspection with respect
to persons or property within facilities and areas in
use by the United States or with respect to property
of the United States in the Republic of Korea is desired
by the Korean authorities, the United States military
authorities will undertake, upon request, to make such
search, seizure, or inspection. In the event of a
judgement concerning such property, except property
owned or utilized by the United States Government or
its instrumentalities, the United States shall in
accordance with its laws turn over such property to
the authorities of the Republic of Korea for disposition
in accordance with the judgement.

The United States military authorities may arrest
or detain in the vicinity of a facility or area any
person in the commission or attempted commission of

- 6 -

0081

an offense against the security of that facility or area.
Any such person whose custody is to be in the hands of
the authorities of the Republic of Korea in accordance
with paragraph 5 of this Article, or any such person who
is not a member of the United States armed forces,
civilian component, or a dependent shall immediately
be turned over to the authorities of the Republic of
Korea.

- 7 -

48

Article (Revision)

Either Government may at any time request
the revision of any article of this Agreement,
in which case the two Governments shall enter
into negotiation through diplomatic channels.

0083-

49

## Agreed Minute

### Re Paragraph 3(a) (ii)

Where a member of the United States armed forces or civilian component is charged with an offense, a certificate issued by a staff judge advocate on behalf of his commanding officer stating that the alleged offense, if committed by him, arose out of an act or omission done in the performance of official duty, shall be sufficient evidence of the fact for the purpose of determining primary jurisdiction, unless the contrary is proved.

If the chief prosecutor of the Republic of Korea considers that there is proof contrary to the certificate of official duty, he will refer the matter to the Joint Committee for decision.

The above statements shall not be interpreted to prejudice in any way Article 308 of the Korean Code of Criminal Procedure.

0084

<u>Agreed Minute</u>

<u>Re Paragraph 3(c)</u>

The authorities of the Republic of Korea will, upon the notification of individual cases falling under the waiver provided in Article ____ paragraph 3(c) from the military authorities of the United States, waive its primary right to exercise jurisdiction under Article ____ except where they determine that it is of particular importance that jurisdiction be exercised by the authorities of the Republic of Korea.

0085

51.

Paragraph 5(d)

   An accused member of the United States Armed Forces
or civilian component over whom the Republic of Korea is
to exercise jurisdiction will, if he is in the hand of the
United States, be under the custody of the United States
during all judicial proceedings and until custody is requested
by the authorities of the Republic of Korea.

   The military authorities of the United States may
transfer custody to the Korean authorities at any time and shall
give sympathetic consideration to any request for the transfer
of custody which may be made by the Korean authorities in
specific cases.

Paragraph 5(e)

   In respect of offenses solely against the security
of the Republic of Korea provided in Paragraph 2(c), custody
shall remain with the authorities of the Republic of Korea.

0086

52

Para. 5(e)(iii)

Every half year, a statement of the sums paid by
the Republic of Korea in the course of the half-yearly
period in respect of every case regarding which the
liability, amount, and proposed distribution on a percentage
basis has been approved by both governments shall be sent
to the appropriate authorities of the United States, together
with a request for reimbursement. Such reimbursement shall
be made in won within the shortest possible time. The
approval by both governments as referred to in this subparagraph shall not prejudice any decision taken by the
arbitrator or adjudication by a competent tribunal of the
Republic of Korea as set forth in paragraphs 2(c) and 5(c)
respectively.

Para. 12
(UNDERSTANDING)
The status of the KSC members will be determined by
other negotiations between the Republic of Korea and the
United States.

Para. A2 of the Agreed Minute
The provisions of paragraphs five, six, seven and
eight will be extended, at the earliest date practicable,
to other areas of the Republic of Korea as determined
by the Joint Committee.

R.O.K

## ARTICLE
## Criminal Jurisdiction

(1)

1. Subject to the provisions of this Article:

(a) the military authorities of the United States shall have the right to exercise within the Republic of Korea criminal and disciplinary jurisdiction conferred on them by the law of the United States over the members of the United States armed forces and the civilian components.

(b) the authorities of the Republic of Korea shall have jurisdiction over the members of the United States armed forces, the civilian component, and their dependents with respect to offenses committed within the territory of the Republic of Korea and punishable by the law of the Republic of Korea.

2. (a) The military authorities of the United States shall have the right to exercise exclusive jurisdiction over members of the United States armed forces and the civilian components with respect to offenses, including offenses relating to its security, punishable by the law of the United States, but not by the law of the Republic of Korea.

(b) The authorities of the Republic of Korea shall have the right to exercise exclusive jurisdiction over members of

0088

of the United States armed forces, the civilian component, and their dependents with respect to offenses, including offenses relating to the security of the Republic of Korea, punishable by its law but not by the law of the United States.

(c) For the purpose of this paragraph and of paragraph 3 of this Article a security offense against a State shall include:

   (i) treason against the State;

   (ii) sabotage, espionage or violation of any law relating to official secrets of that State, or secrets relating to the national defense of that State.

3. In cases where the right to exercise jurisdiction is concurrent the following rules shall apply;

   (a) The military authorities of the United States shall have the primary right to exercise jurisdiction over members of the United States armed forces or the civilian component in relation to:

      (i) offenses solely against the property or security of the United States, or offenses solely against the person or property of another member of the United States armed forces or the civilian component or of a dependent;

0089

2

(ii) offenses arising out of any act or omission

done in the performance of official duty ~~provided~~

~~that such act or omission is directly~~

~~related to the duty" The question as to~~

~~whether offenses were committed in the~~

~~performance of official duty shall be decided by~~

~~a competent district public prosecutor of~~

~~the Republic of Korea.~~

~~In case the offenders commanding officer~~

~~finds otherwise, he may appeal from the~~

~~prosecutor's decision to the Minister of~~

~~Justice within ten days from the receipt of~~

~~the decision of the prosecutor, and the~~

~~decision of the Minister of Justice shall be~~

~~final.~~

비안에없음,

52차회의에서 삭정

1964. 5. 20.

(b) In the case of any other offenses the authorities

of the Republic of Korea shall have the primary right to

exercise jurisdiction.

(c) If the State having the primary right decides

not to exercise jurisdiction, it shall notify the authorities

of the other State as soon as practicable. The authorities

of the State having the primary right shall give sympathetic

consideration to a request from the authorities of the other

0030

3

State for a waiver of its right in cases where that other State considers such waiver to be of particular importance.

4. The foregoing provisions of this Article shall not imply any right for the military authorities of the United States to exercise jurisdiction over persons who are nationals of or ordinarily resident in the Republic of Korea, unless they are members of the United States forces.

5. (a) The military authorities of the United States and the authorities of the Republic of Korea shall assist each other in the arrest of members of the United States armed forces, the civilian component, or their dependents in the territory of the Republic of Korea and in handing them over to the authorities which is to exercise jurisdiction in accordance with the above provisions.

(b) The authorities of the Republic of Korea shall notify the military authorities of the United States of the arrest of any member of the United States armed forces, the civilian component, or their dependents.

(c) The military authority of the United States shall immediately notify the authority of the Republic of Korea of the arrest of a member of the United States armed forces, the civilian component, or a dependent, unless the United States authority has the right to exercise exclusive jurisdiction

0091

over such a person.

(d) An accused member of the United States armed force, the civilian component or a dependent over whom the Republic Korea is to exercise jurisdiction shall, if he is in the hand of the United States, be under the custody of the United State, Upon presentation of a warrant issued by a judge of the Repub Korea he shall be handed over immediately to the Korean Authorities.

6. (a) The authorities of the Republic of Korea and the military authorities of the United States shall assist each other in the carrying out of all necessary investigations into offenses, and in the collection and production of evidenc including the seizure and, in proper case, the handing over of objects connected with an offense. The handing over of such objects may, however, be made subject to their return within the time specified by the authority delivering them.

(b) The authorities of the Republic of Korea and the military authorities of the United States shall notify each other of the disposition of all cases in which there are concurr rights to exercise jurisdiction.

7. (a) A death sentence shall not be carried out in the Republic of Korea by the military authorities of the United States if the legislation of the Republic of Korea does not provide for such punishment in a similar case.

0092

(b) The authorities of the Republic of Korea shall give sympathetic consideration to a request from the military authorities of the United States for assistance in carrying out a sentence of imprisonment pronounced by the military authorities of the United States under the provisions of this Article within the territory of the Republic of Korea.

8. Where an accused has been tried in accordance with the provisions of this Article either by the authorities of the Republic of Korea or the military authorities of the United States and has been acquitted, or has been convicted and is serving, or has served, his sentence or has been pardoned, he may not be tried again for the same offense within the territory of the Republic of Korea by the authorities of the other State. However, nothing in this paragraph shall prevent the military authorities of the United States from trying a member of its forces for any violation of rules of discipline arising from an act or omission which constituted an offense for which he was tried by the authorities of the Republic of Korea.

9. Whenever a member of the United States armed forces, the civilian component or a dependent is prosecuted under the jurisdiction of the Republic of Korea he shall be entitled:

(a) to a prompt and speedy trial;

0093

(b) to be informed, in advance of trial, of the specific charge or charges made against him;

(c) to be confronted with the witnesses against him;

(d) to have compulsory process for obtaining witnesses in his favor, if they are within the jurisdiction of the Republic of Korea;

(e) to have legal representation of his own choice for his defense or to have free or assisted legal representation under the conditions prevailing in the Republic of Korea;

(f) If he considers it necessary, to be provided with the services of a competent interpreter; and

(g) to communicate with a representative of the Government of the United States and to have such a representative present at his trial.

10. (a) Regularly constituted military units or formation of the United States armed forces shall have the right to police any facilities or areas which they use under Article Ⅳ of this Agreement. The military police of such forces may take all appropriate measures to ensure the maintenance of order and security within such facilities and areas.

(b) Outside these facilities and areas such military police shall be employed only subject to arrangements with the authorities of the Republic of Korea and in liaison with these authorities and in so far as such employment is necessary

0094

to maintain discipline and order among the members of the
United States armed forces.

8

## Agreed Minutes

RE Paragraph 2(c)

Both Governments shall inform each other of the details of all the security offenses mentioned in this subparagraph and the provisions governing such offenses in the existing laws of their respective countries.

RE Paragraph 3(a) (ii)

The term "official duty" is not meant to include all acts by members of the United States armed forces or the civilian component during periods while they are on duty. Any departure from acts which are duly required to be done as a normal function of a particular duty shall be deemed as an act outside of his "official duty."

RE Paragraph 3(c)

Mutual procedures relating to waivers of the primary right to exercise jurisdiction shall be determined by the Joint Committee.

Trials of cases in which the authorities of the Republic of Korea waived the primary right to exercise jurisdiction, and trials of cases involving offenses described in paragraph 3(a) (ii) committed against the State or nationals of the Republic of Korea shall be held promptly in the Republic of Korea within a reasonable distance from the places where the offenses are alleged to have taken place unless other arrangements are mutually agreed upon. Representatives of the authorities of the Republic of Korea may be present at such trials.

RE Paragraph 4

Dual nationals, the Republic of Korea and United States, who are the members of the United States armed forces or the civilian component and are brought to the Republic of Korea shall not be considered as nationals of the Republic of Korea, but shall be considered as United States nationals for the purposes of this paragraph.

0096

## RE Paragraph 5(b)

In case the authorities of the Republic of Korea have arrested an offender who is a member of the United States armed forces, the civilian component or a dependent with respect to a case over which the Republic of Korea has the primary right to exercise jurisdiction, the authorities of the Republic of Korea will, unless they deem that there is adequate cause and necessity to retain such offender, release him to the custody of the United States military authorities provided that he shall, on request, be made available to the authorities of the Republic of Korea, if such be the condition of his release. The United States authorities shall, on request, transfer his custody to the authorities of the Republic of Korea at the time he is indicted by the latter.

## RE Paragraph 6

1. A member of the United States armed forces or the civilian component shall, if sommoned by the authorities of the Republic of Korea as a witness in the course of investigations and trials, make himself available to the authorities of the Republic of Korea.

2. If any person sommoned as witness did not make himself available to the authorities of the Republic of Korea, they may take necessary measures in accordance with the provisions of the law of the Republic of Korea. Subject to the foregoing, the military authorities of the United States shall, upon presentation of a warrant issued by a judge of the Republic of Korea, immediately take all appropriate measures to ensure the execution of the warrant by the authorities of the Republic of Korea.

## RE Paragraph 9

1. The rights enumerated in this paragraph are guaranteed to all persons on trial in the Korean courts by the provisions of the Constitu-

0097

tion of the Republic of Korea. In addition to these rights, a member of
the United States armed forces, the civilian component or a dependent
who is prosecuted under the jurisdiction of the Republic of Korea
shall have such other rights as are guaranteed under the Constitution
and laws of the Republic of Korea to all persons on trial in the Korean
courts.

2. Nothing in the provisions of paragraph 9(g) concerning the
presence of a representative of the United States Government at the
trial of a member of the United States armed forces, the civilian
component or a dependent prosecuted under the jurisdiction of the
Republic of Korea, shall be so construed as to prejudice the provisions
of the Constitution of the Republic of Korea with respect to public
trials.

RE Paragraph 10(a) and 10(b)

1. The United States military authorities will normally make
arrests of the members of the United States armed forces and the
civilian component within facilities and areas in use by and guarded
under the authority of the United States armed forces. The authorities
of the Republic of Korea may arrest all persons who are subject to
the jurisdiction of the Republic of Korea within facilities and areas
in cases where the authorities of the United States armed forces have
given consent, or in cases of pursuit of a flagrant offender who has
committed a serious crime.

Where persons whose arrest is desired by the authorities of the
Republic of Korea and who are not subject to the jurisdiction of the
United States armed forces are within facilities and areas in use by
the United States armed forces, the United States military authorities
shall, upon request, promptly arrest such persons. All persons arrested

by the United States military authorities, who are not subject to the jurisdiction of the United States armed forces, shall immediately be turned over to the authorities of the Republic of Korea.

The United States military authorities may, under due process of law, arrest within or in the vicinity of a facility or area any person in the commission of an offense against the security of that facility or area. Any such person not subject to the jurisdiction of the United States armed forces shall immediately be turned over to the authorities of the Republic of Korea.

2. The authorities of the Republic of Korea will normally not exercise the right of seizure, search, or inspection with respect to any person or property within facilities and areas in use by and guarded under the authorities of the United States armed forces or with respect to property of the United States armed forces wherever situated except in cases where the authorities of the United States armed forces consent to such seizure, search, or inspection by the authorities of the Republic of Korea of such persons or property.

Where seizure, search, or inspection with respect to persons or property within facilities and areas in use by the United States armed forces or with respect to property of the United States armed forces in the Republic of Korea is desired by the authorities of the Republic of Korea, the United States military authorities shall, upon request, make such seizure, search, or inspection. In the event of a judgement concerning such property, except property owned or utilized by the United States Government or its instrumentalities, the United States shall turn over such property to the authorities of the Republic of Korea for disposition in accordance with the judgement. 0099

# RATIFICATION OF AGREEMENT

1. This Agreement shall enter into force <u>thirty days</u> after the date of a written notification from the Government of the Republic of Korea to the Government of the United States that it has approved the Agreement <u>in accordance with its legal procedures.</u>

2. <u>The Government of the Republic of Korea shall undertake to seek from its legislature</u> all legislative and budgetary action necessary to give effect to its provisions of this agreement.

3. Subject to the provisions of Article XXII, Paragraph 12, this agreement shall, upon its entry into force, supersede and replace the agreement between the Government of the United States and the Government of the Republic of Korea on jurisdictional matters, effected by an exchange of notes at Taejon on July 12, 1950.

4. <u>The provisions of the present Agreement shall apply to the United States armed forces, their members, civilian component,</u> invited contractors or dependents thereof,

- 1 -

0100

while in the Republic of Korea pursuant to the resolution of the United Nations Security Council or pursuant to the Mutual Defense Treaty. Such provisions will not, however, apply to members of the United States armed forces for whom status is provided in the Agreement for the Establishment of the United States Military Advisory Group to the Republic of Korea, signed on January 26, 1950 and personnel of the United States armed forces attached to the Embassy of the United States.

Article _____ (Local Procurement)

1. The United States may contract for any supplies
or construction work to be furnished or undertaken in
the Republic of Korea for purposes of, or authorized
by, this Agreement, without restriction as to choice
of supplier or person who does the construction work.
Such supplies or construction work may, upon agreement
between the appropriate authorities of the two Governments,
also be procured through the Government of the Republic
of Korea.

2. Materials, supplies, equipment and services which
are required from local sources for the maintenance
of the United States armed forces and the procurement
of which may have an adverse effect on the economy of the
Republic of Korea shall be procured in coordination with,
and, when desirable, through or with the assistance of,
the competent authorities of the Republic of Korea.

3. Materials, supplies, equipment and services
procured for official purposes in the Republic of
Korea by the United States armed forces, or by authorized
procurement agencies of the United States armed forces,
upon appropriate certification shall be exempt from the
following Korean taxes:

0102

(a) Commodity tax

(b) Gasoline tax

(c) Electricity and gas tax

Materials, supplies, equipment and services procured
for ultimate use by the United States armed forces shall
be exempt from commodity and gasoline taxes upon appropriate
certification by the United States armed forces.  With
respect to any present or future Korean taxes not
specifically referred to in this Article which might be
found to constitute a significant and readily identifiable
part of the gross purchase price of materials, supplies, equipment and services procured by the United States armed forces,
or for ultimate use by such forces, the two Governments
will agree upon a procedure for granting such exemption
or relief therefrom as is consistent with the purpose
of this Article.

4.  Neither members of the United States armed
forces, civilian component, nor their dependents,
shall by reason of this Article enjoy any exemption
from taxes or similar charges relating to personal
purchases of goods and services in the Republic of Korea
chargeable under Korean legislation.

5.  Except as such disposal may be authorized by
the Korean and United States authorities in accordance

0103

with mutually agreed conditions, goods purchased
in the Republic of Korea exempt from the taxes
referred to in paragraph 3, shall not be disposed
of in the Republic of Korea to persons not entitled
to purchase such goods exempt from such tax.

76

0104

"4. Regarding para 3, it is understood that "materials, supplies, equipment and services procured for official purposes" refers to direct procurement by the United States armed forces or its authorized procurement agencies from Korean suppliers. "Materials, supplies, equipment and services procured for ultimate use" refers to procurement by contractors of the United States armed forces from Korean suppliers of items to be incorporated into or necessary for the production of the end product of their contracts with the United States Armed Forces".

0105

한·미국 간의 상호방위조약 제4조에 의한 시설과 구역 및 한국에서의 미국군대의 지위에 관한 협정(SOFA)
전59권. 1966.7.9 서울에서 서명 : 1967.2.9 발효(조약 232호) (V.47 한·미국 양측 교섭안)  111

*1964. 2. 14. 새로 제시*

ARTICLE _____

CONTRACTORS

1. Persons, including corporations organized under
the laws of the United States, and their employees, who
are ordinarily resident in the United States and whose
presence in the Republic of Korea is solely for the purpose
of executing contracts with the United States for the
benefit of the United States armed forces or other armed
forces in Korea under the Unified Command receiving
logistical support from the United States armed forces,
who are designated by the Government of the United States
in accordance with the provisions of the paragraph 2 below,
shall, except as provided in this Article, be subject to
the laws and regulations of the Republic of Korea.

2. The designation referred to in paragraph 1 above
shall be made upon consultation with the Government of the
Republic of Korea and shall be restricted to cases where
open competitive bidding is not practicable due to security
considerations, to the technical qualifications of the
contractors involved, to the unavailability of materials
or services required by United States standards, or to
limitations of United States law. The designation shall
be withdrawn by the Government of the United States:

𝑓𝑥

0106

(a) Upon completion of contracts with the United States armed forces or other armed forces in Korea under the Unified Command receiving logistical support from the United States armed forces;

(b) Upon proof that such persons are engaged in business activities in Korea other than those pertaining to the United States armed forces or other armed forces in Korea under the Unified Command receiving logistical support from the United States armed forces;

(c) Upon proof that such persons are engaged in practices illegal in Korea.

3. Upon certification by appropriate United States authorities as to their identity, such persons shall be accorded the following benefits of this Agreement:

(a) Accession and movement, as provided for Article       , paragraph 2;

(b) Entry into Korea in accordance with the provisions of Article          ;

(c) The exemption from customs duties, and other such charges provided for in Article       , paragraph 3, for members of the United States armed forces, the civilian component, and their dependents;

(d) If authorized by the Government of the United States, the use of the services of the organizations provided

55

0107

for in Article     ;

    (e) Those provided in Article     , paragraph 2, for members of the United States armed forces, the civilian component, and their dependents;

    (f) If authorized by the Government of the United States, the use of military payment certificates, as provided for in Article     ;

    (g) The use of postal facilities provided for in Article     ;

    (h) The use of utilities and services in accordance with those priorities, conditions, rates, or tariffs accorded the United States armed forces by Article paragraph 3, relating to utilities and services;

    (i) Exemption from the laws and regulations of Korea with respect to licensing and registration of business and corporations.

    4. The arrival, departure, and place of residence in Korea of such persons shall from time to time be notified by the United States armed forces to the Korean authorities.

    5. Upon certification by an authorized representative of the United States armed forces, depreciable assets, except houses, held, used or transferred by such persons exclusively for the execution of contracts referred to in paragraph 1 shall not be subject to taxes or similar

56

0108

charges of Korea.

6. Upon certification by an authorized representative
of the United States armed forces, such persons shall be
exempt from taxation in Korea on the holding, use, transfer
by death, or transfer to persons or agencies entitled to
tax exemption under this Agreement, of movable property,
tangible or intangible, the presence of which in Korea
is due solely to the temporary presence of these persons
in Korea, provided that such exemption shall not apply to
property held for the purpose of investment or the conduct
of other business than those executing contracts as described
in paragraph 1 of this Article in Korea or to any intangible
property registered in Korea.

7. The persons referred to in paragraph 1 shall
not be liable to pay income or corporation taxes to the
Government of Korea or to any other taxing agency in
Korea on any income derived under a contract with the
Government of the United States in connection with the
construction, maintenance or operation of any of the
facilities or areas covered by this Agreement. Persons
in Korea in connection with the execution of such a
contract with the United States shall not be liable to
pay any Korean taxes to the Government of Korea or to
any taxing agency in Korea on income derived from sources

0109

outside of Korea nor shall periods during which such
persons are in Korea be considered periods of residence
or domicile in Korea for the purposes of Korean taxation.
The provisions of this paragraph do not exempt such
persons from payment of income or corporation taxes on
income derived from Korean sources, other than those
sources referred to in the first sentence of this paragraph,
nor do they exempt such persons who claim Korean residence
for United States income tax purposes from payment of
Korean taxes on income.

8. The Korean authorities shall have the primary
right to exercise jurisdiction over the contractors and
their employees and the dependents of such persons referred to in paragraph 1 of this Article
in relation to offences committed in the Republic of Korea
and punishable by the law of the Republic of Korea. In
those cases in which the Korean authorities decide not to
exercise such jurisdiction they shall notify the military
authorities of the United States as soon as possible.
Upon such notification the military authorities of the
United States shall have the right to exercise such
jurisdiction over the persons referred to as is conferred
on them by the law of the United States.

58

0110

## Agreed Minutes

1. This Article shall not prevent the persons referred to in paragraph 1 from employing third-country nationals who shall, except as provided in paragraph 2, and sub-paragraphs (a), (d), (e), (f), (g) of paragraph 3, be subject to the laws and regulations of the Republic of Korea.

2. The dependents of the persons and their employees, including third-country nationals, shall, except those benefits as provided in sub-paragraphs (d), (f) and (g), be subject to the laws and regulations of the Republic of Korea.

3. There is no obligation under this Article to grant exemption from taxes payable in respect of the use and ownership of private vehicles.

0111

59

Article

1. The United States armed forces and the organizations provided for in Article ___ may employ civilian personnel under this Agreement. Such civilian personnel shall be nationals of the Republic of Korea.

2. ~~Local labour requirements of the United States armed forces and of the said organizations shall be satisfied with the~~ *to the maximum extent practicable* ~~with the assistance of the Korean authorities.~~ *In case the United States Military Authorities exercise* The obligations for the withholding and payment of income tax and social security contributions, and, unless otherwise agreed upon in this article, the conditions of employment and work, such as those relating to wages and supplementary payments, the conditions for the protection of workers, and the rights of workers concerning labour relations shall be those laid down by the legislation of the Republic of Korea.

3. Should the United States armed forces dismiss a worker and a decision of a court or a Labour Commission of the Republic of Korea to the effect that the contract of employment has not terminated become final, the following procedures shall apply:

(a) The United States armed forces shall be informed by the Government of the Republic of Korea of

2. Local labour requirements of the United States armed forces and of the said organizations shall be satisfied to the maximum extent practicable with the assistance of the Korean authorities. In case the United States military authorities exercise direct recruitment and employment of labors, they shall provide the Republic of Korea with the relevant information required for labor administration.

0112

24

the decision of the court or Commission;

(b) Should the United States armed forces not desire to return the worker to duty, they shall so notify the Government of the Republic of Korea within ten days after being informed by the latter of the decision of the court or Commission, and may temporarily withhold the worker from duty;

(c) Upon such notification, the Government of the Republic of Korea and the United States armed forces shall consult together without delay with a view to finding a practical solution of the case;

(d) Should such a solution not be reached within a period of thirty days from the date of commencement of the consultations under (c) above, the worker will not be entitled to return to duty. In such case, the Government of the United States shall pay to the Government of the Republic of Korea an amount equal to the cost of employment of the worker for a period of time to be agreed between the two Governments through the Joint Committee.

4. The United States Government shall ensure that the contractors referred to in Article _____ employ the Korean personnel to the maximum extent practicable in connection with their activities under this Agreement.

0113

The provisions of paragraph 2 of this Article shall be applied to the employment by the contractors of the said Korean personnel.

## AGREED MINUTES

1. It is understood that the Government of the Republic of Korea shall be reimbursed for costs incurred under relevant contracts between appropriate authorities of the Korean Government and the United States armed forces or the organizations provided for in Article _____ in connection with the employment of workers to be provided for the United States armed forces or such organizations.

2. It is understood that the term "the legislation of the Republic of Korea" mentioned in Paragraph 2, Article _____ includes decisions of the courts and the Labour Commissions of the Republic of Korea, subject to the provisions of Paragraph 3, Article _____.

3. It is understood that the provisions of Article ___, Paragraph 3 shall only apply to discharges for security reasons including disturbing the maintenance of military discipline within the facilities and areas used by the United States armed forces.

0114

26

## Labor Article

### Paragraph 2

The employers provided for in the paragraph 1 shall recruit and employ to the maximum extent practicable with the assistance of the authorities of the Republic of Korea. In case employers exercise direct recruitment and employment of employees, employers shall provide such relevant information as may be necessary for labour administration to the Office of Labour Affairs of the Republic of Korea.

### Paragraph 3

The conditions of employment and work, such as those relating to wages and supplementary payments, the conditions for the protection and welfare of employees, compensations, and the rights of employees, concerning labor relations shall, unless otherwise agreed upon in this Article, conform with those laid down by the legislation of the Republic of Korea.

0115

2/7

제65차[회의]( 69. 10. 23)[제10](handwritten) <u>Agreed Minute</u>

With regard to any dispute between the employers
except the persons referred to in Paragraph 1, Article _____,
and employees or labor unions which cannot be settled through
the use of existing procedures of the U.S. armed forces,
settlement shall be accomplished in the following manner.

(a). The dispute shall be referred to the Office of
Labor Affairs, Ministry of Health and Social Affairs, Republic
of Korea, for conciliation.

(b) In the event that the dispute is not settled by
the procedure described in (a) above, the matter may be
referred to a Special Labor Committee appointed by the Office
of Labor Affairs, Ministry of Health and Social Affairs,
Republic of Korea, for mediation. This committee shall be
tri-partite in composition and shall be consisted of equal
representation from Labor Unions, the Office of Labor
Affairs, and the United States armed forces.

(c) In the event that the dispute is not settled
by the procedures described in (a) and (b) above, the dispute
shall be referred to the Joint Committee, or such sub-
committee as may be established thereunder for arbitration
to resolve the dispute. The decisions of the Joint Committee
or sub-committee thereunder shall be binding.

0116

28

Agreed Minute Re Paragraph 3(b)

Revised Paragraph 1

   1.  At the request of the United States, the Government of the Republic of Korea waives in favor of the
United States the primary right granted to the Korean
authorities under sub-paragraph (b) of Paragraph 3 of
this Article in cases of concurrent jurisdiction, in
accordance with Paragraphs 2,3,4,5,6 and 7 of this Minute.

Revised Paragraph 4

   4.  If, pursuant to Paragraph 3 of this Minute, the
competent Korean authorities have recalled the waiver
in a specific case and in such case an understanding
cannot be reached in discussions between the authorities
concerned, the Government of the United States may make
representations to the Government of the Republic of
Korea through diplomatic channels.  The Government of
the Republic of Korea, giving due consideration to the
interests of Korean administration of justice and to
the interests of the Government of the United States,
shall resolve the disagreement in the exercise of its
authority in the field of foreign affairs. The recall
of waiver shall be final and conclusive unless the
statement for recall referred to in Paragraph 3 of this

- 1 -

29

0117

Minute is withdrawn by the Government of the Republic
of Korea through consultation between both Governments.

Paragraph 6

6.  Trials of cases in which the authorities of
the Republic of Korea waive the primary right to
exercise jurisdiction, and trials of cases involving
offenses described in paragraph 3(a) (ii) committed
against the State or nationals of the Republic of Korea
shall be held promptly in the Republic of Korea within
a reasonable distance from the place where the offenses
are alleged to have taken place unless other arrangements are mutually agreed upon.  Representatives of the
Republic of Korea may be present at such trials.
(U.S. draft proposed at the 67th meeting)

- 2 -

0118

30

<u>Agreed Minute #1 Re Paragraph 3(a) (ii)</u>

1. Where a member of the United States armed forces
or civilian component is charged with an offense, a
certificate issued by competent authorities of the United
States armed forces stating that the alleged offense,
if committed by him, arose out of an act or omission
done in the performance of official duty shall be
sufficient evidence of the fact for the purpose of
determining primary jurisdiction.

In those exceptional cases where the chief prosecutor
for the Republic of Korea considers that there is
proof contrary to a certificate of official duty, it
<u>shall</u> be made the subject of review through discussions
between appropriate officials of the Government of the
Republic of Korea and the diplomatic mission of the
United States in the Republic of Korea.

<u>Agreed Minute #2 Re Paragraph 3(a)(ii)</u>

2. The term "official duty" as used in Article ___
and the agreed minute is not meant to include all acts
by members of the Armed Forces and the civilian component
during periods when they are on duty, but is meant to
apply only to acts which are required to be done as

- 1 -

0119

functions of those duties which the individuals are
performing. Thus, a substantial departure from the
acts a person is required to perform in a particular
duty usually will indicate an act outside of his "official
duty." (U.S. draft proposed at the 49th meeting)

- 2 -

0120

5.     (a) The military authorities of the United States
and the authorities of the Republic of Korea shall
assist each other in the arrest of members of the United
States armed forces, the civilian component, or their
dependents in the territory of the Republic of Korea and
in handing them over to the authority which is to have
custody in accordance with the following provisions.

(b) The authorities of the Republic of Korea shall
notify promptly the military authorities of the United
States of the arrest of any member of the United States
armed forces, or civilian component, or a dependent.
The military authorities of the United States shall
promptly notify the authorities of the Republic of Korea
of the arrest of a member of the United States armed
forces, the civilian component, or a dependent in any
case in which the Republic of Korea has the primary
right to exercise jurisdiction.

(c) The custody of an accused member of the United
States armed forces or civilian component, or of a dependent,
over whom the Republic of Korea is to exercise jurisdiction
shall, if he is in the hands of the military authorities
of the United States, remain with the military authorities

- 1 -

0121

of the United States pending the conclusion of all
judicial proceedings and until custody is requested by
the authorities of the Republic of Korea. If he is in
the hands of the Republic of Korea, he shall, on request,
be handed over to the military authorities of the United
States and remain in their custody pending completion
of all judicial proceedings and until custody is requested
by the authorities of the Republic of Korea. When an
accused has been in the custody of the military authorities of the United States, the military authorities of
the United States may transfer custody to the authorities
of the Republic of Korea at any time, and shall give
sympathetic consideration to any request for the transfer
of custody which may be made by the authorities of the
Republic of Korea in specific cases. The military authorities of the United States shall promptly make any such
accused available to the authorities of the Republic
of Korea upon their request for purposes of investigation
and trial, and shall take all appropriate measures to
that end and to prevent any prejudice to the course of
justice. They shall take full account of any special
request regarding custody made by the authorities of
the the Republic of Korea. The authorities of the
Republic of Korea shall give sympathetic consideration

- 2 -

0122

34

to a request from the military authorities of the United
States for assistance in maintaining custody of an accused
member of the United States armed forces, the civilian
component, or a dependent.

(d) In respect of offenses solely against the security
of the Republic of Korea provided in Paragraph 2(c),
an accused shall be in the custody of the authorities
of the Republic of Korea.

0123

35

<u>Revised Korean Draft of Labor Article</u>
(The underlined parts are modification)

1. The United States Armed Forces and the organizations provided for in Article ____ (<u>hereinafter referred to as</u> "employer") may employ civilian personnel (<u>hereinafter referred to as "employee"</u>) under this Agreement. Such civilian personnel shall be nationals of the Republic of Korea.

2. <u>The employers may recruit, employ and administer their personnel. Recruitment services of the Government of the Republic of Korea shall be utilized to the maximum extent practicable.</u> In case employers accomplish direct recruitment of employees, <u>the United States Armed Forces</u> shall provide such relevant information as may be required for labor administration to the Office of Labor Affairs of the Republic of Korea.

3. <u>Except as may otherwise be mutually agreed</u>, the conditions of employment and work, such as those relating to wages and supplementary payments, the conditions for the protection and welfare of employees, compensations, and the rights of employees, concerning labor relations shall conform with those laid down by the legislation of the Republic of Korea.

4. <u>Employers shall insure the just and timely resolution of employee grievances.</u>

5. (a) <u>Should the Republic of Korea adopt measures allocating labor, the United States Armed Forces shall be accorded allocation privileges no less favorable than those enjoyed by the Armed Forces of the Republic of Korea.</u>

0124

21

(b) In the event of a national emergency such as war, hostilities, or other imminent situations, the employees who have acquired skills essential to the mission of the United States Armed Forces may, upon request of the United States Armed Forces, be deferred from Republic of Korea military service or other compulsory services. The United States Armed Forces shall in advance furnish to the Republic of Korea lists of those employees deemed essential.

6. Members of the civilian component shall not be subject to Korean laws or regulations with respect to their terms and conditions of employment.

## AGREED MINUTES

1. The undertaking of the United States to conform with those laid down by the legislation of the Republic of Korea does not imply any waiver by the United States Government of its immunities under international law.

2. Employers shall withhold from the pay of their employees, and pay over to the Government of the Republic of Korea, withholdings required by the income tax legislation of the Republic of Korea.

3. It is understood that the Government of the Republic of Korea shall be reimbursed for direct costs incurred in providing assistance pursuant to Paragraph 2.

4. In case where it is impossible for the employers to conform, on account of the military requirements of the United States Armed Forces, with the Korean labor legislation under the provisions of Paragraph 3, the matter shall in advance be referred to the Joint Committee for mutual agreement.

The Republic of Korea will give due consideration to the military requirements of the United States Armed Forces.

0125

22

5. With regard to any dispute between the employers and any employees or labor unions which cannot be settled through the use of existing procedures of the United States Armed Forces, settlement shall be accomplished in the following manner:

(a) The dispute shall be referred to the Office of Labor Affairs of the Republic of Korea for conciliation.

(b) In the event that the dispute is not settled by the procedures described in (a) above, the dispute shall be referred to a special committee designated by the Joint Committee for further conciliation efforts.

(c) In the event that the dispute is not settled by the procedures outlined above, the Joint Committee will resolve the dispute. The decisions of the Joint Committee shall be binding.

(d) Neither employee organizations nor employees shall engage in any practices disruptive of normal work requirements unless the cooling-off period set forth in Article 14 of the Korean Labor Dispute Law has elapsed after the dispute is referred to the Office of Labor Affairs mentioned in (a) above.

(e) Failure of any employee organization or employee to abide by the decision of the Joint Committee on any dispute, or engaging in practices disruptive of normal work requirements in violation of the provisions of Paragraph (d) above, shall be considered cause for the depriviation of the rights and protection accorded by the relevant laws of the Republic of Korea.

0126

23

## LABOR ARTICLE

(Underlining indicates modifications from Korean
draft of the Labor Article tabled at 69th session)

1.   In this Article the expression:

     (a) "employer" refers to the United States Armed Forces
(including non-appropriated fund activities).

     (b) "employee" refers to any civilian (other than a
member of the civilian component of the United States
Armed Forces) employed by an employer. Such civilian
personnel shall be nationals of the Republic of Korea.

2.   Employers may recruit, employ and administer their
personnel. Recruitment services of the Government of the
Republic of Korea shall be utilized to the maximum extent
practicable. In case employers accomplish direct recruitment of employees, The United States Armed Forces shall
provide such relevant information as may be required for
labor administration to the Office of Labor Affairs of the
Republic of Korea.

3.   To the extent not inconsistent with the provisions of
this Article or except as may otherwise be mutually agreed,
the conditions of employment and work, such as those relating
to wages and supplementary payments, the conditions for the
protection and welfare of employees, compensations, and the
rights of employees, concerning labor relations shall
conform with those laid down by the labor legislation of
the Republic of Korea.

4.   (a) With regard to any dispute between employers and
any employees or labor unions which cannot be settled through
the use of existing procedures of the United States Armed
Forces, settlement shall be accomplished in the following
manner:

0127

17

(1) The dispute shall be referred to the Office of Labor Affairs of the Republic of Korea for conciliation.

(2) In the event that the dispute is not settled by the procedures described in (1) above, the dispute shall be referred to a special committee designated by the Joint Committee for further conciliation efforts.

(3) In the event that the dispute is not settled by the procedures outlined above, the Joint Committee will resolve the dispute. The decisions of the Joint Committee shall be binding.

(4) Neither employee organizations nor employees shall engage in any practices disruptive of normal work requirements unless the cooling-off period set forth in Article 14 of the Korean Labor Dispute Law has elapsed after the dispute is referred to the specially-designated committee mentioned in (2) above.

(5) Failure of any employee organization or employee to abide by the decision of the Joint Committee on any dispute, or engaging in practices disruptive of normal work requirements in violation of the provisions laid down in (4) above, shall be considered cause for the depriviation of the rights and protection accorded by the relevant labor legislation of the Republic of Korea.

(b) The right concerning strike shall be accorded to employees except those whose exercise of the right is prohibited by the Joint Committee.

0128

18

5.    In the event of a national emergency, such as war, hostilities or situations where war or hostilities is imminent, the application of this Article shall be limited in accordance with the emergency measures taken by the Government of the Republic of Korea, and, in addition, the following arrangements will be made:

(a) Should the Government of the Republic of Korea adopt measures allocating labor, the United States Armed Forces shall be accorded allocation privileges no less favorable than those enjoyed by the Armed Forces of the Republic of Korea.

(b) Employees who have acquired skills essential to the mission of the United States Armed Forces will, upon request of the United States Armed Forces and through mutual agreement, be deferred from Republic of Korea military service or other compulsory services. The United States Armed Forces shall in advance furnish to the Government of the Republic of Korea lists of those employees deemed necessary.

6.    Members of the civilian component of the United States Armed Forces shall not be subject to Korean laws or regulations with respect to their terms and conditions of employment.

## AGREED MINUTES

1.    The undertaking of the United States to conform to the labor legislation of the Republic of Korea does not imply any waiver by the United States Government of its immunities under international law.

2.    It is understood that the Government of the Republic of Korea shall be reimbursed for direct costs incurred in providing assistance pursuant to Paragraph 2.

0128-1

13

## LABOR ARTICLE

(Underlining indicates modifications from
the U.S. draft tabled at 89th session)

1. (b) ... Such civilian personnel shall be nationals
of the Republic of Korea.

3. To the extent not inconsistent with the provisions
of this Article or the military requirements of the
United States Armed Forces, the conditions of employment,
compensation, and labor-management relations established
by the United States Armed Forces for their employees
shall conform with provisions of labor legislation
of the Republic of Korea.

4. (a)(5) ..... to the Joint Committee, as stipulated
in subparagraph (2) above.

5. (b) ...... be deferred, through mutual consultation,
from Republic of Korea ....

Agreed Minutes

4. When employers cannot conform with provisions of
labor legislation of the Republic of Korea applicable
under Paragraph 3 on account of the military requirements
of the United States Armed Forces, the matter shall be
referred, in advance whenever possible, to the Joint
Committee for mutual agreement.

5. A union or other employee group shall be recognized unless its objectives are inimical to the common interests of the United States and the Republic of Korea. Membership or non-membership in such group shall not be a factor in employment or other actions affecting employees.

0130

16

## 2. 미측

0131

# PREAMBLE

The United States of America and the Republic of Korea, pursuant to Article IV of the Mutual Defense Treaty between the United States of America and the Republic of Korea signed at Washington on October 1, 1953, have entered into this Agreement regarding facilities and areas and the status of United States armed forces in the Republic of Korea in terms as set forth below:

0132

1.49

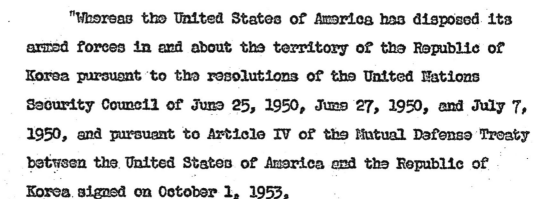

"Whereas the United States of America has disposed its armed forces in and about the territory of the Republic of Korea pursuant to the resolutions of the United Nations Security Council of June 25, 1950, June 27, 1950, and July 7, 1950, and pursuant to Article IV of the Mutual Defense Treaty between the United States of America and the Republic of Korea signed on October 1, 1953.

Therefore, the United States of America and the Republic of Korea, in order to strengthen the close bonds of mutual interest between their two countries, have entered into this Agreement regarding facilities and areas and the status of United States armed forces in the Republic of Korea in terms as set forth below:"

0133

148

October 19, 1962

## ARTICLE I

## DEFINITIONS

In this Agreement the expression

(a)  "members of the United States armed forces" means
the personnel on active duty belonging to the land, sea or
air armed services of the United States of America when in
the territory of the Republic of Korea except for those for
whom status has otherwise been provided.

(b)  "civilian component" means the civilian persons who
are in the employ of, serving with, or accompanying the United
States armed forces in the Republic of Korea, but excludes
persons who are ordinarily resident in the Republic of Korea
or who are mentioned in paragraph                    of Article

(c)  "dependents" means

(1)  Spouse and children under 21;

(2)  Parents, and children over 21, or other relatives
dependent for over half their support upon a
member of the United States armed forces or
civilian component.

0134

143

DEFINITIONS ARTICLE

PROPOSED ADDITIONAL SENTENCE TO SUBPARAGRAPH (b)


For the purposes of the Agreement only, dual nationals, i.e. persons having both United States and Korean nationality, who are brought into the Republic of Korea by the United States shall be considered as United States nationals.

DEFINITIONS ARTICLE

AGREED MINUTE

With regard to Article 1(a), the expression "members of
the United States armed forces" does not include personnel on
active duty belonging to the United States land, sea or air armed
services for whom status has otherwise been provided such as
personnel for whom status is provided in the Military Advisory
Group Agreement signed on January 26, 1950, and personnel of
service attache offices in the Embassy of the United States of
America.

0136

# DEFINITIONS ARTICLE

## AGREED MINUTE

정자로

With regard to subparagraph (b), it is recognized that persons possessing certain skills, not ~~readily~~ available from United States or Korean sources, who are nationals of third states may be brought into Korea by the United States armed forces solely for employment by the United States armed forces. Such persons, and third state nationals who are employed by, serving with, or accompanying the United States armed forces in Korea when this agreement becomes effective, shall be considered as members of the civilian component.

0137

146

## DEFINITIONS ARTICLE

**Agreed Minute:**

"The personnel referred to in subparagraph (a) for whom status has otherwise been provided (include) personnel of the United States armed forces attached to the United States Embassy and personnel for whom status has been provided in the Military Advisory ~~Assistance~~ Group Agreement of January 26, 1950 as amended."

0138

142

*Communications in the facilities & areas.*

SOF B-7

1. A Joint Committee shall be established as the means for consultation between the Government of the United States and the Government of the Republic of Korea on all matters requiring mutual consultation regarding the implementation of this Agreement *except when* ~~shall otherwise provided~~. (In particular, the Joint Committee shall serve as the means for consultation in determining the facilities and areas in the Republic of Korea which are required for the use of the United States in carrying out the purposes of this Agreement.)

2. The Joint Committee shall be composed of a representative of the Government of the United States and a representative of the Government of the Republic of Korea, each of whom shall have one or more deputies and a staff. The Joint Committee shall determine its own procedures, and arrange for such auxiliary organs and administrative services as may be required. The Joint Committee shall be so organized that it may meet immediately at any time at the request of the representative of either the Government of the United States or the Government of the Republic of Korea.

3. If the Joint Committee is unable to resolve any matter, it shall refer that matter to the respective Governments for further consideration through appropriate channels.

0139

138

## ENTRY AND EXIT

1.    The United States may bring into the Republic of Korea persons who are members of the United States armed forces, the civilian component, and their dependents, subject to the provisions of this Article. [ The Government of the Republic of Korea will be notified at regular intervals, in accordance with procedures to be agreed between the two Governments, of numbers and categories of persons entering and departing.

2.    Members of the United States armed forces shall be exempt from Korean passport and visa laws and regulations. Members of the United States armed forces, the civilian component, and their dependents shall be exempt from Korean laws and regulations on the registration and control of aliens, but shall not be considered as acquiring any right to permanent residence or domicile in the territory of the Republic of Korea.

3.    Upon entry into or departure from the Republic of Korea members of the United States armed forces shall be in possession of the following documents:

(a)    personal identity card showing name, date of birth, rank and service number, service, and photograph; and

(b)    individual or collective travel order certifying to the status of the individual or group as a member or members of the United States armed forces and to the travel ordered.

139                                   0140

For purposes of their identification while in the Republic of Korea, members of the United States armed forces shall be in possession of the foregoing personal identity card which must be presented on request to the appropriate Korean authorities.

*not surrender.*

4.  Members of the civilian component, their dependents, and the dependents of members of the United States armed forces shall be in possession of appropriate documentation issued by the United States authorities so that their status may be verified by Korean authorities upon their entry into or departure from the Republic of Korea, or while in the Republic of Korea.

5.  If the status of any person brought into the Republic of Korea under paragraph 1 of this Article is altered so that he would no longer be entitled to such admission, the United States authorities shall notify the Korean authorities and shall, if such person be required by the Korean authorities to leave the Republic of Korea, assure that transportation from the Republic of Korea will be provided within a reasonable time at no cost to the Government of the Republic of Korea.

6.  If the Government of the Republic of Korea has requested the removal from its Territory of a member of the United States armed forces or civilian component or has made an expulsion order

*expulsion order*

*explanatory note.*

0141

140

against an ex-member of the United States armed forces or the
civilian component or against a dependent of a member or an ex-
member, the authorities of the United States shall be responsible
for receiving the person concerned into its own territory or otherwise disposing of him outside the Republic of Korea. ) This paragraph shall apply only to persons who are not ordinarily resident
in the Republic of Korea and have entered the Republic of Korea
as members of the United States armed forces or civilian component
or for the purpose of becoming such members, and to the dependents
of such persons.

*[handwritten: not nationals of Korea]*

*[handwritten: Practical arrangements]*

0142

141

## Agreed Minutes to Article

### (Entry and Exit)

1. With regard to Paragraph 3(a), United States Armed Forces law enforcement personnel (such as MP, SP, AP, CID and CIC), who engage in military police activities in the Republic of Korea, will carry a bilingual identity card containing the bearer's name, position, and the fact that he is a member of a law enforcement agency. This card will be shown upon request to persons concerned when the bearer is in the performance of duty.

2. The United States Armed Forces will furnish, upon request, to Korean authorities the form of the identification cards of the members of the United States Armed Forces, the civilian component, and their dependents and descriptions of the various uniforms of the United States Armed Forces in the Republic of Korea.

3. The final sentence of Paragraph 3 means that members of the United States Armed Forces will display their identity cards upon request but will not be required to surrender them to Korean authorities.

4. Following a change of status pursuant to Paragraph 5, the responsibilities of the United States authorities under Paragraph 6 shall arise only if the expulsion order is issued within a reasonable time after the notice under Paragraph 5 has been communicated to the Korean authorities.

0143

*just too vague*

*142*

ARTICLE    (Customs)

2.    All materials, supplies and equipment imported by the United States armed forces, including their authorized procurement agencies and their non-appropriated fund organizations provided for in Article ___ , for the official use of the United States armed forces or for the use of forces logistically supported by the United States armed forces or for the use of the members of the United States armed forces, the civilian component, or their dependents shall be permitted entry into the Republic of Korea free from customs duties and other such charges. Similarly, materials, supplies and equipment which are imported by others than the United States armed forces but are to be used exclusively by the United States armed forces and/or forces logistically supported by the United States armed forces or are ultimately to be incorporated into articles or facilities to be used by such forces shall be permitted entry into the Republic of Korea free from customs duties and other such charges. Appropriate certification shall be made by the United States armed forces with respect to the importation of materials, supplies and equipment for the foregoing specified purposes.

Tuesday 2/1

Subject to mutually satisfactory

0144

127

ARTICLE    (Customs)

1.    Save as provided in this Agreement, members of the United States armed forces, the civilian component, and their dependents shall be subject to the laws and regulations administered by the customs authorities of the Republic of Korea.

2.    All materials, supplies and equipment imported by the United States armed forces, including their authorized procurement agencies and their non-appropriated fund organizations provided for in Article     , for the official use of the United States armed forces or for the use of the members of the United States armed forces, the civilian component, and their dependents, and materials, supplies and equipment which are to be used exclusively by the United States armed forces or are ultimately to be incorporated into articles or facilities used by such forces, shall be permitted entry into the Republic of Korea; such entry shall be free from customs duties and other such charges. Appropriate certification shall be made that such materials, supplies and equipment are being imported by the United States armed forces, (including their authorized procurement agencies and their non-appropriated fund organizations) provided for in Article )    , or, in the case of materials, supplies and equipment to be used exclusively by the United States armed forces or ultimately to be incorporated into articles or facilities used by such forces, that delivery thereof is to be taken by the United States armed forces for the purposes specified above. The exemptions provided in this paragraph shall extend to materials, supplies and equipment imported by the United States armed forces for the use of other armed forces in Korea which receive logistical support from the United States armed forces.

0145

152   주한미군지위협정(SOFA) 서명 및 발효 18

3.   Property consigned to and for the personal use of members of the United States armed forces, the civilian component, and their dependents, shall be subject to customs duties and other such charges, except that no duties or charges shall be paid with respect to:

(a)   Furniture, household goods, and personal effects for their private use imported by the members of the United States armed forces or civilian component when they first arrive to serve in the Republic of Korea or by their dependents when they first arrive for reunion with members of such forces or civilian component;

(b)   Vehicles and parts imported by members of the United States armed forces or civilian component for the private use of themselves or their dependents;

(c)   Reasonable quantities of personal effects and household goods of a type which would ordinarily be purchased in the United States for the private use of members of the United States armed forces, civilian component, and their dependents, which are mailed into the Republic of Korea through United States military post offices.

4.   The exemptions granted in paragraphs 2 and 3 shall apply only to cases of importation of goods and shall not be interpreted as refunding customs duties and domestic excises collected by the customs authorities at the time of entry in cases of purchase of goods on which such duties and excises have already been collected.

0146

129

5.    Customs examination shall not be made in the following cases:

(a)    Members of the United States armed forces under orders entering or leaving the Republic of Korea;

(b)    Official documents under official seal and mail in United States military postal channels;

(c)    Military cargo consigned to the United States armed forces, ~~including their authorized procurement agencies and their non-appropriated fund organizations provided for in Article~~ .

6.    Except as such disposal may be authorized by the United States and Korean authorities in accordance with mutually agreed conditions, goods imported into the Republic of Korea free of duty shall not be disposed of in the Republic of Korea to persons not entitled to import such goods free of duty.

7.    Goods imported into the Republic of Korea free from customs duties and other such charges pursuant to paragraphs 2 and 3, may be re-exported free from customs duties and other such charges.

8.    The United States armed forces, in cooperation with Korean authorities, shall take such steps as are necessary to prevent abuse of privileges granted to the United States armed forces, members of such forces, the civilian component, and their dependents in accordance with this Article.

9. (a)    In order to prevent offenses against laws and regulations administered by the customs authorities of the Government of the Republic of Korea, the Korean authorities and the United States armed forces shall assist each other in the conduct of inquiries and the collection of evidence.

(b)    The United States armed forces shall render all assistance within their power to ensure that articles liable to seizure by, or on behalf of, the customs authorities of the Government of the Republic of Korea are handed to those authorities.

(c)    The United States armed forces shall render all assistance within their power to ensure the payment of duties, taxes, and penalties payable by members of such forces or of the civilian component, or their dependents.

(d)    Vehicles and articles belonging to the United States armed forces seized by the customs authorities of the Government of the Republic of Korea in connection with an offense against its customs or fiscal laws or regulations shall be handed over to the appropriate authorities of the forces concerned.

0148

(3)

## AGREED MINUTES TO ARTICLE _____ (Customs)

1. The quantity of goods imported under paragraph 2 by non-appropriated fund organisations of the United States armed forces for the use of the members of the United States armed forces, the civilian component, and their dependents shall be limited to the extent reasonably required for such use.

2. Paragraph 3(a) does not require concurrent shipment of goods with travel of owner nor does it require single loading or shipment. In this connection, members of the United States armed forces or civilian component and their dependents may import free of duty their personal and household effects during a period of six months from the date of their first arrival.

3. The term "military cargo" as used in paragraph 5(c) is not confined to arms and equipment but refers to all cargo consigned to the United States armed forces, (including their authorized procurement agencies and their non-appropriated fund organizations provided for in Article _____).

4. The United States armed forces will take every practicable measure to ensure that goods will not be imported into the Republic of Korea by or for the members of the United States armed forces, the civilian component, or their dependents, the entry of which would be in violation of Korean customs laws and regulations. The United States armed forces will promptly notify the Korean customs authorities whenever the entry of such goods is discovered.

0149

132

5.   The Korean customs authorities may, if they consider
that there has been an abuse or infringement in connection with
the entry of goods under Article      , take up the matter with
the appropriate authorities of the United States armed forces.

6.   The words "The United States armed forces shall render
all assistance within their power," etc., in paragraph  9(b) and
(c) refer to reasonable and practicable measures by the United
States armed forces authorized by United States law and service
regulations.

*delete*

0150

133

*Customs*

## Agreed Minute — No- 7.

7. It is understood that the duty free treatment provided in paragraph 2 shall apply to materials, supplies, and equipment imported for sale through commissaries and non-appropriated fund organizations, under such regulations as the United States armed forces may promulgate, to those individuals and organizations referred to in Article _____ and its Agreed Minute.

0151

134

Proposed additional sentence, Agreed Minute #3:

"Pertinent information on cargo consigned to non-appropriated fund organizations will be furnished authorities of the Republic of Korea upon request through the Joint Committee."

*promptly*

AGREED MINUTE 3 (Revised)

55th session
June 19, '64

The term "military cargo" as used in paragraph 5(c) is not confined to arms and equipment but refers to all cargo consigned to the United States armed forces (including their authorized procurement agencies and their non-appropriated fund organizations provided for in Article_____). Pertinent information on cargo consigned to non-appropriated fund organizations will be furnished on a routine basis to authorities of the Republic of Korea. The extent of the pertinent information will be determined by the Joint Committee.

0153

136

5. Customs examinations shall not be made in the following cases:

    a. Members of the US armed forces under orders, other than leave orders, entering or leaving the Republic of Korea.

tabled 1964. 7. 8.

Accepted 1964. 7. 8. (57th Session)

0154

137

*and communication systems*

1. All civil and military air traffic control shall be developed in close coordination and shall be integrated to the extent necessary for the operation of this Agreement. Procedures, and any subsequent changes thereto, necessary to effect this coordination and integration will be established by arrangement between the appropriate authorities of the two Governments.

2. The United States is authorized to establish, construct and maintain aids to navigation for vessels and aircraft, both visual and electronic as required, throughout the Republic of Korea and in the territorial waters thereof. Such navigation aids shall conform generally to the system in use in Korea. The United States and Korean authorities which have established navigation aids shall duly notify each other of their positions and characteristics and shall give advance notification where practicable before making any changes in them or establishing additional navigation aids.

*Air Traffic control our proposal* — *yes*

*through mutual Agreement*

*# through arrangement between appropriate authorities of the both Governments*

125

# NAVIGATIONAL AIDS ARTICLE

<u>Agreed Minute:</u>

"Installation by the United States Armed Forces of
/permanent/ navigational aids for vessels and aircraft outside of areas and facilities in use by the United States
Armed Forces ~~will~~ shall be effected in accordance with the ~~pro~~
~~cedures established under paragraph 1 of Article △]~~"

arrangements between the two governments
through the joint committee provided for
in article ____.

126

'0156

한·미국 간의 상호방위조약 제4조에 의한 시설과 구역 및 한국에서의 미국군대의 지위에 관한 협정(SOFA)
전59권. 1966.7.9 서울에서 서명 : 1967.2.9 발효(조약 232호) (V.47 한·미국 양측 교섭안)  163

ARTICLE _____

    1. Each Party waives all its claims against the other Party for damage to any property owned by it and used by its land, sea or air armed forces, if such damage:

    (a) was caused by a member or an employee of the armed forces of the other Party in the performance of his official duties; or

    (b) arose from the use of any vehicle, vessel or aircraft owned by the other Party and used by its armed forces, provided either that the vehicle, vessel or aircraft causing the damage was being used for official purposes, or that the damage was caused to property being so used.

    Claims by one Party against the other Party for maritime salvage shall be waived provided that the vessel or cargo salvaged was owned by a Party and being used by its armed forces for official purposes.

    2. In the case of damage caused or arising as stated in paragraph 1 to other property owned by a Party:

    (a) each Party waives its claim up to the amount of $1400 or its equivalent in Korean currency at the rate of exchange provided for in the Agreed

0157

Minute to Article ＿＿＿ at the time the claim is filed.

(b) claims in excess of the amount stated in subparagraph (a) shall be settled by the Party against which the claim is made in accordance with its domestic law.

3. For the purpose of paragraphs 1 and 2 of this Article, the expression "owned by a Party" in the case of a vessel includes a vessel on bare boat charter to that Party or requisitioned by it on bare boat charter terms or seized by it in prize (except to the extent that the risk of loss or liability is borne by some other person than such Party).

4. Each Party waives all its claims against the other Party for injury or death suffered by any member of its armed forces while such member was engaged in the performance of his official duties.

5. Claims (other than contractual claims) arising out of acts or omissions of members or employees of the United States armed forces done in the performance of official duty, or out of any other act, omission or occurrence for which the United States armed forces are legally responsible, and causing damage in the

75

0158

Republic of Korea to third parties other than the
two Governments shall be processed and settled in
accordance with the applicable provisions of United
States law. The United States Government shall
entertain other non-contractual claims against members
of the United States armed forces or of the civilian
component and may offer an ex gratia payment in such
cases and in such amount as is determined by the appropriate United States authorities.

6. (a) A member or employee of the United States
armed forces shall not be afforded immunity from the
jurisdiction of the civil courts of Korea except: (1)
in a matter arising out of acts or omissions done in
the performance of official duty; or (2) in respect
to any claim where there has been payment in full
satisfaction of the claim.

(b) In the case of any private movable property,
excluding that in use by the United States armed forces,
which is subject to compulsory execution under Korean
law, and is within the facilities and areas in use by
the United States armed forces, the United States
authorities shall, upon the request of the Korean

0159

courts, render all assistance within their power to
see that such property is turned over to the Korean
authorities.

7. The authorities of the United States and Korea
shall cooperate in the procurement of evidence for a
fair disposition of claims under this Article.

8. Paragraphs 2 and 5 of this Article shall
apply only to claims arising incident to noncombat
activities.

9. For the purposes of this Article, each Party
shall have the right to determine whether a member or
employee of its armed forces was engaged in the
performance of official duties and whether property
owned by it was being used by its armed forces for
official purposes.

10. For the purposes of this Article, members of
the Korean Augmentation to the United States Army
(KATUSA) shall be considered as members of the United
States armed forces, and members of the Korean Service
Corps (KSC) shall be considered as employees of the
armed forces of the Republic of Korea.

11. The provisions of this Article shall not
apply to any claims which arose before the entry into
force of this Agreement.

# ARTICLE

## Health and Sanitation

Consistent with the right of the United States to furnish medical support for its armed forces, civilian component and their dependents, matters of mutual concern pertaining to the control and prevention of diseases and the coordination of other public health, medical, sanitation, and veterinary services shall be resolved by the authorities of the two Governments in the Joint Committee established under Article ____.

0161

78

# ARTICLE

## MILITARY PAYMENT CERTIFICATES

1.    (a)    United States military payment certificates denominated in dollars may be used by persons authorized by the United States for internal transactions. The Government of the United States will take appropriate action to insure that authorized personnel are prohibited from engaging in transactions involving military payment certificates except as authorized by United States regulations. The Government of Korea will take necessary action to prohibit unauthorized persons from engaging in transactions involving military payment certificates and with the aid of United States authorities will undertake to apprehend and punish any person or persons under its jurisdiction involved in the counterfeiting or uttering of counterfeit military payment certificates.

    (b)    It is agreed that the United States authorities will (to the extent authorized by United States law,) apprehend and punish members of the United States armed forces, the civilian component, or their dependents, who tender military payment certificates to unauthorized persons and that no obligation will be due to such unauthorized persons or to the Government of Korea or its agencies from the United States or any of its agencies as a result of any unauthorized use of military payment certificates within Korea.

0162

2.     In order to exercise control of military payment
certificates the United States may designate certain American
financial institutions to maintain and operate, under United
States supervision, facilities for the use of persons authorized
by the United States to use military payments certificates.
Institutions authorized to maintain military banking facilities
will establish and maintain such facilities physically separated
from their Korean commercial banking business, with personnel
whose sole duty is to maintain and operate such facilities   Such
facilities shall be permitted to maintain   United States currency
bank accounts and to perform all financial transactions in connection therewith including receipt and remission of funds to the extent
provided by Article . . . . . paragraph 2, of this Agreement.

0163

80

## ARTICLE XIX - Military Payment Certificates
### AGREED MINUTE

Inasmuch as United States Military Payment Certificates are property of the United States Government, any Military Payment Certificates which are in, or come into, the possession of the Government of the Republic of Korea shall be returned without componsation to the authorities of the United States armed forces as expeditiously as practicable.

81

0164

## PROPOSED STATEMENT FOR JOINT AGREED SUMMARY

The ROK and U.S. negotiators agree that nothing in the Status of Forces Agreement in any way prevents the appropriate authorities of either the Republic of Korea or the U.S. from raising any appropriate matter at any time with each other. The U.S. negotiators recognize the desire of the ROK authorities to discuss the disposal of MPC's under custody of the ROK Government. However, both the ROK and U.S. negotiators have agreed to remove from the SOFA text any reference to the question of compensation for MPC's held by unauthorized persons. This agreement does not prejudice the position of either party in connection with discussion of this question through other channels.

0165

82

# ARTICLE

1. Members of the United States armed forces, the civilian component and their dependents, shall be subject to the foreign exchange controls of the Government of the Republic of Korea.

2. The preceding paragraph shall not be construed to preclude the transmission into or out of Korea of United States dollars or dollar instruments representing the official funds of the United States or realized as a result of service or employment in connection with this Agreement by members of the United States armed forces and the civilian component, or realized by such persons and their dependents from sources outside Korea.

3. The United States authorities shall take suitable measures to preclude the abuse of the privileges stipulated in the preceding paragraphs or circumvention of the Korean foreign exchange controls.

83

0166

# FOREIGN EXCHANGE CONTROLS

## AGREED MINUTE

Payment in Korea by the United States armed forces including those activities provided in Article _____, to persons other than members of the United States armed forces, civilian component, their dependents and those persons referred to in Article _____ shall be effected in accordance with the Korean Foreign Exchange Control Law and regulations. The funds to be used for these transactions shall be convertible into currency of the Republic of Korea at the highest rate in terms of the number of Korean Won per United States dollar which, at the time the conversion is made, is not unlawful in the Republic of Korea.

84

0167

1. The United States may contract for any materials, supplies, equipment and services (including construction work) to be furnished or undertaken in the Republic of Korea for purposes of, or authorized by, this Agreement, without restriction as to choice of contractor, supplier or person who provides such services. Such materials, supplies, equipment and services may, upon agreement between the appropriate authorities of the two Governments, also be procured through the Government of the Republic of Korea.

0168

85

## Article

## Local Procurement

1. The United States may contract for any supplies or construction work to be furnished or undertaken in the Republic of Korea for purposes of, or authorized by, this Agreement, without restriction as to choice of supplier or person who does the construction work. Such supplies or construction work may, upon agreement between the appropriate authorities of the two Governments, also be procured through the Government of the Republic of Korea.

2. Materials, supplies, equipment and services which are required from local sources for the maintenance of the United States armed forces and the procurement of which may have an adverse effect on the economy of the Republic of Korea shall be procured in coordination with, and, when desirable, through or with the assistance of, the competent authorities of the Republic of Korea.

3. Materials, supplies, equipment and services procured for official purposes in the Republic of Korea by the United States armed forces, including their authorized procurement agencies, or procured

86

0169

for ultimate use by the United States armed forces
shall be exempt from the following Korean taxes upon
appropriate certification by the United States armed
forces:

      (a) Commodity tax:

      (b) Traffic tax:

      (c) Petroleum tax:

      (d) Electricity and gas tax:

      (e) Business tax.

With respect to any present or future Korean taxes not
specifically referred to in this Article which might be
found to constitute a significant and readily identifiable
part of the gross purchase price of materials, supplies,
equipment and services procured by the United States
armed forces, or for ultimate use by such forces, the
two Governments will agree upon a procedure for granting
such exemption or relief therefrom as is consistent
with the purpose of this Article.

    4. Neither members of the United States armed
forces, civilian component, nor their dependents,
shall by reason of this Article enjoy any exemption
from taxes or similar charges relating to personal
purchases of goods and services in the Republic of Korea

87

0170

chargeable under Korean legislation.

5. Except as such disposal may be authorized by the United States and Korean authorities in accordance with mutually agreed conditions, goods purchased in the Republic of Korea exempt from taxes referred to in paragraph 3, shall not be disposed of in the Republic of Korea to persons not entitled to purchase such goods exempt from such tax.

### AGREED MINUTE

1. The United States armed forces will furnish the Korean authorities with appropriate information as far in advance as practicable on anticipated major changes in their procurement program in the Republic of Korea.

2. The problem of a satisfactory settlement or difficulties with respect to procurement contracts arising out of differences between Korean and United States economic laws and business practices will be studied by the Joint Committee or other appropriate persons.

3. The procedures for securing exemptions from taxation on purchases of goods for ultimate use by the United States armed forces will be as follows:

0171

88

(a) Upon appropriate certification by the United States armed forces that materials, supplies and equipment consigned to or destined for such forces, are to be used, or wholly or partially used up, under the supervision of such forces, exclusively in the execution of contracts for the construction, maintenance or operation of the facilities and areas referred to in Article or for the support of the forces therein, or are ultimately to be incorporated into articles or facilities used by such forces, an authorized representative of such forces shall take delivery of such materials, supplies and equipment directly from manufacturers thereof. In such circumstances the collection of taxes referred to in Article , paragraph 3, shall be held in abeyance.

(b) The receipt of such materials, supplies and equipment in the facilities and areas shall be confirmed by an authorized agent of the United States armed forces to the Korean authorities.

(c) Collection of the taxes on such materials, supplies and equipment shall be held in abeyance until.

0172

89

(1) The United States armed forces confirm and certify the quantity or degree of consumption of the above referred to materials, supplies and equipment, or

(2) The United States armed forces confirm and certify the amount of the above referred to materials, supplies, aid equipment which have been incorporated into articles or facilities used by the United States armed forces.

(d) Materials, supplies, and equipment certified under (e) (1) or (2) shall be exempt from taxes referred to in Article        , paragraph 3, insofar as the price thereof is paid out of United States Government appropriations or out of funds contributed by the Government of the Republic of Korea for disbursement by the United States.

0173

90

"4. Regarding para 3, it is understood that "materials, supplies, equipment and services procured for official purposes" refers to direct procurement by the United States armed forces or its authorized procurement agencies from Korean suppliers. "Materials, supplies, equipment and services procured for ultimate use" refers to procurement by contractors of the United States armed forces from Korean suppliers of items to be incorporated into or necessary for the production of the end product of their contracts with the United States Armed Forces".

0174

91

## ARTICLE

## SECURITY MEASURES

"The United States and the Republic of Korea will cooperate in taking such steps as may from time to time be necessary to ensure the security of the United States armed forces, the members thereof, the civilian component, the persons who are present in the Republic of Korea pursuant to Article ____, their dependents and their property. The Government of the Republic of Korea agrees to seek such legislation and to take such other action as may be necessary to ensure the adequate security and protection within its territory of installations, equipment, property, records, and official information of the United States, of the persons referred to in this paragraph, and their property and, consistent with Article ____, to ensure the punishment of offenders under the applicable laws of the Republic of Korea."

0175

92

In cooperating with each other under this Article the
two governments agree that each will take such measures  *legislal*. 어도 포함
as may be necessary to ensure the security and protection
of the U. S. Armed Forces, the members thereof, the
civilian component, the persons who are present in the
Republic of Korea pursuant to the article dealing with
Invited Contractors, their dependents and their property.

0176

93

ARTICLE _____

## TAXATION

1. The United States armed forces shall not be subject to taxes or similar charges on property held, used or transferred by such forces in Korea.

2. Members of the United States armed forces, the civilian component, and their dependents shall not be liable to pay any Korean taxes to the Government of Korea or to any other taxing agency in Korea on income received as a result of their service with or employment by the United States armed forces, including the activities provided for in Article      . Persons in Korea solely by reason of being members of the United States armed forces, the civilian component, or their dependents shall not be liable to pay any Korean taxes to the Government of Korea or to any taxing agency in Korea on income derived from sources outside of Korea, nor shall periods during which such persons are in Korea be considered as periods of residence or domicile in Korea for the purpose of Korean taxation. The provisions of this Article do not exempt such persons

0177

94

from payment of Korean taxes on income deriv~~

Korean sources, other than those sources referred to
in the first sentence of this paragraph, nor do they
exempt United States citizens who claim Korean residence
for United States income tax purposes from payment of
Korean taxes on income.

3. Members of the United States armed forces, the
civilian component, and their dependents shall be exempt
from taxation in Korea on the holding, use, transfer
_inter se_, or transfer by death of movable property,
tangible or intangible, the presence of which in Korea
is due solely to the temporary presence of these persons
in Korea, provided that such exemption shall not apply
to property held for the purpose of investment or
the conduct of business in Korea or to any ihtangible
property registered in Korea.

0178

95

## ARTICLE

## LICENSING OF MOTOR VEHICLES

1. Korea shall accept as valid, without a driving
tnst or fee, the driving permit or license or military
driving permit issued by the United States, or political
subdivision thereof, to a member of the United States
armed forces, the civilian component, and their dependents,

2. Official vehicles of the United States armed
forces and the civilian component shall carry distinctive
numbered plates or individual markings which will
readily identify them.

3. Privately owned vehicles of members of the
United States armed forces, the civilian component
and their dependents may be licensed or registered,
and shall be provided with license plate or other
identification as appropriate, by the United States.
The authorities of the United States shall take adequate
safety measures for, and shall assure the technical
supervision of, the vehicles licensed by them and
shall, where necessary, and at the request of the
Government of the Republic of Korea, furnish the name
and address of the owner of a vehicle licensed by them.

0179

96

# ARTICLE

3.  The Government of the Republic of Korea will
license and register those vehicles privately owned by
members of the United States armed forces, the civilian
component, or dependents.  The names of the owners of
such vehicles and such other pertinent information as
is required by Korean law to effect the licensing
and registration of such vehicles, shall be furnished
to the Government of the Republic of Korea by officials
of the United States Government through the Joint
Committee.  Except for the actual cost of the issuance
of license plates, members of the United States armed
forces, the civilian component, and their dependents
shall be exempt from the payment of all fees and charges
relating to the licensing, registration, or operation
of vehicles in the Republic of Korea and, in accordance
with the provisions of Article _____, from the payment
of all taxes relating thereto.

0180

97

# ARTICLE

## Non-Appropriated Fund Activities

1. Military exchanges, messes, social clubs, theaters, newspapers and other non-appropriated fund activities authorized and regulated by the United States military authorities may be established by the United States armed forces for the use of members of such forces, the civilian component, and their dependents. Except as otherwise provided in this Agreement, such activities shall not be subject to Korean regulations, licenses, fees, taxes, or similar controls.

2. No Korean tax shall be imposed on sales of merchandise or services by such activities. Purchases within Korea of merchandise and supplies by such activities shall be subject to the Korean taxes to which other purchasers of such merchandise and supplies are subject (and at rates no less favorable than those imposed on other purchasers.)

3. Except as such disposal may be permitted by the United States and Korean authorities in accordance with mutually agreed conditions, goods which are sold by such activities shall not be disposed of in Korea to persons not authorized to make purchases from such activities.

4. The activities referred to in this Article shall, after consultation between the representatives of the two

b. — through

0181

98

governments in the Joint Committee, provide such information to the Republic of Korea tax authorities as is required by Korean tax legislation.

5. The activities referred to in paragraph 1 may be used by other officers or personnel of the United States Government ordinarily accorded such privileges, by non-Korean persons whose presence in Korea is solely for the purpose of providing contract services financed by the United States Government, by the dependents of the foregoing, by organizations which are present in the Republic of Korea primarily for the benefit and service of the United States armed forces personnel, such as the American Red Cross and the United Service Organizations, and by the non-Korean personnel of such organizations and their dependents.

0182

99

<u>Non-Appropriated Fund Activities Article</u>

<u>Suggested Paragraph 1 (b)</u>:

(b) When a newspaper authorized and regulated by
the United States military authorities is sold to the
general public, it shall be subject to Korean regulations,
licenses, fees, taxes or similar controls so far as such
circulation is concerned.

0183

/00

# AGREED MINUTE

The United States Armed Forces may grant the use of the organizations referred to in paragraph 1 of Article    to: (a) other officers or personnel of the United States Government ordinarily accorded such privileges; (b) those other non-Korean Armed Forces in Korea under the Unified Command which receive logistical support from the United States Armed Forces, and their members; (c) those non-Korean persons whose presence in the Republic of Korea is solely for the purpose of providing contract services financed by the United States Government; (d) those organizations which are present in the Republic of Korea primarily for the benefit and service of the United States Armed Forces, such as the American Red Cross and the United Service Organizations, and their non-Korean personnel; (e) dependents of the foregoing; and (f) other persons and organizations with the express consent of the Government of the Republic of Korea.

0184

/ 0 /

2. No Korean tax shall be imposed on sales of merchandise or services by such organizations, except as provided in paragraph 1 (b) of this article. Purchases within the Republic of Korea of merchandise and supplies by such organizations shall be subject to the Korean taxes to which other purchasers of such merchandise and supplies are subject unless otherwise agreed between the two Governments.

/ 02

# ARTICLE
## MILITARY POST OFFICES

1. The United States may establish and operate, within the facilities and areas in use by the U.S. armed forces, United States military post offices for the use of members of the United States armed forces, the civilian component, and their dependents, for the transmission of mail between United States military post offices in Korea and between such military post offices and other United States post offices.

2. United States military post offices may be used by other officers and personnel of the United States Government, and their dependents, ordinarily accorded such privileges abroad.

0186

한·미국 간의 상호방위조약 제4조에 의한 시설과 구역 및 한국에서의 미국군대의 지위에 관한 협정(SOFA)
전59권. 1966.7.9 서울에서 서명 : 1967.2.9 발효(조약 232호) (V.47 한·미국 양측 교섭안) 193

## ARTICLE

The United States may enroll in its reserve forces and train, in Korea, eligible United States citizens who are in the Republic of Korea. ✗

- stationing in ROK
- a certain length of period

- Residing in ROK

✗ except for ordinary tourists

0187.

104

It is the duty of members of the United States Armed Forces, the civilian component, (the persons who are present in the Republic of Korea pursuant to Article _____) and their dependents, to respect the law of Korea and to abstain from any activity inconsistent with the spirit of this Agreement, and, in particular, from any political activity in Korea.

0188

105

## Meteorological Services
### Article ____

The Government of Korea undertakes to furnish the United States armed forces with the following meteorological services in accordance with arrangements between the appropriate authorities of the two Governments:

(a) Meteorological observations from land and ocean areas including observations from ships;

(b) Climatological information including periodic summaries and historical data wherever available;

(c) Telecommunications service to disseminate meteorological information;

(d) Seismographic data.

0189

/06

D

<u>Facilities and Areas</u>

Article ____

3. (a) The United States armed forces shall have the use
of all utilities and services, ~~which are~~ owned, controlled or regulated by the Government of
the Republic of Korea or ~~political~~ local administrative subdivisions thereof. The
term "utilities and services" shall include, but not be limited
to, transportation and communications facilities and systems,
electricity, gas, water, steam, heat, light, power, (however
produced,) and sewage disposal. (The use of utilities and
services as provided herein shall not prejudice the right of
the United States to operate military transportation, communication, power and such other services and facilities deemed
necessary for the operations of the United States armed forces.)

(b) The use of such utilities and services by the
United States shall be in accordance with priorities, conditions,
and rates or tariffs no less favorable than those accorded any
other user, ~~...~~ (Should the
emergency operating needs of the United States armed forces so
require, the Republic of Korea shall, (upon notification thereof,)
take appropriate measures to assure provision of utilities and services
necessary to meet these needs.)

Emergency Clause

0100

4.     It is agreed that arrangements will be effected between the Governments of the United States and the Republic of Korea for accounting applicable to financial transactions arising out of this Agreement.

0191

108

Agreed Minutes to Article _____

*agreed*

1.    It is understood that any change in priority or (increase in utility or service rates applicable to the United States armed forces) shall be the subject of prior consultation in the Joint Committee.

2.    Paragraph 3 of Article _____ will not be construed as in any way abrogating the Utilities and Claims Settlement Agreement of December 18, 1958 which continues in full force and effect.

3. (

0192

109

## UTILITIES AND SERVICES

### Proposed new third and fourth sentences, Paragraph 3 (a)

### Article "D"

The use of utilities and services as provided herein

shall not prejudice the right of the United States to operate

military transportation, communication, power and such other

utilities and services deemed necessary for the operations

of the United States armed forces. This right shall not be

exercised in a manner inconsistent with the operation by the

Government of the Republic of Korea of its utilities and

services.

0193

/ / 0

Minutes:

This article will not be construed as in any way abrogating the Utilities and Claims Settlement Agreement of December 18, 1958 which continues in full force and effect. Existing arrangements under that Agreement for the use of utilities and services by the United States armed forces and the payment therefor continue in effect. Changes in priorities or rates applicable to the United States armed forces shall be the subject of prior consultation in the Joint Committee.

AG. 1

Agreed Minute #1

The application of

It is understood that any changes determined by the
Korean authorities in priorities, conditions, and rates or
tariffs, applicable to the United States armed forces shall
be the subject of consultation in the Joint Committee prior
to their effective date.

0195

112

Agreed Minute #3

In an emergency the Republic of Korea agrees to take appropriate measures to assure provision of utilities and services necessary to meet the needs of the United States armed forces.

0196

113.

# ARTICLE

1. (a) The United States is granted, under Article IV of the Mutual Defense Treaty, the use of facilities and areas in the Republic of Korea. Agreements as to specific facilities and areas shall be concluded by the two Governments through the Joint Committee provided for in Article    of this Agreement. "Facilities and Areas" include existing furnishings, equipment and fixtures, wherever located, used in the operation of such facilities and areas.

   (b) The facilities and areas of which the United States has the use at the effective date of this Agreement shall be considered as facilities and areas agreed upon between the two Governments in accordance with sub-paragraph (a) above.

2. At the request of either Government, the Governments of the United States and the Republic of Korea shall review such arrangements and may agree that such facilities and areas or portions thereof shall be returned to the Republic of Korea or that additional facilities and areas may be provided.

3. The facilities and areas used by the United States shall be returned to the Republic of Korea under such conditions as may be agreed through the Joint Committee whenever they are no longer needed for the purposes of this Agreement and the United States agrees to keep the needs for facilities and areas under continual observation with a view toward such return.

0197

114

4.  ((a)) When facilities and areas are temporarily not
being used and the Government of the Republic of Korea is so
advised, the Government of the Republic of Korea may make, or
permit Korean nationals to make, interim use of such facilities
and areas provided that it is agreed between the two Governments
through the Joint Committee that such use would not be harmful
to the purposes for which the facilities and areas are normally
used by the United States armed forces.

(b) With respect to facilities and areas which are
to be used by United States armed forces for limited periods of
time, the Joint Committee shall specify in the agreements covering
such facilities and areas the extent to which the provisions of
this Agreement shall apply.

0198

115

한·미국 간의 상호방위조약 제4조에 의한 시설과 구역 및 한국에서의 미국군대의 지위에 관한 협정(SOFA)
전59권. 1966.7.9 서울에서 서명 : 1967.2.9 발효(조약 232호) (V.47 한·미국 양측 교섭안)　205

<u>Article II - Facilities and Areas (Grant of and Return)</u>

1. .......

(b) The facilities and areas of which the United States armed forces have the use at the effective date of this agreement together with those areas and facilities which the United States armed forces have returned to the Republic of Korea with the reserved right of re-entry, when these facilities and areas have been re-entered by U.S. forces, shall be considered as the facilities and areas agreed upon between the two Governments in accordance with subparagraph (a) above. Records of facilities and areas of which the United States armed forces have the use or right of re-entry shall be maintained through the Joint Committee after this Agreement comes into force.

0199

116

1. Within the facilities and areas, the United States may take all the measures necessary for their establishment, operation, safeguarding and control. In an emergency, measures necessary for their safeguarding and control may also be taken in the vicinity thereof. In order to provide access for the United States armed forces to the facilities and areas for their support, safeguarding and control, the Government of the Republic of Korea shall, at the request of the United States armed forces, and upon consultation between the two Governments through the Joint Committee, take necessary measures within the scope of applicable laws and regulations over land, territorial waters and airspace adjacent to, or in the vicinities of the facilities and areas. The United States may also take necessary measures for such purposes upon consultation between the two Governments through the Joint Committee.

2. (a) The United States agrees not to take the measures referred to in paragraph 1 in such a manner as to interfere unnecessarily with navigation, aviation, communication, or land travel to or from or within the territories of the Republic of Korea.

(b) All questions relating to telecommunications including radio frequencies for electromagnetic radiating devices, or like matters, shall continue to be resolved expeditiously in the utmost spirit of coordination and cooperation by arrangement between the designated military communications authorities of the two Governments.

(c) The Government of the Republic of Korea shall, within the scope of applicable laws, regulations and agreements, take all reasonable measures to avoid or eliminate interference with electromagnetic radiation sensitive devices, telecommunications devices, or other apparatus required by the United States armed forces.

0200

OK

12. 3. Operations in the facilities and areas in use by the United States armed forces shall be carried on with due regard for the public safety.

Same

## ARTICLE III — Facilities and Areas

### (Security Measures In)

### AGREED MINUTE

It is agreed that in the event of an emergency, the United States armed forces shall be authorized to take such measures in the vicinity of the areas and facilities as may be necessary to provide for their safeguarding and control.

0202

/19

## ARTICLE

1. The United States is not obliged, when it returns facilities and areas to the Republic of Korea on the expiration of this Agreement or at an earlier date, to restore the facilities and areas to the condition in which they were at the time they became available to the United States armed forces, or to compensate the Republic of Korea in lieu of such restoration.

2. All removable facilities erected or constructed by or on behalf of the United States at its expense and all equipment, materials and supplies brought into or procured in the Republic of Korea by or on behalf of the United States in connection with the construction, development, operation, maintenance, safeguarding and control of the facilities and areas will remain the property of the United States Government and may be removed from the Republic of Korea.

3. The foregoing provisions shall not apply to any construction which the Government of the United States may undertake under special arrangements with the Government of the Republic of Korea.

AREAS AND FACILITIES ARTICLE
PROPOSED ADDITIONAL PARAGRAPH TO
AREAS AND FACILITIES ARTICLE PERTAINING
TO RETURN OF FACILITIES AND AREAS


The Republic of Korea is not obligated to compensate
the United States for improvements made in United States
facilities and areas or for the buildings structures,
remaining thereon upon the return of the facilities
and areas.

/2/

0204    비료

# ARTICLE

5.   1. It is agreed that the United States will bear for the duration of the Agreement without cost to the Republic of Korea all expenditures incident to the maintenance of the United States armed forces in the Republic of Korea, (except those to be borne by the Republic of Korea as provided in paragraph 2.)

4.   2. It is agreed that the Republic of Korea will furnish for the duration of this Agreement without cost to the United States and make compensation where appropriate to the owners and suppliers thereof all facilities and areas and rights of way, including facilities and areas jointly used such as those at airfields and ports as provided in Articles II and III. The Government of the Republic of Korea assures the use of such facilities and areas to the United States Government and will hold the United States Government as well as its agencies and employees harmless from any third party claims which may be advanced in connection with such use.

     3. /Use of public utilities and services to be inserted later.7

## ARTICLE

1. United States and foreign vessels and aircraft operated by, for, or under the control of the United States for official purposes shall be accorded access to any port or airport of Korea free from toll or landing charges. When cargo or passengers not accorded the exemptions of this Agreement are carried on such vessels and aircraft, notification shall be given to the appropriate Korean authorities, and their entry into and departure from Korea shall be according to the laws and regulations of Korea.

2. The vessels and aircraft mentioned in paragraph 1, United States Government-owned vehicles including armor, and members of the United States armed forces, the civilian component, and their dependents shall be accorded access to and movement between facilities and areas in use by the United States armed forces and between such facilities and areas and the ports or airports of Korea. Such access to and movement between facilities and areas by United States military vehicles shall be free from toll and other charges.

3. When the vessels mentioned in paragraph 1 enter Korean ports, appropriate notification shall, under normal conditions, be made to the proper Korean authorities. Such vessels shall have freedom from compulsory pilotage, but if a pilot is taken pilotage shall be paid for at appropriate rates.

OK

0206

/23

## AGREED MINUTES TO ARTICLE

1. "United States and foreign vessels...operated by, for, or under the control of the United States for official purposes" mean United States public vessels and chartered vessels (bare boat charter, voyage charter and time charter). Space charter is not included. Commercial cargo and private passengers are carried by them only in exceptional cases.

2. The Korean ports mentioned herein will ordinarily mean "open ports".

3. An exception from making the "appropriate notification" referred to in paragraph 3 will apply only in unusual cases where such is required for security of the United States armed forces or similar reasons.

4. The laws and regulations of Korea will be applicable except as specifically provided otherwise in this Article.

0207

124

56th Session (1964. 6. 26,)에서 피측이 제안하고
동회의 석상에서 양해사항으로 우리 측이 수락

"If the US authorities determine that there would be

significant advantage for US-ROK mutual defense to utilize one

or more third-country corporations as USFK-invited contractor,

the authorities of the Government of the Republic of Korea shall

give sympathetic consideration to a US request to extend the

benefits of this agreement to such non-US corporations. "

0208

68

# ARTICLE

Either Government may at any time request the revision of any Article of this Agreement, in which case the two Governments shall enter into negotiations through appropriate channels.

0209

69

*Revised U.S. Draft*

*I ← Waiver of Primary Right to exercise Jurisdiction*

<u>Re Paragraph 3(b)</u>

1. The Government of the Republic of Korea waives in favor of the United States the primary right granted to the Korean authorities under sub-paragraph (b) of Paragraph 3 of this Article in cases of concurrent jurisdiction, in accordance with Paragraphs 2, 3, 4, 5, 6, and 7 of this Minute.

2. Subject to any particular arrangements which may be made under Paragraph 7 of this Minute, the military authorities of the United States shall notify the competent Korean authorities of individual cases falling under the waiver provided in Paragraph 1 of this Minute.

3. Where the competent Korean authorities hold the view that, by reason of special circumstances in a specific case, major interests of Korean administration of justice make imperative the exercise of Korean jurisdiction, they may recall the waiver granted under Paragraph 1 of this minute by a statement to the competent military authorities of the United States within a period of twenty-one days after receipt of the notification envisaged in Paragraph 2 of this Minute or any shorter period which may be provided in arrangements made under Paragraph 7 of this Minute. The Korean authorities may also submit the statement prior to receipt of such notification.

0210

*3¹*

(a) Subject to a careful examination of each specific case and to the results of such examination, major interests of Korean administration of justice within the meaning of Paragraph 3 above may make imperative the exercise of Korean jurisdiction, in particular, in the following cases:

(i) Security offenses against the Republic of Korea;

(ii) Offenses causing the death of a human being, robbery, and rape, except where the offenses are directed against a member of the United States Armed Forces or the civilian component, or a dependent; and

(iii) Attempts to commit such offenses or participation therein.

(b) In respect of the offenses referred to in Subparagraph (a) of this Paragraph, the authorities concerned shall proceed in particularly close cooperation from the beginning of the preliminary investigation in order to provide the mutual assistance envisaged in Paragraph 6 of this Article.

0211

32

4. If, pursuant to Paragraph 3 of this Minute, the competent Korean authorities have recalled the waiver in a specific case and in such case an understanding cannot be reached in discussions between the authorities concerned, the Government of the United States may make representations to the Government of the Republic of Korea through diplomatic channels. The Government of the Republic of Korea, giving due consideration to the interests of Korean administration of justice and to the interests of the Government of the United States, shall resolve the disagreement in the exercise of its authority in the field of foreign affairs.

5. With the consent of the competent Korean authorities, the military authorities of the United States may transfer to the Korean courts or authorities for investigation, trial and decision, particular criminal cases in which jurisdiction rests with the United States.

With the consent of the military authorities of the United States, the competent Korean authorities may transfer to the military authorities of the United States for investigation, trial and decision, particular criminal cases in which jurisdiction rests with the Republic of Korea.

0212

33

6. (a) Where a member of the United States Armed Forces or civilian component, or a dependent, is arraigned before a court of the United States, for an offense committed in the Republic of Korea against Korean interests, the trial shall be held within the Republic of Korea.

(i) Except where the law of the United States requires otherwise, or

(ii) Except where, in cases of military exigency or in the interests of justice, the military authorities of the United States intend to hold the trial outside the Republic of Korea. In this event they shall afford the Korean authorities timely opportunity to comment on such intention and shall give due consideration to any comments the latter may make.

(b) Where the trial is held outside of the Republic of Korea the military authorities of the United States shall inform the Korean authorities of the place and date of the trial. A Korean representative shall be entitled to be present at the trial, except where his presence is incompatible with the rules of the court of the United States or with the security requirements of the United States, which

0213

34

are not at the same time the security requirements of the
Republic of Korea. The authorities of the United States shall inform
the Korean authorities of the judgment and the final outcome of the
proceedings.

7. In the implementation of the provisions of this Article and
this agreed minute, and to facilitate the expeditious disposal of
offenses of minor importance, arrangements may be made between
the military authorities of the United States and the competent
Korean authorities. These arrangements may also extend to dispensing with notification and to the period of time referred to in
Paragraph 3 of this Minute, within which the waiver may be
recalled.

0214

35

## Labor Article

### Paragraph 2

Employers may accomplish the recruitment, employment and management of employees directly and, upon request by the employer, with the assistance of the authorities of the Republic of Korea. In case employers accomplish direct recruitment of employees, employers will provide available relevant information as may be required for labor administration to the Office of Labor Affairs of the Republic of Korea.

(64th, Oct. 16, '64)

0215

25

Labor Article

Paragraph 3

To the extent not inconsistent with the provisions of this article or the basic management needs of the United States Armed Forces, the conditions of employment, compensation, and labor-management practices established by the United States Armed Forces for their employees will conform with the labor laws, customs, and practices of the Republic of Korea.

(64th, Oct 16, '64)

0216

한·미국 간의 상호방위조약 제4조에 의한 시설과 구역 및 한국에서의 미국군대의 지위에 관한 협정(SOFA) 전59권. 1966.7.9 서울에서 서명 : 1967.2.9 발효(조약 232호) (V.47 한·미국 양측 교섭안) 223

## Labor Article

### Agreed Minute

Employers will withhold from the pay of their employees, and pay over to the Government of the Republic of Korea, withholdings required by the income tax legislation of the Republic of Korea.

*( 64대, Oct 16, '64)*

0217

I would like first to make a general comment on the Labor Article.
In 1945 both Japan and Germany were conquered enemy countries. US
forces occupied those countries in a military occupation. As a defeated
enemy country the Japanese Government, in so far as it was allowed to
govern, did so only as an agent of the Supreme Commander of the Allied
Powers. As for labor, the Japanese government was simply called upon
to provide it wherever the Supreme Commander required it. It was
provided free, without any cost to the United States. In both Japan
and Germany the wages of this labor were paid by the Japanese or German
governments, without any reimbursement by the United States. They were
part of the Occupation Costs paid by a defeated enemy country. This was
the origin of the system of indirect hire we have today in Japan. As both
Japan and Germany went through successive stages and were converted
from enemies to allies, the nature of the US military presence changed
from military occupiers to visiting forces and the occupation costs
came to be shared between us with the United States taking over the
payment of some of them, including labor costs. But the system of
indirect hire, which still exists in Japan, in which the Japanese
government obtains our labor force for us, is a carryover from our
military occupation of a defeated enemy country. We do not have such
an arrangement with any of the other free countries in the Pacific
area. In China, in the Philippines, in Australia, in Okinawa, in
Vietnam, in Thailand, and here in Korea, we hire labor directly in
the free labor market. We do not have it impressed for us by the
host government. It would not be proper for us to do so. Such an
arrangement would be typical of a military occupation. We of course
are not here as military occupiers but are here at your invitation and
in response to the call of the United Nations. Our relationship with
you is that of guest and host. We are free and equal allies in a
common cause. Our employment of labor here has been that typical of
a free employer on the one hand and a free labor force on the other.
We have tried to be a good employer in conformity with your labor
laws and practice. We will continue to be such. But it would be
grossly improper and a very backward step after 19 years of free labor
practice for us here to adopt the Japanese labor article based on
an impressed labor system imposed (also 19 years ago) upon a defeated
enemy nation.

All of this is the reason that our draft labor article is worded
as it is and is not based on the Japanese article. At the last session
in which this article was discussed you raised certain objections to
our draft and in consequence of your suggestions we have obtained
authority to make certain changes in our draft which we believe you
desire. These changes are not taken from the Japanese article with

28                                    0218

its entirely different origin but instead are designed to make our free labor draft more fully representative of your stated preferences.

First, in paragraph 1 (b), we offer to delete the phrase "who is an employee of the Government of Korea." This was suggested by your side.

Second, in paragraph 2, we offer to add the words, "and upon request by the employer, with the assistance of the authorities of the Republic of Korea." This is based upon a suggestion from your side. It is not, we realize, exactly what you suggested, but it is absolutely as far as we can go in this direction. We simply can not be bound to obtain no employees at all except through your governmental agencies. In an agreement designed to create a status for our forces somewhat better than that of mere tourists and businessmen we cannot accept a limitation on employing a labor force which is more restrictive than those placed upon such businessmen, whether Korean or third-national who do business here. This would seem so obvious on the face of it that we ask you to give serious consideration to our proposed language. This language which we are proposing today is very similar to that in the labor article of our new SOFA with Australia. Australia is certainly an important ally of the United States and is a first-class power in the Pacific area and in your consideration of this proposal we ask you to give weight to that fact.

Third, in paragraph 3, we offer to delete the words "provided, however that an employer may terminate employment whenever the continuation of such employment would materially impair the accomplishment of the mission of the United States armed forces" and to place them instead in the agreed minutes as the second sentence of agreed minute 2 where they would read: "Moreover the United States government may terminate employment whenever the continuation of such employment would materially impair the accomplishment of the mission of the United States armed forces." This proposal of our side is designed to meet an objection from your side.

Fourth, we offer to add a new agreed minute as follows: "It is understood that the Government of the Republic of Korea shall be reimbursed for direct costs incurred in providing assistance requested pursuant to paragraph 2." This offer is made to comply with a suggestion made by your side at our last discussion of this article.

Fifth, we are authorized to convey to you that the principle of US forces withholding employee contributions to social security and income tax is acceptable to the United States. We consider that such an obligation is included in our commitment of general conformity with

2

0210

27

the labor laws, customs, and practices of the Republic of Korea.
Should you desire a specific reference in the agreement to this
obligation to withhold taxes, suitable language may be worked out.
I would like to add one additional comment about the language in our
paragraph 3 calling for general conformity with Korean labor laws,
customs, and practices. The United States fully recognizes the
sovereignty of the Republic of Korea within Korean territory. At
the same time it should be remembered that the United States is also
a sovereign nation and under accepted principles of international law
it is not proper for one sovereign to hail another sovereign into its
courts as a defendant or before its administrative tribunals as a
respondent. It is precisely for this reason that we cannot now nor
at any time in the future agree to comply with any law which requires
the United States to appear when summoned before a court or board.
I may say that this is not done, either, in Japan or Germany but that
in those states the judicial or administrative actions brought by
employees or their representatives are defended or responded to by
the governments of Japan and Germany, not by the government of the
United States. We are most willing to be helped and advised by the
competent ministries of your government in the settlement of any labor
dispute but we cannot agree that the United States give up a right
inherent in every sovereign state not to be brought against its will
before the tribunals of another sovereign. Out position on this point
cannot change, here or anywhere else in the world. It is a universal
principle of international law.

Now we ask you to consider our five proposals, all made in a
desire on our part to be responsive to your legitimate requirements.
They do not fully meet your position as expressed in our previous
discussion but they are as far as we can go toward meeting you.
Please give them full consideration and convey your views to us at
the next meeting.

3

30

AGREED MINUTE RE PARAGRAPH 3

The Republic of Korea, recognizing that it is the primary responsibility of the United States authorities to maintain good order and discipline where persons subject to United States law are concerned, waives its primary right to exercise jurisdiction under paragraph 3b. In accordance therewith, the United States authorities shall notify the authorities of the Republic of Korea of their intention to exercise jurisdiction in such cases through the Joint Committee. When the authorities of the Republic of Korea, after consultation with United States authorities, are of the opinion that, by reason of special circumstances in a specific case involving an offense against the security of the Republic of Korea, or of forcible rape, or of a malicious killing, the exercise of Korean jurisdiction is of vital importance to the Republic of Korea in that case, they will notify the United States authorities of that opinion within fifteen days after receipt of notification that the United States intends to exercise jurisdiction. The United States shall not have the right to exercise jurisdiction within those fifteen days. If any question arises concerning who is to exercise jurisdiction, the United States diplomatic mission will be afforded an opportunity to confer with the proper authorities of the Republic of Korea before a final determination of this matter is made.

Trials of cases in which the authorities of the Republic of Korea waive the primary right to exercise jurisdiction, and trials of cases involving offenses described in para 3(a)(ii) committed against the state or nationals of the Republic of Korea will be held within a reasonable distance from the place where the offenses are alleged to have taken place unless other arrangements are mutually agreed upon. Representatives of the Republic of Korea may be present at such trials.

In the implementation of the provisions of Article ___ and this Minute, and to facilitate the expeditious disposal of offenses, arrangements may be made between the authorities of the United States and the Republic of Korea to dispense with notification.

OK/

0222

39

Agreed Minute Re Paragraph 3(a)

2. Where a member of the United States armed forces or civilian component is charged with an offense, a certificate issued by competent authorities of the United States forces stating that the alleged offense, if committed by him, arose out of an act or omission done in the performance of official duty shall be sufficient evidence of the fact for the purpose of determining primary jurisdiction.

In those exceptional cases where the chief prosecutor for the Republic of Korea considers that there is proof contrary to a certificate of official duty, it may be made the subject of review through discussions between appropriate officials of the Government of the Republic of Korea and the diplomatic mission of the United States in Korea.

→ shall 로써 표현하도라

The term "official duty" as used in Article _____ and the
Agreed Minutes is not meant to include all acts by members of
the Armed Forces and the civilian component during periods
when they are on duty, but is meant to apply only to acts which
are required to be done as functions of those duties which the
individuals are performing. Thus, a substantial departure from
the acts a person is required to perform in a particular duty
usually will indicate an act outside of his "official duty".

41

0224

ARTICLE ---

1. Subject to the provisions of this Article,

(a) the authorities of the United States shall have the right to exercise within the Republic of Korea all criminal and disciplinary jurisdiction conferred on them by the law of the United States over members of the United States armed forces or civilian component, and their dependents.

(b) the civil authorities of the Republic of Korea shall have the right to exercise jurisdiction over the members of the United States armed forces or civilian component, and their dependents, with respect to offenses committed within the territory of the Republic of Korea and punishable by the law of the Republic of Korea.

2. (a) The authorities of the United States shall have the right to exercise exclusive jurisdiction over members of the United States armed forces or civilian component, and their dependents, with respect to offenses, including offenses relating to its security, punishable by the law of the United States, but not by the law of the Republic of Korea.

(b) The authorities of the Republic of Korea shall have the right to exercise exclusive jurisdiction over members of the United States armed forces or civilian component, and their dependents, with respect to offenses, including offenses relating to the security of the Republic of Korea, punishable by its law but not by the law of the United States.

(c) For the purpose of this paragraph and of paragraph 3 of this Article, a security offense against a State shall include:

(i) treason against the State;

42

0225

(ii)  sabotage, espionage or violation of any law relating to

official secrets of that State, or secrets relating to the

national defense of that State.

3.  In cases where the right to exercise jurisdiction is concurrent the following

rules shall apply:

(a)  The authorities of the United States shall have the primary right to

exercise jurisdiction over members of the United States armed forces or civilian

component, and their dependents, in relation to:

(i)  offenses solely against the property or security of the United

States, or offenses solely against the person or property of

another member of the United States armed forces or civilian

component or of a dependent;

(ii)  offenses arising out of any act of omission done in the

performance of official duty;

(b)  In the case of any other offense, the authorities of the Republic of

Korea shall have the primary right to exercise jurisdiction.

(c)  If the State having the primary right decides not to exercise

jurisdiction, it shall notify the authorities of the other State as soon as

practicable.  The authorities of the State having the primary right shall give

sympathetic consideration to a request from the authorities of the other State

for a waiver of its right in cases where that other State considers such waiver

to be of particular importance.

0226

43

4. The foregoing provisions of this Article shall not imply any right for the authorities of the United States to exercise jurisdiction over persons who are, nationals of or ordinary resident in the Republic of Korea, unless they are members of the United States armed forces.

5. (a) The authorities of the United States and the authorities of the Republic of Korea shall assist each other in the arrest of members of the United States armed forces, the civilian component, or their dependents in the territory of the Republic of Korea and in handing them over to the authority which is to have custody in accordance with the following provisions.

(b) The authorities of the Republic of Korea shall notify promptly the authorities of the United States of the arrest of any member of the United States armed forces, or civilian component, or a dependent.

(c) The custody of an accused member of the United States armed forces or civilian component, or of a dependent, over whom the Republic of Korea is to exercise jurisdiction shall, if he is in the hands of the United States, remain with the United States pending the conclusion of all judicial proceedings and until custody is requested by the authorities of the Republic of Korea. If he is in the hands of the Republic of Korea, he shall be promptly handed over to the authorities of the United States and remain in their custody pending completion of all judicial proceedings and until custody is requested by the authorities of the Republic of Korea. The United States authorities will make any such accused available to the authorities of the Republic of Korea upon their request for purposes of investigation and trial. The authorities of the Republic of Korea shall give sympathetic consideration to a request from the authorities of the United States

44

0227

for assistance in maintaining custody of an accused member of the United States armed forces, the civilian component, or a dependent.

6. (a) The authorities of the United States and the authorities of the Republic of Korea shall assist each other in the carrying out of all necessary investigations into offenses, and in the collection and production of evidence, including the seizure and, in proper cases, the handing over of objects connected with an offense. The handing over of such objects may, however, be made subject to their return within the time specified by the authority delivering them.

(b) The authorities of the United States and the authorities of the Republic of Korea shall notify each other of the disposition of all cases in which there are concurrent rights to exercise jurisdiction.

7. (a) A death sentence shall not be carried out in the Republic of Korea by the authorities of the United States if the legislation of the Republic of Korea does not provide for such punishment in a similar case.

(b) The authorities of the Republic of Korea shall give sympathetic consideration to a request from the authorities of the United States for assistance in carrying out a sentence of imprisonment pronounced by the authorities of the United States under the provisions of this Article within the territory of the Republic of Korea. The authorities of the Republic of Korea shall also give sympathetic consideration to a request from the authorities of the United States for the custody of any member of the United States armed forces or civilian component or a dependent, who is serving a sentence of confinement imposed by a court of the Republic of Korea. If such custody is released to the

45-

0228

authorities of the United States, the United States shall be obligated to continue
the confinement of the individual in an appropriate confinement facility of the
United States until the sentence to confinement shall have been served
in full or until release from such confinement shall be approved by competent
Korean authority.

8. Where an accused has been tried in accordance with the provisions of
this Article either by the military authorities of the United States or the authorities of
the Republic of Korea and has been acquitted, or has been convicted and is
serving, or has served, his sentence, or his sentence has been remitted or
suspended, or he has been pardoned, he may not be tried again for the same
offense within the territory of the Republic of Korea by the authorities of the
other State. However, nothing in this paragraph shall prevent the authorities
of the United States from trying a member of its armed forces for any violation
of rules of discipline arising from an act or omission which constituted an
offense for which he was tried by the authorities of the Republic of Korea.

9. Whenever a member of the United States armed forces or civilian
component or a dependent is prosecuted under the jurisdiction of the Republic
of Korea he shall be entitled:

(a) to a prompt and speedy trial;

(b) to be informed, in advance of trial, of the specific charge or
charges made against him;

(c) to be confronted with the witnesses against him;

(d) to have compulsory process for obtaining witnesses in his favor, if
they are within the jurisdiction of the Republic of Korea;

0229

46

(e) to have legal representation of his own choice for his defense or to have free or assisted legal representation under the conditions prevailing for the time being in the Republic of Korea;

(f) if he considers it necessary, to have the services of a competent interpreter; and

(g) to communicate with a representative of the Government of the United States and to have such a representative present at his trial.

10. (a) Regularly constituted military units or formations of the United States armed forces shall have the right to police any facilities or areas which they use under Article    of this Agreement.  The military police of such forces may take all appropriate measures to ensure the maintenance of order and security within such facilities and areas.

(b) Outside these facilities and areas, such military police shall be employed only subject to arrangements with the authorities of the Republic of Korea and in liaison with those authorities, and in so far as such employment is necessary to maintain discipline and order among the members of the United States armed forces, or ensure their security.

11. In the event of hostilities to which the provisions of Article II Of the Treaty of Mutual Defense apply, the provisions of this Agreement pertaining to criminal jurisdiction shall be immediately suspended and the authorities of the United States shall have the right to exercise exclusive jurisdiction over members of the United States armed forces, the civilian component, and their dependents.

0230

47

12.  The provisions of this Article shall not apply to any offenses committed before the entry into force of this Agreement.  Such cases shall be governed by the provisions of the Agreement between the United States of America and the Republic of Korea effected by an exchange of notes at Taejon, Korea on July 12, 1950.

<u>AGREED MINUTES</u>

The provisions of this Article shall not affect existing agreements, arrangements, or practices, relating to the exercise of jurisdiction over personnel of the United Nations forces present in Korea other than forces of the United States.

<u>RE Paragraph 1(b)</u>

1.  The authorities of the United States shall have the right to exercise exclusive jurisdiction over members of the United States armed forces or civilian component, and their dependents, if any, in the combat zone.  The extent of the combat zone shall be defined by the Joint Committee and shall include the area from the demilitarization zone to the rear boundaries of the United States corps (group) and the Republic of Korea army-size unit deployed in that zone.

2.  In the event that martial law is declared by the Republic of Korea, the provisions of this Article shall be immediately suspended in the part of the Republic of Korea under martial law, and the authorities of the United States shall have the right to exercise exclusive jurisdiction over members of the United States armed forces or civilian component, and their dependents, in such part until martial law is ended.

48

0231

3.  The jurisdiction of the authorities of the Republic of Korea over members of the United States armed forces or civilian component, and their dependents, shall not extend to any offenses committed outside the Republic of Korea.

RE Paragraph 2 (b)

The Republic of Korea, recognizing the effectiveness in appropriate cases of the administrative and disciplinary sanctions which may be imposed by the United States authorities over members of the United States armed forces or civilian component, and their dependents, will give sympathetic consideration in such cases to requests in the Joint Committee for waivers of its right to exercise jurisdiction under paragraph 2.

RE Paragraph 2 (c)

Each Government shall inform the other of the details of all security offenses mentioned in this subparagraph, and of the provisions regarding such offenses in its legislation.

RE Paragraph 3

The Republic of Korea, recognizing that it is the primary responsibility of the United States authorities to maintain good order and discipline among the members of the United States Armed Forces and civilian component, and their dependents, waives the right of the authorities of the Republic of Korea to exercise jurisdiction under paragraph 3.  The United States authorities shall notify the competent authorities of the Republic of Korea of individual cases falling under the waiver thus provided.  If, by reason of special circumstances in a specific case, the authorities of the Republic of Korea consider that it is

49

0232

of particular importance that jurisdiction be exercised by the Republic of Korea in that case, they shall, within 15 days of receipt of the notification envisaged above, seek agreement of the Joint Committee to recall the waiver for that particular case.

Subject to the foregoing, the waiver granted by the Republic of Korea shall be unconditional and final for all purposes and shall bar both the authorities and the nationals of the Republic of Korea from instituting criminal proceedings.

To facilitate the expeditious disposal of offenses of minor importance, arrangements may be made between United States authorities and the competent authorities of the Republic of Korea to dispense with notification.

RE Paragraph 3 (a)

1. The authorities of the United States shall have the primary right to exercise juridiction over members of the United States armed forces in relation to offenses which, if committed by a member of the armed forces of the Republic of Korea, would be tried by court-martial rather than by a civilian court.

2. Where a member of the United States armed forces or civilian component is charged with an offense, a certificate issued by or on behalf of his commanding officer stating that the alleged offense, if committed by him, arose out of an act or omission done in the performance of official duty, shall be conclusive for the purpose of determining primary jurisdiction.

RE Paragraph 6

1. The authorities of the United States and the authorities of the Republic of Korea shall assist each other in obtaining the appearance of witnesses

0233

necessary for the proceedings conducted by such authorities within the Republic of Korea.

When a member of the United States armed forces in Korea is summoned to appear before a Korean court, as a witness or as a defendant, United States authorities shall, unless military exigency requires otherwise, secure his attendance provided such attendance is compulsory under Korean law. If military exigency prevents such attendance, the authorities of the United States shall furnish a certificate stating the estimated duration of such disability.

Service of process upon a member of the United States armed forces or civilian component, or a dependent required as a witness or a defendant must be personal service in the English language. Where the service of process is to be effected by a Korean process server upon any person who is inside a military installation or area, the authorities of the United States shall take all measures necessary to enable the Korean process server to effect such service.

In addition, the Korean authorities shall promptly give copies of all criminal writs (including warrants, summonses, indictments, and subpoenas) to an agent designated by the United States authorities to receive them in all cases of Korean criminal proceedings involving a member of the United States armed forces or civilian component, or a dependent.

When citizens or residents of the Republic of Korea are required as witnesses or experts by the authorities of the United States, the courts and authorities of the Republic of Korea shall, in accordance with Korean law, secure the attendance of such persons. In these cases the authorities of the United States shall act

51
0234

through the Attorney General of the Republic of Korea, or such other agency as is designated by the authorities of the Republic of Korea.

Fees and other payments for witnesses shall be determined by the Joint Committee established under Article

2. The privileges and immunities of witnesses shall be those accorded by the law of the court, tribunal or authority before which they appear. In no event shall a witness be required to provide testimony which may tend to incriminate him.

3. If, in the course of criminal proceedings before authorities of the United States or the Republic of Korea, the disclosure of an official secret of either of these States or the disclosure of any information which may prejudice the security of either appears necessary for the just disposition of the proceedings, the authorities concerned shall seek written permission to make such disclosure from the appropriate authority of the State concerned.

RE Paragraph 9 (a)

The right to a prompt and speedy trial by the courts of the Republic of Korea shall include public trial by an impartial tribunal composed exclusively of judges who have completed their probationary period. A member of the United States armed forces or civilian component, or a dependent, shall not be tried by a military tribunal of the Republic of Korea.

RE Paragraph 9 (b)

A member of the United States armed forces or civilian component, or a dependent, shall not be arrested or detained by the authorities of the Republic of Korea without adequate cause, and he shall be entitled to an immediate

52

0235

hearing at which such cause must be shown in open court in his presence and the presence of his counsel. His immediate release shall be ordered if adequate cause is not shown. Immediately upon arrest or detention he shall be informed of the charges against him in a language which he understands.

He shall also be informed a reasonable time prior to trial of the nature of the evidence that is to be used against him. Counsel for the accused shall, upon request, be afforded the opportunity before trial to examine and copy the statements of witnesses obtained by authorities of the Republic of Korea which are included in the file forwarded to the court of the Republic of Korea scheduled to try the case.

RE Paragraph 9 (c) and (d)

A member of the United States armed forces or civilian component, or a dependent, who is prosecuted by the authorities of the Republic of Korea shall have the right to be present throughout the testimony of all witnesses, for and against him, in all judicial examinations, pretrial hearings, the trial itself, and subsequent proceedings, and shall be permitted full opportunity to examine the witnesses.

RE Paragraph 9 (e)

The right to legal representation shall exist from the moment of arrest or detention and shall include the right to have counsel present, and to consult confidentially with such counsel, at all preliminary investigations, examinations, pretrial hearings, the trial itself, and subsequent proceedings, at which the accused is present.

0236

53

RE Paragraph 9 (f)

The right to have the services of a competent interpreter shall exist from the moment of arrest or detention.

RE Paragraph 9 (g)

The right to communicate with a representative of the Government of the United States shall exist from the moment of arrest or detention, and no statement of the accused taken in the absence of such a representative shall be admissible as evidence in support of the guilt of the accused. Such representative shall be entitled to be present at all preliminary investigations, examinations, pretrial hearings, the trial itself, and subsequent proceedings, at which the accused is present.

RE Paragraph 9

A member of the United States armed forces or civilian component, or a dependent, tried by the authorities of the Republic of Korea shall be accorded every procedural and substantive right granted by law to the citizens of the Republic of Korea. If it should appear that an accused has been, or is likely to be, denied any procedural or substantive right granted by law to the citizens of the Republic of Korea, representatives of the two Governments shall consult in the Joint Committee on the measures necessary to prevent or cure such denial of rights.

In addition to the rights enumerated in items (a) through (g) of paragraph 9 of this Article, a member of the United States armed forces or civilian component, or a dependent, who is prosecuted by the authorities of the Republic of Korea:

0237

(a) shall be furnished a verbatim record of his trial in English;

(b) shall have the right to appeal a conviction or sentence; in addition, he shall be informed by the court at the time of conviction or sentencing of his right to appeal and of the time limit within which that right must be exercised;

(c) shall have credited to any sentence of confinement his period of pretrial confinement in a United States or Korean confinement facility;

(d) shall not be held guilty of a criminal offense on account of any act or omission which did not constitute a criminal offense under the law of the Republic of Korea at the time it was committed;

(e) shall not be subject to a heavier penalty than the one that was applicable at the time the alleged criminal offense was committed or was adjudged by the court of first instance as the original sentence;

(f) shall not be held guilty of an offense on the basis of rules of evidence or requirements of proof which have been altered to his prejudice since the date of the commission of the offense.

(g) shall not be compelled to testify against or otherwise incriminate himself;

(h) shall not be subject to cruel or unusual punishment;

(i) shall not be subject to prosecution or punishment by legislative or executive act;

(j) shall not be prosecuted or punished more than once for the same offense.

(k) shall not be required to stand trial if he is physically or mentally unfit to stand trial and participate in his defense;

(l) shall not be subjected to trial except under conditions consonant with the dignity of the United States armed forces, including appearing in appropriate

0238

-55-

military or civilian attire and unmanacled.

No confession, admission, or other statement, or real evidence, obtained by illegal or improper means will be considered by courts of the Republic of Korea in prosecutions under this Article.

In any case prosecuted by the authorities of the Republic of Korea under this Article no appeal will be taken by the prosecution from a judgment of not guilty or an acquittal nor will an appeal be taken by the prosecution from any judgment which the accused does not appeal, except upon grounds of errors of law.

The authorities of the United States shall have the right to inspect any Korean confinement facility in which a member of the United States armed forces, civilian component, or dependent is confined, or in which it is proposed to confine such an individual.

In the event of hostilities, the Republic of Korea will take all possible measures to safeguard mrembers of the United States armed forces, members of the civilian component, and their dependents who are confined in Korean confinement facilities, whether awaiting trial or serving a sentence imposed by the courts of the Republic of Korea. The Republic of Korea shall give sympathetic consideration to requests for release of these persons to the custody of responsible United States authorities. Necessary implementing provisions shall be agreed upon between the two governments through the Joint Committee.

Facilities utilized for the execution of a sentence to death or a period of confinement, imprisonment, or penal servitude, o r for the detention of members of the United States armed forces or civilian component or dependents, will

56

0230

meet minimum standards as agreed by the Joint Committee. The United States authorities shall have the right upon request to have access at any time to members of the United States armed forces, the civilian component, or their dependents who are confined or detained by authorities of the Republic of Korea. During the visit of these persons at Korean confinement facilities, United States authorities shall be authorized to provide supplementary care and provisions for such persons, such as clothing, food, bedding, and medical and dental treatment.

RE Paragraph 10 (a) and 10 (b)

The United States authorities will normally make all arrests within facilities and areas in use by the United States armed forces. The Korean authorities will normally not exercise the right of search, seizure, or inspection with respect to any person or property within facilities and areas in use by the authorities of the United States or with respect to property of the United States wherever situated, except in cases where the competent authorities of the United States consent to such search, seizure, or inspection by the Korean authorities of such persons or property.

Where search, seizure, or inspection with respect to persons or property within facilities and areas in use by the United States or with respect to property of the United States in Korea is desired by the Korean authorities, the United States authorities will undertake, upon request, to make such search, seizure, or inspection. In the event of a judgment concerning such property, except property owned or utilized by the United States Government or its instrumentalities, the United States will in accordance with its laws turn over such property to the

57

0240

Korean authorities for disposition in accordance with the judgment.

The United States authorities may arrest or detain in the vicinity of a facility or area any person in the commission or attempted commission of an offense against the security of that facility or area. Any such person who is not a member of the United States armed forces or civilian component or a dependent shall immediately be turned over to the Korean authorities.

0241

58

# ARTICLE ____

## CONTRACTORS

*+ Who are ordinarily Resident in the United States*

1. Persons, including corporations, their employees, and the dependents of such persons, present in Korea solely for the purpose of executing contracts with the United States for the benefit of the United States armed forces or other armed forces in Korea under the Unified Command receiving logistical support from the United States armed forces, who are designated by the Government of the United States in accordance with the provisions of paragraph 2 below, shall, except as provided in this Article, be subject to the laws and regulations of Korea.

2. The designation referred to in paragraph 1 above shall be made upon consultation with the Government of Korea and shall be restricted to cases where open competitive bidding is not practicable due to security considerations, to the technical qualifications of the contractors involved, to the unavailability of materials or services required by United States standards, or to limitations of United States law. The designation shall be withdrawn by the Government of the United States:

69

0242

(a) Upon completion of contracts with the United States
for the United States armed forces or other armed forces in
Korea under the Unified Command receiving logistical support
from the United States armed forces;

(b) Upon proof that such persons are engaged in business
activities in Korea other than those pertaining to the United
States armed forces or other armed forces in Korea under the
Unified Command receiving logistical support from the United
States armed forces;

(c) Upon proof that such persons are engaged in practices
illegal in Korea.

3. Upon certification by appropriate United States authorities
as to their identity, such persons shall be accorded the following
benefits of this Agreement:

(a) Rights of accession and movement, as provided for in
Article     , paragraph 2;

(b) Entry into Korea in accordance with the provisions of
Article     ;

(c) The exemption from customs duties, and other such
charges provided for in Article     , paragraph 3, for members

0243

60

of the United States armed forces, the civilian component, and their dependents;

(d) If authorized by the Government of the United States, the right to use the services of the activities provided for in Article    ;

(e) Those rights provided in Article    , paragraph 2, for members of the United States armed forces, the civilian component, and their dependents;

(f) If authorized by the Government of the United States, the right to use military payment certificates, as provided for in Article    ;

(g) The use of postal facilities provided for in Article    ;

(h) Those rights accorded the United States armed forces by Article    , paragraph 3, relating to utilities and services;

(i) Those rights provided to members of the United States armed forces, the civilian component, and their dependents by Article    , relating to driving permits and registration of vehicles;

(j) Exemption from the laws and regulations of Korea with respect to terms and conditions of employment, and licensing and registration of businesses and corporations.

4. The arrival, departure, and place of residence in Korea of such persons shall from time to time be notified by the United States armed

61

0244

forces to the Korean authorities.

5.  Upon certification by an authorized representative of the United States armed forces, depreciable assets, except houses, held, used or transferred by such persons exclusively for the execution of contracts referred to in paragraph 1 shall not be subject to taxes or similar charges of Korea.

6.  Upon certification by an authorized representative of the United States armed forces, such persons shall be exempt from taxation in Korea on the holding, use, transfer by death, or transfer to persons or agencies entitled to tax exemption under this Agreement, of movable property, tangible or intangible, the presence of which in Korea is due solely to the temporary presence of these persons in Korea, provided that such exemption shall not apply to property held for the purpose of investment or the conduct of other business in Korea or to any intangible property registered in Korea.

7.  The persons referred to in paragraph 1 shall not be liable to pay income or corporation taxes to the Government of Korea or to any other taxing agency in Korea on any income derived under a contract with the Government of the United States in connection with the construction, maintenance or operation of any of the facilities or areas covered by this

62

0245

Agreement.  Persons in Korea in connection with the execution of such a contract with the United States shall not be liable to pay any Korean taxes to the Government of Korea or to any taxing agency in Korea on income derived from sources outside of Korea, nor shall periods during which such persons are in Korea be considered periods of residence or domicile in Korea for the purposes of Korean taxation.  The provisions of this paragraph do not exempt such persons from payment of income or corporation taxes on income derived from Korean sources, other than those sources referred to in the first sentence of this paragraph, nor do they exempt such persons who claim Korean residence for United States income tax purposes from payment of Korean taxes on income.

8.

Agreed Minute:

1.  The execution of contracts with the United States in addition to those specified in paragraph 1 of Article      shall not exclude the persons provided for in Article    from the application of that Article.

*except para .(1) .?*

0246

63

## AGREED MINUTE - 2

2. Contractor employees who are present in Korea on the effective date of this agreement and who would qualify for the privileges contained in Article _____ but for the fact that they are not ordinarily resident in the United States shall be entitled to enjoy such privileges so long as their presence is for the purpose stated in paragraph 1 of Article _____.

67

0247

8.  The persons referred to in paragraph 1 shall be subject to those provisions of Article 제6계 and the Agreed Minutes thereto which pertain to members of the civilian component, and to dependents.

(C.J. 조항이 합의 될 대까지) 보류

66

0248

ARTICLE _____

3.  Upon certification by appropriate United
States authorities as to their identity, such persons
shall be accorded the following benefits of this
Agreement:

(a) Accession and movement, as provided for
in Article _____, paragraph 2;

(b) Entry into Korea in accordance with the
provisions of Article _____;

(c) The exemption from customs duties and other
such charges provided for in Article _____, paragraph
3, for members of the United States armed forces,
the civilian component, and their dependents;

(d) If authorized by the Government of the
United States, the use of the services of the
activities provided for in Article _____;

(e) Those provided in Article _____, paragraph
2, for members of the United States armed forces,
the civilian component, and their dependents;

(f) If authorized by the Government of the
United States, the use of military payment certificates,
as provided in Article _____;

0249

64

(g) The use of postal facilities provided
for in Article _____;

(h) The use of utilities and services in
accordance with those priorities, conditions,
rates, or tariffs accorded the United States
armed forces by Article ____, paragraph 3, relating
to utilities and services;

(i) Those provided to members of the United
States armed forces, the civilian component, and
their dependents by Article _____, relating to
driving permits and registration of vehicles;

(j) Exemption from the laws and regulations
of Korea with respect to terms and conditions
of employment, and licensing and registration of
businesses and corporations.

65

<u>REVISED US DRAFT OF PARAGRAPH 5</u>

5. (a) The authorities of the United States and the authorities of the Republic of Korea shall assist each other in the arrest of members of the United States armed forces, the civilian component, or their dependents in the territory of the Republic of Korea and in handing them over to the authority which is to have custody in accordance with the following provisions.

(b) The authorities of the Republic of Korea shall notify promptly the authorities of the United States of the arrest of any member of the United States armed forces, or civilian component, or a dependent. The military authorities of the United States shall promptly notify the authorities of the Republic of Korea of the arrest of a member of the United States armed forces, the civilian component, or a dependent in any case in which the Republic of Korea has the primary right to exercise jurisdiction.

(c) The custody of an accused member of the United States armed forces or civilian component, or of a dependent, over whom the Republic of Korea is to exercise jurisdiction shall, if he is in the hands of the United States, remain with the United States pending the conclusion of all judicial proceedings and until custody is requested by the authorities of the Republic of Korea. If he is in the hands of the Republic of Korea, he shall be promptly handed over to the authorities of the United States and remain in their custody pending completion of all judicial proceedings and until custody is requested by the authorities of the Republic of Korea. When an accused has been in the custody of the military authorities of the United States, they shall give sympathetic consideration to any request for the transfer of custody which may be made by the authorities of the Republic of Korea in specific cases. The United States authorities will make any such accused available to the authorities of the

0251

*and shall take all appropriate measures to the end and*
*to prevent any prejudice to the ~~court~~, ~~use~~ of Justice.*
*They shall take full* *account of any special* ~~repre~~
*regarding custody made by the authorities of the Republic of Korea.*

Republic of Korea upon their request for purposes of investigation and trial.

The authorities of the Republic of Korea shall give sympathetic consideration to a request from the ~~authorities~~ *military* of the United States for assistance in maintaining custody of an accused member of the United States armed forces, the civilian component, or a dependent.

(d) In respect of offenses solely against the security of the Republic of Korea provided in Paragraph 2(c), an accused shall be in the custody of the authorities of the Republic of Korea. (Subject US-ROK agreement on two understandings.)

2

3/7

ARTICLE____

## Labor Procurement

1. In this Article the expression:

(a) "employer" refers to the United States armed forces (including nonappropriated fund activities) and the persons referred to in the first paragraph of Article _____.

(b) "employee" refers to any civilian (other than a member of the civilian component) employed by an employer, except (1) a member of the Korean Service Corps, ~~who is an employee of the Government of Korea,~~ 삭제 (17개조6) and (2) a domestic employed by an individual member of the United States armed forces, civilian component or dependent thereof.

2. Employers may accomplish the recruitment, employment and management of employees directly and upon request by the employer, with the assistance of the authorities of the Republic of Korea (추가, 45차제의 1964.3.6)

3. The condition of employment, the compensation, and the labor-management practices shall be established by the United States armed forces for their employees in general conformity with the labor laws, customs and practices of the Republic of Korea; ~~provided however, that an employer may terminate employment whenever the continuation of such employment would materially impair the accomplishment of the mission of the United States armed forces.~~ → 삭제 1964. 3.6. (록구 1964. 3. 13)

4. (a) An employee shall have the same right to strike as an employee in a comparable position in the employment of the armed forces of the Republic of Korea. Such an employee may voluntarily organize and join a union or other employee group whose objectives are not inimical to the interests of the United States. Membership or nonmembership in such groups shall not be a cause for discharge or non-employment.

0253

2/

(b) Employers will maintain procedures designed to assure the just and timely resolution of employee grievances.

5. (a) Should the Republic of Korea adopt measures allocating labor, the United States armed forces shall be accorded employment privileges no less favorable than those enjoyed by the armed forces of the Republic of Korea.

(b) In the event of a national emergency, employees who have acquired skills essential to the mission of the United States armed forces shall be exempt from Republic of Korea military service or other compulsory service. The United States armed forces shall furnish to the Republic of Korea lists of those employees deemed essential.

6. Members of the civilian component shall not be subject to Korean laws or regulations with respect to their terms and conditions of employment.

AGREED MINUTES

1. The Republic of Korea will make available, at designated induction points, qualified personnel for Korean Service Corps units in numbers sufficient to meet the requirements of United States armed forces. The employment of a domestic by an individual member of the United States armed forces, civilian component or dependent thereof shall be governed by applicable Korean law and in addition by wage scales and control measures promulgated by the United States armed forces.

2. The undertaking of the United States Government to conform to Korean labor laws, customs, and practices, does not imply any waiver by the United States Government of its immunities under international law.

0254

## AGREED MINUTE

2. The undertaking of the United States Government to conform to Korean labor laws, customs, and practices, does not imply any waiver by the United States Government of its immunities under international law. Moreover, the United States Government may terminate employment whenever the continuation of such employment would materially impair the accomplishment of the mission of the United States armed forces.

0255

23

## AGREED MINUTE

3.  It is understood that the Government of the Republic of Korea shall be reimbursed for direct costs incurred in providing assistance requested pursuant to paragraph 2.

0256

24

1. It is recalled that we have discussed to work out agreement on the labor article through the 8 consecutive negotiating sessions durin the past ten months. It is the firm belief of the Korean negotiators that we have considerably made progressed ~~to reach the points of~~ toward agreement on certain matters except ~~minor~~ some divergencies ~~which we are to adjust and to compromise each other.~~ In this regard, Korean negotiators appreciate to the U.S. negotiators for their endeavors in making this progress and particularly in proposing significant modifications made at the previous session.

2. The Korean negotiators have carefully reviewed the revised draft of U.S. side and considered the views of U.S. negotiators as well, ~~to draw out our detailed comments on U.S. modifications as promised last session and to make concessions as far as possible.~~ As were clearly expressed ~~in several occasions~~ in the past ~~sessions, it is~~ it held position the real ~~hope~~ of the Korean negotiating team, ~~in the past and in the future~~ that the status including rights and privileges of Korean employees working for the U.S. armed forces, which presently enjoyed by them, will be enhanced and up-graded to the extent practicable. But, we are not to stick at realizing do not intend this standards ~~with~~ at the sacrifice of the U.S. armed forces. We are prepared to compromise to the ~~maximum~~ extent ~~possible~~ (at least) can have the same that the Korean employees keep ~~their~~ rights and privileges as ~~which~~ they are presently enjoying. ~~that is to say, we are not in a position to down-grade their status or to diminish their rights and privileges.~~

3. With this basic requirements and position ~~in mind,~~ we have made most significant modifications ~~out~~ of our former

0257

13

draft, ~~which are designed to comply with the views of the~~ *we table*
~~U.S. negotiators to the maximum extent possible. The table~~
~~of~~ our new revised draft ~~is~~ before you for your consideration.
As you see, the ~~underlined parts in most of pages are~~ *are underlined.*
modifications ~~by~~ the Korean side, which comprise twelve (12)
paragraphs including 6 sub-paragraphs. These modifications
include 6 paragraphs as well as 3 sub-paragraphs of U.S. draft
in part or as a whole ~~⊕~~ which Korean negotiators are now
prepared to accept, (in some cases), with minor ~~understanding~~ *reservation.*
~~It is very hopeful on the part of~~ Korean negotiators *hope* that the
U.S. side will accept those remaining paragraphs which
Korean side has ~~again renewed taking~~ *carefully revised in light of* views of U.S.
negotiators expressed at former session ~~into full consideration.~~

   4. ~~For the convenience of the meeting,~~ We are going to
explain, ~~with your permission,~~ our modifications paragraph
by paragraph and *at the same time* ~~to~~ comments on U.S. draft as well, ~~whenever~~
~~deemed necessary.~~ *With regard to* ~~As~~ the first paragraph ~~is concerned,~~ our
revised draft ~~provides the harmonized incorporation of~~ *designed to incorporate* both
Korean and U.S. drafts, except a deletion of "the Korean
Service Corps" for which both sides had already ~~agreed~~ *proposed* not
to raise ~~or include this question~~ within *the framework of* the present SOFA
negotiation. We therefore foresee no difficulty to agree ~~on~~ *on*
this paragraph.

   5. With regard to Paragraph 2, it is recalled that
the U.S. negotiators proposed at the 64th Session the
revised table which were designed, inter alia, to withhold
the right of direct employment and management, and the
Korean side counter-proposed at the 65th Session, revision
of the Paragraph to the effect that ~~implicitly~~ *article* enabling the
U.S. armed forces to accomplish direct employment and manage-

0258

2

ment, the assistance of the Korean authorities should be made use of to the maximum extent practicable. At that time, U.S. negotiators held the view that a literal wording should explicitly ~~be~~ made on the availability of direct employment and management by the U.S. armed forces and, again, at the previous session, the U.S. negotiators renewed a draft ~~to that effect, which appeared to be too broad and very flexible~~ _revised_ ~~newly substituted~~ de administration _for the word "manage"._ In order to meet the desire of the U. . side ~~to the maximum extent~~ and keeping our basic requirements to the minimum extent, we are now proposing the present draft paragraph for ~~adoption~~ _consideration._ In proposing this revision, the Korean negotiators wish to make it clear, ~~as an understanding between the both sides,~~ (N) that the employers shall endeavour to recruit and employ to the maximum extent practible with the assistance of the Korean authorities and may employ directly such skilled labor and specially trained technical personnel ~~as are unable to provide for by the Korean authorities,~~ ~~and~~ (N) that the employers may establish personnel administration practice for their employees, ~~(but shall not exercise severe disciplinary consure as well as the right to dismiss employees in certain circumstances and especially when disputes are involved.) Since the intention and purpose of this amendment were in full length reiterated at the previous sessions, the Korean negotiators would not repeat them here again.)~~ ~~As for~~ The third sentence of the paragraph, it is designed to have the relevant information on Korean employees, preferably ~~(on periodical basis, say annually or quarterly)~~ as may be required for labor administration by the Korean authorities, to which we presume no objection by the U.S. side.

0259

15-3

6. Turning to the Paragraph 3, there has been no great differences at the previous session with regard to the principle of conform by the employers with those conditions of employment laid down in the Korean labor legislation. The Korean negotiators expressed discussion was, however, centred on the inclusion of phrase "basic management needs" which was replaced by the phrase "military requirements" at the 68th session. At later time, the Korean negotiators expressed the view that the phrase was still ambiguous and too broad, which might have defined or explained. In that regard, Mr. Habib stated that "the interpretation of the phrase in individual cases would be referred to the Joint Committee." Again, the Korean negotiators maintained that "the phrase be defined before reaching agreement on this Article."

With these views expressed by both sides during, the Korean side has now tables them Agreed Minute #5 to which the Korean side attaches great importance. It is logical, we agree consider, that any action or measures taken in virtue of on account of 6 "the military requirements" shall be referred to the Joint Committee for clear interpretation, in case Korean side raises objection as and whenever disputes arise inconsistent with the Korean labor legislation. At this moment, We would like to make it clear that the Korean authorities would not raise objections to refer the matter every action or measure, unless the rights and privileges of Korean employees are deprived or diminished greatly. Of course, naturally we hope such cases would not occur.

With the condition that the U.S. side accept this Agreed Minute #5, the Korean side is ready prepared to accept the phrase "the military requirements" stipulated in Paragraph 3.

0260

It is added, in this connection, that the Korean negotiators still maintain ~~to hold~~ that the main clause of Paragraph 3 ~~exhibited~~ of proposal is preferable draft. ~~by the Korean side, which appears to be clearly conclusive and inclusive of all employment conditions so far.~~

7. As regards the Paragraph 4, of the U.S. draft it is the opinion of the Korean negotiators that the provisions of its sub-paragraph (a) relating to strike, labor union, and so on, are already covered with by the Paragraph 3 which stipulates that employer ~~employee~~ relations ~~to~~ conform with the existing Korean labor legislation. It is also our view that the sub-paragraph (a) is an unnecessary duplication and, therefore, we propose to delete it from the present Article. As for the sub-paragraph (b), we are prepared to accept ~~without reservation~~ it.

8. Turning to the Paragraph 5, we are pleased to accept the sub-paragraph (a), of the U.S. draft ~~without raising any objection~~.

As for the sub-paragraph (b), it is legally established practice that ~~any~~ all eligible Korean youths can't be exempted from their military service ~~under whatsoever qualifications~~ so far, for it is imperative duty of all youths under the provisions of the Constitution ~~as in the case of the United States~~ but some may be granted deferment, not exemption, of their military service under very special circumstances in accordance with the Korean Draft Law. On this matter, Korean negotiators have ~~nothing~~ but to reiterate the ~~standing~~ regulations of the Republic of Korean legislation. It is to be known that in Korea, no word "exemption" is applicable in-so-far as the military service is concerned, except to those who are the disabled or the crippled. Therefore, the Korean negotiators propose to adopt the sub-paragraph (b), as amended in the present Revised Korean Draft.

0261

17

9. May we invite your attention to the Paragraph 6 regarding the employment by the contractors, which was appeared in the original Korean draft. Since there have been no provisions relating to local employment by the contractors, Korean negotiators deem it necessary to maintain this clause (with ~~minor~~ *an* addition) that the employment conditions shall be governed in accordance with the Korean labor legislation. *We take it for granted* It is our ~~understanding~~ that the U.S. side ~~agreed~~ *would* ~~implicitly~~ on this points in principle.

With regard to the Paragraph 7 which is shown in the U.S. draft as Paragraph 6, we *have* no objection ~~to adopting this~~.

10. ~~Allow me to~~ Turn to the Agreed Minutes, the Para. 1 contains the second part of the U.S. draft, whereas the first part of the Para. is deleted in the light of our previous ~~understanding~~ *contention* that the matters concerning Korean Service Corps should be eliminated from the SOFA deliberation. With this understanding ~~in mind~~, this Paragraph would be accepted by both sides.

11. We are ~~very glad~~ *ready* to accept *the first sentence of* the Agreed Minutes #2. But, in so far as the second part is concerned, the Korean negotiators are firmly against the inclusion of it in the present Agreed Minutes. In this regard, the Korean negotiators held the view at the previous meeting that this addition would be unnecessary duplication of the revised Paragraph 3 of U.S. draft and would imply a retreat by the U.S. negotiators to a rigid position in the application of the phrase "military requirements". In this connection, the revised (Korean draft in its) Agreed Minutes #5 provides a proper *procedures* ~~manner~~ by which this sort of matters may be referred to the Joint Committee.

0262

18.

12. As for Agreed Minutes #3 and #4 containing the identical versions of the U.S. draft, Korean negotiators are willing to accept without any change. As regards the Agreed Minutes #5, full explanation was already made when we discussed the Paragraph 3.

Turning to the last question to establish procedures for the settlement of labor disputes which cannot be settled through the use of existing procedures of the U.S. armed forces, the Korean negotiators are now ready to agree on adopting a three stage procedures for settling any labor disputes as proposed by the U.S. negotiators at the 68th session. The Korean negotiators also agree with the views expressed by the U.S. side that the Joint Committee will resolve the disputes and its decisions shall be binding. In the opinion of the Korean negotiators, any practice disruptive of normal work requirements shall be minimized to the maximum extent possible, for which the Korean authorities would exert their utmost efforts to that end in cooperation with the U.S. military authorities as in the past and in the future, unless the Korean laws otherwise preclude to do so. That is to say, the Korean authorities are obliged to prevent the Korean employees from indulging in any practice disruptive of normal work requirements in case such practices are in violation of the relevant provisions of Korean legislation. This is logical and normal manner in any case. It is, therefore, proposed that any disruptive practices during the settlement procedures shall be regulated in accordance with the applicable provisions of Korean labor law which accommodates every possible circumstances to be arisen in respect of labor disputes. It is illogical, and against

0263

common sense, to preclude the exercise of fundamental rights of laborers for a indefinite period of time in ~~the name~~ of "settlement procedures ~~being proceeded~~". By this, Korean negotiators do not ~~insist~~ that the employers shall be able to engage in disruptive practice at any time they feel like. Our assertion is simply based on the necessity that their interests shall be protected in such a reasonable manner as are provided for in the Korean labor legislation. Whereas the employment conditions will be governed by the Korean labor regulations, ~~may not~~ employees' rights to strike be governed under the same Korean laws. With this, nothing ~~deceives~~ the ~~intention and~~ accomplishment of the mission of the United States armed forces. ~~Moreover, nothing would prevent the U.S. armed forces from promoting and maintaining good employer-employee relations.~~ In this sence, it is our conceived hope that the U.S. side will find our proposals acceptable ~~for the sake of~~ Korean employees ~~who are assisting the U.S. armed forces for carrying out~~ common mission of defense and security as a whole.

8

20

한·미국 간의 상호방위조약 제4조에 의한 시설과 구역 및 한국에서의 미국군대의 지위에 관한 협정(SOFA) 전59권. 1966.7.9 서울에서 서명 : 1967.2.9 발효(조약 232호) (V.47 한·미국 양측 교섭안) 271

# Revised ~~Nonagreement of Labor~~ Article

(The underlined parts are modifications)

1. The United States armed forces and the organizations provided for in Article _____ (hereinafter referred to as "employer") may employ civilian personnel (hereinafter referred to as "employee") under this Agreement. Such civilian personnel shall be nationals of the Republic of Korea.

2. The employers provided for in Paragraph 1 shall recruit and employ to the maximum extent practicable with the assistance of the authorities of the Republic of Korea. The employers may accomplish such recruitment, employment and administration directly as may be essentially required. The United States military authorities shall provide such relevant information on Korean employees as may be required for labor administration to the Office of Labor Affairs of the Republic of Korea.

3. To the extent not inconsistent with the provision of this article or the military requirements of the United States armed forces, the conditions of employment and work, such as those relating to wages and supplementary payments, the conditions for the protection and welfare of employees, compensations, and the rights of employees, concerning labor relations shall conform with those laid down by the legislation of the Republic of Korea.

4. Employers will maintain procedures designed to assure the just and timely resolution of employee grievances.

5. (a) Should the Republic of Korea adopt measures allocating labor, the United States Armed Forces shall be accorded employment privileges no less favorable than those enjoyed by the armed forces of the Republic of Korea.

*9*

0265

(b) In the event of a national emergency such as war, hostilities, or other imminent situations, the employees who have acquired skills essential to the mission of the United States Armed Forces may, upon request of the United States Armed Forces, be deferred from Republic of Korea military service or other compulsory services. The United States armed forces shall in advance furnish to the Republic of Korea lists of those employees deemed essential.

6. The United States Government shall ensure that the contractors referred to in Article _____ employ the Korean personnel to the maximum extent practicable in connection with their activities under this Agreement and the conditions of employment, compensation, and labor-management practices established by the contractors for their employees conform with those laid down by the legislation of the Republic of Korea.

7. Members of the civilian component shall not be subject to Korean laws or regulations with respect to their terms and conditions of employment.


AGREED MINUTES

1. The employment of a domestic by an individual member of the United States armed forces, civilian component or dependent thereof shall be governed by applicable Korean legislation and in addition by wage scales and control measures promulgated by the United States armed forces.

2. The undertaking of the United States to conform with those laid down by the legislation of the Republic of Korea does not imply any waiver by the United States Government of its immunities under international law.

0266

3. Employers shall withhold from the pay of their employees, and pay over to the Government of the Republic of Korea, withholdings required by the income tax legislation of the Republic of Korea.

4. It is understood that the Government of the Republic of Korea shall be reimbursed for direct costs incurred in providing assistance made pursuant to Paragraph 2.

5. Any action and measures, to be taken by the employers on the account of "military requirements" provided for in Paragraph 3, and to be inconsistent with the Korean labor legislation, shall be referred in prior for consultation to the Joint Committee and be subject to the decision thereof.

6. With regard to any dispute between the employers and any employees or labor unions which cannot be settled through the use of existing procedures of the United States Armed Forces, settlement shall be accomplished in the following manner:

(a) The dispute shall be referred to the Office of Labor Affairs, Ministry of Health and Social Affairs, Republic of Korea, for conciliation.

(b) In the event that the dispute is not settled by the procedures described in (a) above, the dispute shall be referred to the Joint Committee, which may refer the matter to the Labor Sub-Committee or specially designated Committee for arbitration to resolve the dispute.

(c) In the event that the dispute is not settled by the procedures outlined above, the Joint Committee will resolve the dispute. The decisions of the Joint Committee shall be binding.

0267

(d) During the period in which a dispute is being handled by the procedures mentioned in paras (a), (b) and (c) above, neither employee organizations nor employees shall indulge in any practice disruptive of normal work requirements in violation of the provisions laid down in the Korean labor legislation.

(e) Failure of any recognized employee organization or employee to abide by the decision of the Joint Committee on any dispute, or indulging in practice disruptive of normal work requirements during settlement procedure in violation of the provisions laid down in the Korean labor legislation, shall be considered cause for the deprivation of the rights and protection accorded by the relevant laws of the Republic of Korea.

0268

12

15 December 1964

<u>Revised US Draft of Labor Article</u>

(The underlined parts are modifications authorized by State-Defense
    in Dec 1964)

1.  In this Article the expression:

    (a)  "employer" refers to the United States Armed Forces
(including nonappropriated fund activities) and the persons referred to in
the first paragraph of Article _____.

    (b)  "employee" refers to any civilian (other than a member
of the civilian component) employed by an employer, except (1) a member of
the Korean Service Corps and (2) a domestic employed by an individual member
of the United States Armed Forces, civilian component or dependent thereof.

2.  <u>Employers may recruit, employ and administer their personnel.</u>
<u>Recruitment services of the Government of the Republic of Korea will be</u>
<u>utilized insofar as is practicable.</u>  In case employers accomplish direct
recruitment of employees, employers will provide available relevant
information as may be required for labor administration to the Office of
Labor Affairs of the Republic of Korea.

3.  To the extent not inconsistent with the provisions of this article or
the military requirements the United States Armed Forces, the conditions of
employment, compensation, and labor-management practices established by the
United States Armed Forces for their employees will conform with the labor
laws, customs and practices of the Republic of Korea.

4.  (a)  An employee shall have the same right to strike as an employee
in a comparable position in the employment of the Armed Forces of the
Republic of Korea.  Such an employee may voluntarily organize and join a
union or other employee group whose objectives are not inimical to the

0269

276  주한미군지위협정(SOFA) 서명 및 발효 18

interests of the United States. Membership or nonmembership in such groups shall not be a cause for discharge or nonemployment.

(b) Employers will maintain procedures designed to assure the just and timely resolution of employee grievances.

5. (a) Should the Republic of Korea adopt measures allocating labor, the United States Armed Forces shall be accorded employment privileges no less favorable than those enjoyed by the armed forces of the Republic of Korea.

(b) In the event of a national emergency, employees who have acquired skills essential to the mission of the United States Armed Forces shall be exempt from Republic of Korea military service or other compulsory service. The United States armed forces shall furnish to the Republic of Korea lists of those employees deemed essential. *in advance*

6. Members of the civilian component shall not be subject to Korean laws or regulations with respect to their terms and conditions of employment.

AGREED MINUTES

1. The Republic of Korea will make available, at designated induction points, qualified personnel for Korean Service Corps units in numbers sufficient to meet the requirements of United States Armed Forces. The employment of a domestic by an individual member of the United States Armed Forces, civilian component or dependent thereof shall be governed by applicable Korean law and in addition by wage scales and control measures promulgated by the United States Armed Forces.

2. The undertaking of the United States Government to conform to Korean labor laws, customs, and practices, does not imply any waiver by the United

6

0270

States Government of its immunities under international law. The United States Government may terminate employment at any time the continuation of such employment is inconsistent with the military requirements of the United States Armed Forces.

3. Employers will withhold from the pay of their employees, and pay over to the Government of the Republic of Korea withholdings required by the income tax legislation of the Republic of Korea.

4. It is understood that the Government of the Republic of Korea shall be reimbursed for direct costs incurred in providing assistance requested pursuant to paragraph 2.

5. With regard to any dispute between employers and any recognized employee organization or employees which cannot be settled through the use of existing procedures of the United States Armed Forces, settlement shall be accomplished as provided below. During such disputes neither employee organizations nor employees shall engage in any practices disruptive of normal work requirements:

(a) The dispute shall be referred to the Office of Labor Affairs, Ministry of Health and Social Affairs, Republic of Korea, for conciliation.

(b) In the event that the dispute is not settled by the procedure described in (a) above, the matter may be referred to the Joint Committee, which may refer the matter to the Labor Sub-Committee or specially designated Committee, for further fact-finding, review and conciliation efforts.

(c) In the event that the dispute is not settled by the procedures outlined above, the Joint Committee will resolve the dispute. The decisions

7

0271

of the Joint Committee shall be binding.

(d) Failure of any recognized employee organization or employee to abide by the decision of the Joint Committee on any dispute, or engaging in practices disruptive of normal work requirements during settlement procedures, shall be considered just cause for the withdrawal of recognition of that organization and the discharge of that employee.

0272

8

4

(Underlining indicates changes from U.S. draft of the Labor Article tabled on December 23, 1964)

1. In this Article the expression:

(a) "employer" refers to the United States Armed Forces (including nonappropriated fund activities) and the persons referred to in the first paragraph of Article (_____).

(b) "employee" refers to any civilian (other than a member of the civilian component) employed by an employer, except (1) a member of the paramilitary Korean Service Corps and (2) a domestic employed by an individual member of the United States Armed Forces, civilian component or dependent thereof.

2. Employers may recruit, employ and administer their personnel. Recruitment services of the Government of the Republic of Korea will be utilized insofar as is practicable. In case employers accomplish direct recruitment of employees, employers will provide such relevant information as may be required for labor administration to the Office of Labor Affairs of the Republic of Korea.

3. To the extent not inconsistent with the provisions of this Article or the military requirements of the United States Armed Forces, the conditions of employment, compensation, and labor-management practices established by the United States Armed Forces for their employees will conform with the labor laws, customs and practices of the Republic of Korea.

4. (a) Employers will maintain procedures designed to assure the just and timely resolution of employee grievances.

U.S.—1

0273

(b)  An employee may voluntarily organize and join a union or other employee group whose objectives are not inimical to the interests of the United States.  Membership or non-membership in such groups shall not be a factor in employment or other actions affecting employees.

(c)  Unions or other employee groups recognized by the armed forces of the United States, pursuant to sub-paragraph (b) above, will be accorded the right of consultation with appropriate authorities of the United States armed forces.

(d)  Any dispute between employers and employees or any recognized employee organization, which cannot be settled through the use or procedures of the United States armed forces, shall be settled as follows:

(1)  The dispute shall be referred to the Office of Labor Affairs, Ministry of Health and Social Affairs, Republic of Korea for conciliation.

(2)  In the event that the dispute is not settled by the procedure described in (1) above, the matter will be referred to the Joint Committee, which may refer the matter to the Labor Sub-Committee or to a specially-designated committee, for further fact-finding, review, and conciliation efforts.

(3)  In the event that the dispute is not settled by the procedures outlined above, the Joint Committee will resolve the dispute. The decisions of the Joint Committee shall be binding.

(4)  Failure of any recognized employee organization or employee to bide by the decision of the Joint Committee on any dispute,

2

0274

2

or engaging in practices disruptive of normal work requirements during settlement procedures, shall be considered just cause for the withdrawal of recognition of that organization and the discharge of that employee.

(e) An employee shall be subject to the same legal provisions concerning strikes and other work stoppages as an employee in a comparable position in the employment of the armed forces of the Republic of Korea.

5. (a) Should the Republic of Korea adopt measures allocating labor, the United States Armed Forces shall be accorded allocation privileges no less favorable than those enjoyed by the Armed Forces of the Republic of Korea.

(b) In the event of a national emergency, such as war, hostilities, or situations where war or hostilities may be imminent, employees who have acquired skills essential to the mission of the United States Armed Forces shall, upon request of the United States Armed Forces, be deferred from Republic of Korea military service or other compulsory service. The United States Armed Forces shall furnish in advance to the Republic of Korea lists of those employees deemed essential.

6. Members of the civilian component shall not be subject to Korean laws or regulations with respect to their terms and condition of employment.

3

after agreement thereon
consultation

0275

## AGREED MINUTES

1. The Republic of Korea will make available, at designated induction points, qualified personnel for Korean Service Corps units in numbers sufficient to meet the requirements of United States Armed Forces.

2. It is understood that the Government of the Republic of Korea shall be reimbursed for direct costs incurred in providing assistance requested pursuant to paragraph 2.

3. The undertaking of the United States Government to conform to Korean labor laws, customs, and practices, does not imply any waiver by the United States Government of its immunities under international law. The United States Government may terminate employment at any time the continuation of such employment is inconsistent with the military requirements of the United States Armed Forces.

4. Employers will withhold from the pay of their employees, and pay over to the Government of the Republic of Korea withholdings required by the income tax legislation of the Republic of Korea.

5. When employers cannot conform with provisions of labor legislation of the Government of the Republic of Korea applicable under this Article on account of the military requirements of the United States Armed Forces, the matter shall be reported, in advance whenever possible, to the Joint Committee for its consideration and review.

4

0276

<u>Claims Article</u>

<u>Proposed Changes in Korean Draft</u>

1. <u>Paragraph 2(a)</u>

Delete "and located in the Republic of Korea"

2. <u>Paragraph 2(f)</u>

"Each party waives its claim in any such case up to the amount
of 1,400 United States dollars or its equivalent in Korean currency
at the rate of exchange provided for in the Agreed Minute to Article ___
at the time the claim is filed."

3. <u>Paragraph 5(e)(i)</u>

"Where the United States alone is responsible, the amount awarded
or adjudged shall be distributed in the proportion of 25 percent
chargeable to the Republic of Korea and 75 percent chargeable to the
United States."

4. <u>Paragraph 5(e)(iii)</u>

"Every half year, a statement of the sums paid by the Republic of
Korea in the course of the half-yearly period in respect of every case
regarding which the liability, amount and proposed distribution on a
percentage basis has been approved by the United States shall be sent
to the appropriate authorities of the United States, together with a
request for reimbursement. Such reimbursement shall be made in won
within the shortest possible time."

5. <u>Paragraph 5(f)</u>

Change "excluding" to "including".

6. <u>Paragraph 9(b)</u>

"In the case of any private movable property, excluding that in
use by the United States armed forces, which is subject to compulsory
execution under Korean law, and is within the facilities and areas in
use by the United States armed forces, the United States authorities
shall, upon the request of the Korean courts, render all assistance
within their power to see that such property is turned over to the
Korean authorities."

0277

70

7.  Paragraph 9(c)

    "The authorities of the United States and the Republic of Korea shall cooperate in the procurement of evidence for a fair disposition of claims under this Article."

8.  Paragraph 12   (new)

    "For the purposes of this Article, members of the Korean Augmentation to the United States Army (KATUSA) shall be considered as members of the United States armed forces, and members of the Korean Service Corps (KSC) shall be considered as employees of the armed forces of the Republic of Korea."

9.  Paragraph 13   (new) ( 別添 11 참조 )

    "The provisions of this Article shall not apply to any claims which arose before the entry into force of this Agreement."

10. Proposed Agreed Minute

    Tabled separately

11. In order to make this article conform to the rest of the Agreement:

    a. Substitute "armed forces" for "armed services"

    b. Substitute "performance of his official duties" for "execution of his official duties"

    c. Substitute "for official purposes" for "in the execution of its official duty"

    d. Substitute "counter claims" for "counter measures"

    wherever appropriate.

0278

7/

## 12. Paragraph 9(a)

The United States shall not claim immunity from the jurisdiction of the courts of the Republic of Korea for members or employees of the United States armed forces in respect of the civil jurisdiction of the courts of the Republic of Korea except in respect of proceedings for the enforcement of any judgment given against them in the Republic of Korea in a matter arising from the performance of their official duties or except after payment in full satisfaction of a claim.

0279

172

## Agreed Minute

A. Unless otherwise provided,

    1. The provisions of paragraphs five, six, seven and eight of this article will become effective six months from the date of entry into force of this agreement as to claims arising from incidents in the Seoul Special City area.

    2. The provisions of paragraphs five, six, seven and eight will be progressively extended to other areas of Korea as determined and defined by the Joint Committee.

B. Until such time as the provisions of paragraphs five, six, seven and eight become effective in any given area

    1. The United States shall process and settle claims (other than contractual claims) arising out of the acts or omissions of members or employees of the United States armed forces done in the performance of official duty or out of any other act, omission or occurence for which the United States armed forces are legally responsible, which cause damage in the Republic of Korea to parties other than the two governments;

    2. The United States shall entertain other non-contractual claims against members or employees of the armed forces and may offer an ex gratia payment in such cases and in such amount as is determined by the appropriate United States authorities; and

    3. Each party shall have the right to determine whether a member or employee of its armed forces was engaged in the performance of official duties and whether property owned by it was being used by its armed forces for official purposes.

C. For the purposes of subparagraph 2(d), subparagraph 5(e) shall be effective throughout Korea from the date of entry into force of this agreement.

0280

73

# 정/리/보/존/문/서/목/록

| 기록물종류 | 문서-일반공문서철 | 등록번호 | 946 9619 | | 등록일자 | 2006-07-27 |
|---|---|---|---|---|---|---|
| 분류번호 | 741.12 | 국가코드 | US | | 주제 | |

| 문서철명 | 한.미국 간의 상호방위조약 제4조에 의한 시설과 구역 및 한국에서의 미국군대의 지위에 관한 협정 (SOFA) 전59권. 1966.7.9 서울에서 서명 : 1967.2.9 발효 (조약 232호) *원본 |
|---|---|

| 생산과 | 미주과/조약과 | 생산년도 | 1952 - 1967 | 보존기간 | 영구 |
|---|---|---|---|---|---|

| 담당과(그룹) | 조약 | 조약 | | 서가번호 | -- |
|---|---|---|---|---|---|

| 참조분류 | |
|---|---|

| 권차명 | V.48 의제 및 초안 |
|---|---|

**내용목차**

1. 의제 (p.2~101)
2. 초안 (p.102~309)

\* 일지 :

| | |
|---|---|
| 1953.8.7 | 이승만 대통령-Dulles 미국 국무장관 공동성명 |
| | - 상호방위조약 발효 후 군대지위협정 교섭 약속 |
| 1954.12.2 | 정부, 주한 UN군의 관세업무협정 체결 제의 |
| 1955.1월, 5월 | 미국, 제의 거절 |
| 1955.4.28 | 정부, 군대지위협정 제의 (한국측 초안 제시) |
| 1957.9.10 | Hurter 미국 국무차관 방한 시 각서 수교 (한국측 제의 수락 요구) |
| 1957.11.13, 26 | 정부, 개별 협정의 단계적 체결 제의 |
| 1958.9.18 | Dawling 주한미국대사, 형사재판관할권 협정 제외 조건으로 행정협정 체결 의사 전달 |
| 1960.3.10 | 정부, 토지, 시설협정의 우선적 체결 강력 요구 |
| 1961.4.10 | 장면 국무총리-McConaughy 주한미국대사 공동성명으로 교섭 개시 합의 |
| 1961.4.15, 4.25 | 제1, 2차 한.미국 교섭회의 (서울) |
| 1962.3.12 | 정부, 교섭 재개 촉구 공한 송부 |
| 1962.5.14 | Burger 주한미국대사, 최규하 장관 면담 시 형사재판관할권 문제 제기 않는 조건으로 교섭 재개 통고 |
| 1962.9.6 | 한.미국 간 공동성명 발표 (9월 중 교섭 재개 합의) |
| 1962.9.20~ 1965.6.7 | 제1-81차 실무 교섭회의 (서울) |
| 1966.7.8 | 제82차 실무 교섭회의 (서울) |
| 1966.7.9 | 서명 |
| 1967.2.9 | 발효 (조약 232호) |

## 마/이/크/로/필/름/사/항

| 촬영연도 | *롤 번호 | 화일 번호 | 후레임 번호 | 보관함 번호 |
|---|---|---|---|---|
| 2006-11-24 | I-06-0072 | 01 | 1-309 | |

0001

# 1. 의제

0002

SOFA NEGOTIATION

Agenda for 5th Session

14:00 Nov. 1, 1962

1. Continuation of Discussion on:

    a. Preamble

    b. Definition

    c. Entry and Exit

2. Consideration of Subsequent Subject

3. Other Business

4. Agenda and Date of Next Meeting

5. Press Release

0003

8-10

SOFA NEGOTIATION

Agenda for 12th Session

15:00 January 24,1963

1. Continuation of Discussion on:

      (a) Customs Duties

      (b.) Utilities and Services ✓

2. Discussion on:

      a. Meteorological Services ✓

      (b) Respect for Local Law ✓

      (c) Enrollment and Training of ✓
         Reservists

3. Other Business

4. Agenda and Date of Next Meeting

5. Press Release

0004

Agenda for 13th Session

14:00 February 5, 1963

1. Continuation of Discussion on:

    a. Customs Duties

    b. Respect for Local Law

    c. Enrollment and Training of Reservists.

*( the persons who are ----- pursuant to Article .)*

*① 9(c) 4호m 7(e) ROK을 挿入*
*② AH. 1. 4 及 5 ── OK*
*2 m free q duty 아 之m reasonable quantity 을 挿入*
*● but excluding NON-AFO 3. 을 挿入*
*● 6. authorized by US Law and service Reg. 削附조*

2. Other Business

3. Agenda and Date of Next Meeting → Feb 14,

4. Press Release

0005

Agenda for 14th Session

14:00 February 14, 1963

1. Continuation of Discussion on:

    a. Utilities and Services

    b. Enrollment and Training of

       Reservists

2. Discussion on:

    Currency Control

3. Other Business

4. Agenda and Date of Next Meeting

5. Press Release

0006

SOFA NEGOTIATION

Agenda for 15th Session

1400: February 25, 1963

1. Continuation of Discussion on:

    a. Currency Control Article

    b. Enrollment and Training of Reservists Article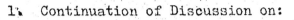

    c. Joint Committee Article

    d. Definitions Article

    e. Control of Air Traffic and Navigations Article

2. Other Business

3. Agenda and Date of Next Meeting

4. Press Release

0007

<u>SOFA NEGOTIATION</u>

<u>Agenda for 16th Session</u>

14:00 March 8, 1963

1. Continuation of Discussion on:

    a. Control of Air Traffic and Navigations Article

    b. Currency Control Article

    c. Facilities and Areas Article

2. Discussion on:

    Military Payment Certificate Article

3. Other Business

4. Agenda and Date of Next Meeting 3/19th. 2:00 pm,

5. Press Release

0008

Agenda for 17th Session

14:00 March 19, 1963

1. Continuation of Discussion on:

    a. Currency Control Article

    b. Military Payment Certificates
       Article

    c. Definitions Article ── 定義條文

    d. Facilities and Areas Article

2. Other Business

3. Agenda and Date of Next Meeting

4. Press Release

0009

SOFA NEGOTIATION

Agenda for 18th Session

14:00 March 29, 1963

1. Continuation of Discussion on:

    Facilities and Areas Article

2. Discussion on:

    Army Post Offices Article

3. Other Business

4. Agenda and Date of Next Meeting

5. Press Release

*11th. April. 1963*

0010

<u>SOFA NEGOTIATION</u>

<u>Agenda for 19th Session</u>

14:00 April 11, 1963

1. Continuation of Discussion on:

    b a.  Customs Duties Article

    a b.  Military Post Offices Article

    c.  Facilities and Areas Article

2. Other Business ( Col. Solf 대개 되어 유감이다 )

3. Agenda and Date of Next Meeting

4. Press Release

0011

<u>SOFA NEGOTIATION</u>

<u>Agenda for 20th Session</u>

14:00 April 24, 1963

1. Continuation of Discussion on:

    a. Utilities and Services Article

    b. Meteorological Services Article

2. Discussion on:

    a. Armed Forces Contractors Article

    b. Non-appropriated Fund Organizations Article

3. Other Business

4. Agenda and Date of Next Meeting

5. Press Release

0012

SOFA NEGOTIATION

Agenda for 21st Session

14:00 May 2, 1963

1. Continuation of Discussion on:

   a. Armed Forces Contractors Article → 討議하지못했음

   b. Non-appropriated Fund Organizations
      Article

2. Other Business

3. Agenda and Date of Next Meeting

4. Press Release

0013

<u>SOFA NEGOTIATION</u>

<u>Agenda for 22nd Session</u>

14:00 May 17, 1963

1. Continuation of Discussion on:

    a. Non-Appropriated Fund Organizations/ ~~Korean Draft~~
       Activities Article               1 (b)

    b. Armed Forces Contractors Article

2. Other Business

3. Agenda and Date of Next Meeting

4. Press Release

0014

SOFA NEGOTIATION

Agenda for 23rd Session

14:00 May 31, 1963

1. Continuation of Discussion on:
   a. Contractors Article
   b. Respect for Local Law Article

2. Discussion on:
   Vehicle and Driver Licenses Article

3. Other Business

4. Agenda and Date of Next Meeting

5. Press Release

0015

_Col. Amigelow_

## SOFA NEGOTIATION

### Agenda for 24th Session

14:00 June 12, 1963

1. Continuation of Discussion on:

    a. Vehicle and Driver Licenses Article

    b. Respect for Local Law Article ━━ 회호

    c. Utilities and Services Article

2. Discussion on:

    Taxation Article

3. Other Business

4. Agenda and Date of Next Meeting

5. Press Release

_25th Session_

_1. Texation_

_2. Health & Sanitation_

_3. Local Procurements_

_4. Security Measures_

0016

<u>SOFA NEGOTIATION</u>

<u>Agenda for 26th Session</u>

14:00 July 10, 1963

1. Continuation of Discussion on:

    a. Health and Sanitation Article

    b. Local Procurement Article

    c. Safety and Security Measures for U.S. Armed Forces, Its Members, Dependents, and Property Article

2. Other Business

3. Agenda and Date of Next Meeting *July 25, 2:00*

4. Press Release

0017

<u>SOFA NEGOTIATION</u>

<u>Agenda for the 27th Session</u>

14:00 July 25, 1963

1. Continuation of Discussion on:

   a. Health and Sanitation Article  ──→ 1. Coordination 반영程.
                                          2. 처리法 등 9. C 예비회의

   b. Local Procurement Article

   c. Foreign Currency Control Article

2. Other Business

3. Agenda and Date of Next Meeting  ──→ Aug. 8.  2:00 PM
                                            (木)

4. Press Release

0018

## SOFA NEGOTIATION
## Agenda for the 28th Session

14:00 August 8, 1963

1. Continuation of Discussion on:

    a. Contractors Article

    b. Vehicle and Drvier Licenses Article

2. Discussion on:

    Claims Article

3. Other Business

4. Agenda and Date of Next Meeting 8/22. ~~

5. Press Release

0019

SOFA NEGOTIATION

Agenda for the 29th Session

15:00 August 22, 1963

1. Continuation of Discussion on:

   a. Vehicle and Driver Licenses Article

   b. Claims Article

2. Other Business

3. Agenda and Date of Next Meeting

4. Press Release

0020

<u>SOFA NEGOTIATION</u>

<u>Agenda for the 29th Session</u>

15:00 August 22, 1963

1. Continuation of Discussion on:

   a.  Vehicle and Driver Licenses Article — 完全合意

   b.  Claims Article

2. Other Business

3. Agenda and Date of Next Meeting

4. Press Release

0021

<u>SOFA NEGOTIATION</u>
Agenda for the 29th Session

14:00 September 5, 1963

*Col. Nye.*
*Col. drucker*
*M. Ford → 轄屬*
*last time*

1. Continuation of Discussion on:

   Claims article

2. Other Business

3. Agenda and Date of Next Meeting *Sept. 20*
   *2.00 P.M*

4. Press Release

0022

SOFA NEGOTIATION

Agenda for the 31st Session

14:00 September 20, 1963

1. Continuation of Discussion on:

a. Facilities and Areas Article (B & C)

b. Contractors Article ~ next time

c. Military Payment Certificates Article

d. Local Procurement Article

2. Other Business

3. Agenda and Date of Next Meeting 10/4. 2:00

4. Press Release

0023

<u>SOFA NEGOTIATION</u>

<u>Agenda for the 32nd Session</u>

14:00 October 4, 1963

1. Continuation of Discussion on:

   a. Facilities and Areas Article (A,B & C)

   b. Contractors Article

2. Other Business

3. Agenda and Date of Next Meeting 10/18 (金)

4. Press Release

0024

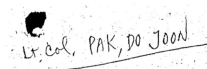

Lt. Col. PAK, DO JOON

<u>SOFA NEGOTIATION</u>

<u>Agenda for the 33rd Session</u>

14:00 October 18, 1963

1. Continuation of Discussion on:
   ✓ a. Facilities and Areas Article  4(b) — OK
     b. Contractors Article
   ✓ c. Taxation Article ——— 승인(完了)

2. Other Business

3. Agenda and Date of Next Meeting

4. Press Release

0025

발언 허승... 대학교 이정민 (로... 총... 조광정... 사무상 이름... 이번... 하기 회의... 부치.

<u>SOFA NEGOTIATION</u>

<u>Agenda for the 34th Session</u>

14;00 October 30,1963

1. Continuation of Discussion on:

    (a.) Air Traffic Control and Navigational Aids ___ 완습보류
        Article

    (b.) Customs Article

    c. Military Post Offices Article

    d. Utilities and Services Article ___

2. Discussion on:

    Revision of the Agreement Article — *tabled*

3. Other Business

4. Agenda and Date of Next Meeting

5. Press Release

0026

# SOFA NEGOTIATION

## Agenda for the 35th Session

14:00 November 14, 1963

1. Continuation of Discussion on:

    a.  Customs Article

    b.  Military Post Offices Article

    c.  Utilities and Services Article

    d.  Revision of the Agreement Article

2. Other Business

3. Agenda and Date of Next Meeting

4. Press Release

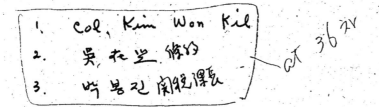

한·미국 간의 상호방위조약 제4조에 의한 시설과 구역 및 한국에서의 미국군대의 지위에 관한 협정(SOFA)
전59권. 1966.7.9 서울에서 서명 : 1967.2.9 발효(조약 232호) (V.48 의제 및 초안)　315

SOFA NEGOTIATION

Agenda for the 36th Session

15:00, December 5, 1963

1. Continuation of Discussions on:

   a. Customs Article

   b. Non-Appropriated Fund Organization/Activities
      Article

   √ c. Revision of the Agreement Article — 含위台度 (36)

2. Other Business

3. Agenda and Date of the Next Meeting

4. Press Release

Col. Kim Won Kil

Mr. Oh, Jae 個인

0028

SOFA NEGOTIATION

Agenda for the 37th Session

15:00, December 27, 1963

1. Continuation of Discussions on:
    a. Non-Appropriated Fund Organizations Article
    b. Customs Article
    c. Military Post Offices Article
2. Other Business
3. Agenda and Date of the Next Meeting
4. Press Release

0029

<u>SOFA NEGOTIATION</u>

<u>Agenda for the 38th Session</u>

15:30, January 9, 1963

1. Continuation of Discussions on:
   b. Customs Article
   b. Non-Appropriated Fund Organizations Article
   c. Military Post Offices Article
2. Other Business
3. Agenda and Date of the Next Meeting
4. Press Release

Capt. Brownlie — 離韓
Capt. Wayne — Welcome,

_____

Utilities & Services.

0030

<u>SOFA NEGOTIATION</u>

Agenda for the 39th Session

14:00 January 17, 1964

1.  Continuation of Discussions on:

    a. Customs Article

    b. Military Post Offices Article

    c. Utilities and Services Article

2.  Other Business

3.  Agenda and Date of the Next Meeting

4.  Press Release

0031

<u>SOFA NEGOTIATION</u>

Agenda for the 40th Session

14:00 January 24, 1964

1. Continuation of Discussions on:

   a. Military Post Offices Article

   b. Customs Article

   c. Non-Appropriated Fund Organizations Article

2. Other Business

3. Agenda and Date of the Next Meeting

4. Press Release

0032

SOFA NEGOTIATION

Agenda for the 41st Session

14:00 Feb. 6, 1964

1. Continuation of Discussions on:

    a. Customs Article

    b. Non-Appropriated Fund Organizations Article

    c. Contractors Article

    d. Labor Article

2. Other Business

3. Agenda and Date of the Next Meeting

4. Press Release

*Chung Woo Young 部分 － 한미간의 합의됨*

0033

<u>SOFA NEGOTIATION</u>

Agenda for the 42nd Session

14:00 Feb. 14, 1964

1.  Continuation of Discussions on:

    a.  Facilities and Areas Article - "C"

    b.  Contractors Article ──→ Revised Draft 金文手交

    c.  Labor Article

    d.  Criminal Jurisdiction Article ── 草案은 22方이 提示

2.  Agenda and Date of the Next Meeting

3.  Press Release

Col. Crawford — Replacement of Col. Fuller
m. Hernandez ⟩ Labor 關係
m. Read

<u>SOFA NEGOTIATION</u>

Agenda for the 43rd Session

14:00 Feb. 20, 1964

1. Continuation of Discussions on:

    a. Contractors Article

    b. Security Measures Article

2. Other Business

3. Agenda and Date of the Next Meeting

4. Press Release

New Members

ROK

Ham, Juhg Ho — Justice

Lee, Jae Sup — Finance

Kim, Nai Sung — Foreign Ministry

0035

SOFA NEGOTIATION

Agenda for the 44th Session

14:00 Feb. 28, 1964

1. Continuation of Discussions on:

    a. Criminal Jurisdiction Article

    b. Utilities and Services Article

2. Other Business

3. Agenda and Date of the Next Meeting

4. Press Release

① Col. Fuller ── promotion 축하 ⟶ Gen.

② 윤두식 模範勞組長
   정태훈  " 課長  } 悳務部
   이명희 樓?

0036

SOFA NEGOTIATION

Agenda for the 45th Session

14:00 March 6, 1964

1. Continuation of Discussions on:

   a. Utilities and Services Article ⟶ 完全合意

   b. Labor Article

   c. Criminal Jurisdiction Article

2. Other Business

3. Agenda and Date of the Next Meeting

4. Press Release

심상섭 當鄉亦 職운영등

<u>SOFA NEGOTIATION</u>

Agenda for the 46th Session

14:00 March 13, 1964

1. Continuation of Discussions on:

    a. Accounting Procedures Article ⟶ 完全合意

    b. Local Procurement Article ⟶

    c. Labor Article

    d. Criminal Jurisdiction Article

    e. Security Measures Article ⟶ 반드시 ROK입장을 고려하겠음

2. Other Business

3. Agenda and Date of the Next Meeting

4. Press Release

0038

<u>SOFA NEGOTIATION</u>

Agenda for the 47th Session

14:00 March 20, 1964

1.  Continuation of Discussions on:

    a. Criminal Jurisdiction Article

2.  Other Business

3.  Agenda and Date of the Next Meeting

4.  Press Release

Gen. Tuller — last meeting

Mr. Kang — ½

0039

<u>SOFA NEGOTIATION</u>

Agenda for the 48th Session

15:30 April 3, 1964

1. Continuation of Discussions on:

    a. Labor Article

    b. Contractors Article

    c. Security Measures Article

2. Other Business

3. Agenda and Date of the Next Meeting

4. Press Release

0040

## SOFA NEGOTIATION

### Agenda for the 49th Session

14:00 April 10, 1964

1. Continuation of Discussions on:

   a. Contractors Article

   b. Criminal Jurisdiction Article

2. Other Business

3. Agenda and Date of the Next Meeting

4. Press Release

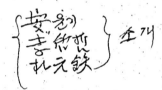

0041

<u>SOFA NEGOTIATION</u>

Agenda for the 50th Session

15:00 April 23,

1. Continuation of Discussions on:

    a. Criminal Jurisdiction Article

2. Other Business

3. Agenda and Date of the Next Meeting

4. Press Release

Maj. Lee, Kye Hoon 소령

0042

<u>SOFA NEGOTIATION</u>

Agenda for the 51st Session

14:00 May 5, 1964

1. Continuation of Discussions on:

a. Customs Article

b. Claims Article

c. Local Procurement Article

2. Other Business

3. Agenda and Date of the Next Meeting

4. Press Release

1. 趙忠勲, Cho, CHOONG HOON,

1. 黃永在, Whang, Young Jae,

0043

<u>SOFA NEGOTIATION</u>

Agenda for the 52nd Session

14:00 May 20, 1964.

1. Continuation of Discussions on:

    a. Local Procurement Article

    b. Criminal Jurisdiction Article

2. Other Business

3. Agenda and Date of the Next Meeting 5/28 (木)

4. Press Release

Col. Wright — Maj. Reokham 代位.

辛亨九 — 換蒙課長

0044

<u>SOFA NEGOTIATION</u>

Agenda for the 53rd Session

14:00 May 28,

1. Continuation of Discussions on:
   ✓ a. Local Procurement Article 一定金合意
   b. Foreign Exchange Controls Article
   c. Military Payment Certificates Article
   d. Customs Article
2. Other Business
3. Agenda and Date of the Next Meeting
4. Press Release

0045

<u>SOFA NEGOTIATION</u>

Agenda for the 54th Session

15:00 June 9, 1964

1. Continuation of Discussion on:

   a. Military Payment Certificates Article

   b. Foreign Exchange Controls Article

   c. Customs Article

2. Other Business

3. Agenda and Date of the Next Meeting

4. Press Release

0046

Agenda for the 55th Session

15:00 June 19, 1964

1. Continuation of Discussions on:

   a. Security Measures Article

   b. Military Payment Certificates Article

   c. Customs Article

   d. Foreign Exchange Controls Article

2. Other Business

3. Agenda and Date of the Next Meeting

4. Press Release

*56th Session    6/26 3:00*

*1. Invited Contractor*
*2. Security Measures*
*3. Customs*

0047

<u>SOFA NEGOTIATION</u>

Agenda for the 57th Session

15:00 July 8, 1964

1. Continuation of Discussions on:

    a. Criminal Jurisdiction Article

    b. Customs Article

    c. Invited Contractors Article

2. Other Business

3. Agenda and Date of the Next Meeting

4. Press Release

0048

<u>SOFA NEGOTIATION</u>

Agenda for the 58th Session

15:00 July 16, 1964

1. Continuation of Discussions on:

   a. Non-Appropriated Fund Organizations Article

   b. Criminal Jurisdiction Article

2. Other Business

3. Agenda and Date of the Next Meeting

4. Press Release

0049

<u>SOFA NEGOTIATION</u>

Agenda for the 59th Session

15:00 July 28, 1964

1. Continuation of Discussions on:

   a. Criminal Jurisdiction Article

2. Other Business

3. Agenda and Date of the Next Meeting

4. Press Release

0050

# SOFA NEGOTIATION

## Agenda for the 60th Session

15:00 August 7, 1964

1. Continuation of Discussions on:

   a. Criminal Jurisdiction Article

2. Other Business

3. Agenda and Date of the Next Meeting

4. Press Release

0051

<u>SOFA NEGOTIATION</u>

Agenda for the 61st Session

15:00 August 14, 1964

1. Continuation of Discussions on:

    a. Claims Article

    b. Criminal Jurisdiction Article

2. Other Business

3. Agenda and Date of the Next Meeting

4. Press Release

0052

<u>SOFA NEGOTIATION</u>

Agenda for the 62nd Session

16:00 August 28, 1964

1. Continuation of Discussions on:

   a. Claims Article

   b. Security Measures Article

2. Other Business

3. Agenda and Date of the Next Meeting

4. Press Release

0053

## SOFA NEGOTIATION

### Agenda for the 63rd Session

15:00 Sept. 11, 1964

1. Continuation of Discussions on:
   a. Claims Article
   b. Security Measures Article
2. Other Business
3. Agenda and Date of the Next Meeting
4. Press Release

ROK                                U.S   Colonel Thompson

Kim SAE KWON 검사
( Claim Section)

Kim Yiu Taik
(Interpreter)

0054

## SOFA NEGOTIATION

Agenda for the 64th Session

16:00 October 16, 1964

1. Continuation of Discussions on:

   a. Labor Procurement Article

2. Other Business

3. Agenda and Date of the Next Meeting

4. Press Release

0055

SOFA NEGOTIATION

Agenda for the 65th Session

16:00 October 23, 1964

1. Continuation of Discussions on:

   a. Labor Procurement Article

2. Other Business

3. Agenda and Date of the Next Meeting

4. Press Release

(U)

0056

SOFA NEGOTIATION

Agenda for the 66th Session

15:00 November 24, 1964

1. Continuation of Discussions on:
   a. Criminal Jurisdiction Article
   b. Civil Claims Article
2. Other Business
3. Agenda and Date of the Next Meeting
4. Press Release

SOFA NEGOTIATION

Agenda for the 67th Session

15:00 December 16, 1964

1. Continuation of Discussions on
   a. Criminal Jurisdiction Article
2. Other Business
3. Agenda and Date of the Next Meeting
4. Press Release

0058

SOFA NEGOTIATION

Agenda for the 68th Session

15:00 December 23, 1964

1. **Continuation** of Discussions on:

   a. Labor Procurement Article

2. Other Business

3. Agenda and Date of the Next Meeting

4. Press Release

0059

SOFA NEGOTIATION

Agenda for the 69th Session

15:00 January 25, 1965

1. Continuation of Discussions on:

   a. Labor Procurement Article

2. Other Business

3. Agenda and Date of the Next Meeting

4. Press Release

0060

SOFA NEGOTIATION

Agenda for the 70th Session

15:00 February 12, 1965

1. Continuation of Discussions on:

   a. Criminal Jurisdiction Article

2. Other Business

3. Agenda and Date of the Next Meeting

4. Press Release

0061

SOFA NEGOTIATION

Agenda for the 71st Session

16:00 February 26, 1965

1. Continuation of Discussions on:

    a. Criminal Jurisdiction Article

    b. Labor Article

2. Other Business

3. Agenda and Date of the Next Meeting

4. Press Release

0062

# SOFA NEGOTIATION

## Agenda for the 72nd Session

15:: March 2, 1965

1. Continuation of Discussions on:
   a. Civil Claims Article
   b. Labor Article
2. Other Business
3. Agenda and Date of the Next Meeting
4. Press Release

0063

SOFA NEGOTIATION

Agenda for the 73rd Session

10:30 April 20, 1965

1. Continuation of Discussions on:

   a. Labor Article

2. Other Business

3. Agenda and Date of the Next Meeting

4. Press Release

0064

SOFA NEGOTIATION


Agenda for the 74th Session

10:00 Apirl 23, 1965


1.  Continuation of Discussions on:

    a. Criminal Jurisdiction Article.

2.  Other Business

3.  Agenda and Date of the Next Meeting

4.  Press Release

0065

SOFA NEGOTIATION

Agenda for the 75th Session

15:30 April 28, 1965

1.  **Continuation** of Discussions on:

    a. **Labor** Article

    b. **Criminal** Jurisdiction Article.

2.  **Other** Business

3.  Agenda and Date of the Next Meeting

4.  **Press** Release

0066

SOFA NEGOTIATION

Agenda for the 76th Session

14:30 April 30, 1965

1. Continuation of Discussions on:

   a. Civil Claims Article

2. Other Business

3. Agenda and Date of the Next Meeting

4. Press Release

SOFA NEGOTIATION

Agenda for the 77th Session

15:00 May 6, 1965

1. Continuation of Discussions on:

    a. Criminal Jurisdiction Article

2. Other Business

3. Agenda and Date of the Next Meeting

4. Press Release

0068

SOFA NEGOTIATION

Agenda for the 78th Session

15:00 May 7, 1965

1. Continuation of Discussions on:
   a. Criminal Jurisdiction Article
   b. Labor Article
2. Other Business
3. Agenda and Date of the Next Meeting
4. Press Release

0069

SOFA NEGOTIATION


Agenda for the 79th Session


16:00 May 12, 1965


1. Continuation of Discussions on:

   a. Labor Article

   b. Claims Article

2. Other Business

3. Agenda and Date of the next Meeting

4. Press Release


0070

# SOFA NEGOTIATIONS

## Agenda for the 80th Session

14 : 00   May 28, 1965.

1. Continuation of Discussions on:

   a. Criminal Jurisdiction Article

   b. Labor Article

   c. Claims Article

2. Other Business

3. Agenda and Date of the Next Meeting

4. Press Release

0071

SOFA NEGOTIATION

Agenda for the 81st Session

16:00 June 7, 1965

1.  Continuation of Discussions on:

    a. Criminal Jurisdiction Article

    b. Labor Article

    c. Civil Claims Article

    d. Other Unsolved Articles

2.  Agenda and Date of the Next Meeting

3.  Press Release

0072

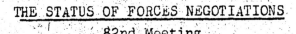

## THE STATUS OF FORCES NEGOTIATIONS
### 82nd Meeting

1. Date and Time:  July 8, 1966, 8:30 a.m.

2. Place:        : Conference Room, Ministry of Foreign Affairs

3. Agenda        : a.  Criminal Jurisdiction Article

                      b.  Labor Article

                      c.  Claims Article, and

                      d.  Other Unsolved Articles

4. Other Business:

5. Press Release :

- E N D -

0073

The Preamble article as agreed upon during the eight
session of the SOFA negotiation held on December 4, 1962:

## PREAMBLE

Whereas the United States of America has disposed
its armed forces in and about the territory of the Republic
of Korea pursuant to the resolutions of the United Nations
Security Council of June 25, 1950, June 27, 1950, and
July 7, 1950, and pursuant to Article IV of the Mutual
Defense Treaty between the United States of America and
the Republic of Korea signed on October 1, 1953.

Therefore, the United States of America and the
Republic of Korea, in order to strengthen the close
bonds of mutual interest between their two countries, have
entered into this Agreement regarding facilities and
areas and the status of United States armed forces in
the Republic of Korea in terms as set forth below:

0074

The text of Access by Vessels and Aircraft and agreed
minutes thereto as agreed upon during the 10th session
of the SOFA negotiation held on January 7, 1963:

## Access by Vessels and Aircraft

1. United States and foreign vessels and aircraft
operated by, for, or under the control of the United
States for official purposes shall be accorded access
to any port or airport of Korea free from toll or landing
charges. When cargo or passengers not accorded the
exemptions of this Agreement are carried on such vessels
and aircraft, notification shall be given to the appropriate Korean authorities, and their entry into and
departure from Korea shall be according to the laws and
regulations of Korea.

2. The vessels and aircraft mentioned in paragraph
1, United States Government-owned vehicles including
armor, and members of the United States armed forces, the
civilian component, and their dependents shall be accorded
access to and movement between facilities and areas in
use by the United States armed forces and between such
facilities and areas and the ports or airports of Korea.
Such access to and movement between facilities and areas
by United States military vehicles shall be free from toll
and other charges.

3. When the vessels mentioned in paragraph 1 enter
Korean ports, appropriate notification shall, under
normal conditions, be made to the proper Korean authorities.
Such vessels shall have freedom from compulsory pilotage,
but if a pilot is taken pilotage shall be paid for at
appropriate rates.

한·미국 간의 상호방위조약 제4조에 의한 시설과 구역 및 한국에서의 미국군대의 지위에 관한 협정(SOFA)
전59권. 1966.7.9 서울에서 서명 : 1967.2.9 발효(조약 232호) (V.48 의제 및 초안) 363

## Agreed Minutes

1. "United States and foreign vessels operated by, for, or under the control of the United States for official purposes" mean United States public vessels and chartered vessels (bare boat charter, voyage charter and time charter). Space charter is not included. Commercial cargo and private passengers are carried by them only in exceptional cases.

2. The Korean ports mentioned herein will ordinarily mean "open ports".

3. An exception from making the "appropriate notification" referred to in paragraph 3 will apply only in unusual cases where such is required for security of the United States armed forces or similar reasons.

4. The laws and regulations of Korea will be applicable except as specifically provided otherwise in this Article.

0076

The entry and exit article and the four agreed
minutes thereto as agreed upon during the tenth
session of SOFA negotiation held on January 7,
1963:

### Entry and Exit

1. The United States may bring into the Republic
of Korea persons who are members of the United States
armed forces, the civilian component, and their dependents, subject to the provisions of this Article. The
Government of the Republic of Korea will be notified at
regular intervals, in accordance with procedures to be
agreed between the two Governments, of numbers and
categories of persons entering and departing.

2. Members of the United States armed forces shall
be exempt from Korean passport and visa laws and regulations. Members of the United States armed forces, the
civilian component, and their dependents shall be
exempt from Korean laws and regulations on the registration and control of aliens, but shall not be considered
as acquiring any right to permanent residence or domicile
in the territory of the Republic of Korea.

3. Upon entry into or departure from the Republic
of Korea members of the United States armed forces shall
be in possession of the following documents:

(a) personal identity card showing name, date
of birth, rank and service number, service, and
photograph; and

0077

(b) individual or collective travel order certifying to the status of the individual or group as a member or members of the United States armed forces and to the travel ordered.

For purposes of their identification while in the Republic of Korea, members of the United States armed forces shall be in possession of the foregoing personal identity card which must be presented on request to the appropriate Korean authorities.

4. Members of the civilian component, their dependents, and the dependents of members of the United States armed forces shall be in possession of appropriate documentation issued by the United States authorities so that their status may be verified by Korean authorities upon their entry into or departure from the Republic of Korea, or while in the Republic of Korea.

5. If the status of any person brought into the Republic of Korea under paragraph 1 of this Article is altered so that he would no longer be entitled to such admission, the United States authorities shall notify the Korean authorities and shall, if such person be required by the Korean authorities to leave the Republic of Korea, assure that transportation from the Republic of Korea will be provided within a reasonable time at no cost to the Government of the Republic of Korea.

6. If the Government of the Republic of Korea has requested the removal from its Territory of a member of the United States armed forces or civilian component or has made an expulsion order against an ex-member of the United States armed forces or the civilian component

0078

or against a dependent of a member or an ex-member,
the authorities of the United States shall be responsible for receiving the person concerned into its own
territory or otherwise disposing of him outside the
Republic of Korea. This paragraph shall apply only
to persons who are nor nationals of the Republic of
Korea and have entered the Republic of Korea as members
of the United States armed forces or civilian component
or for the purpose of becoming such members, and to
the dependents of such persons.

### Agreed Minutes to Entry and Exit Article

1. With regard to Paragraph 3(a), United States
Armed Forces law enforcement personnel (such as MP, SP,
AP, CID and CIC), who engage in military police activities
in the Republic of Korea, will carry a bilingual identity
card containing the bearer's name, position, and the
fact that he is a member of a law enforcement agency.
This card will be shown upon request to persons concerned
when the bearer is in the performance of duty.

2. The United States Armed Forces will furnish,
upon request, to Korean authorities the form of the
identification cards of the members of the United States
Armed Forces, the civilian component, and their dependents
and descriptions of the various uniforms of the United
States Armed Forces in the Republic of Korea.

3. The final sentence of Paragraph 3 means that
members of the United States Armed Forces will display
their identity cards upon request but will not be required
to surrender them to Korean authorities.

0079

4. Following a change of status pursuant to
Paragraph 5, the responsibilities of the United
States authorities under Paragraph 6 shall arise only
if the expulsion order is issued within a reasonable
time after the notice under Paragraph 5 has been
communicated to the Korean authorities.

0080

The text of a Joint Committee article and an agreed minute
thereto as agreed upon during the 15th session of the
SOFA negotiation held on February 25, 1963:

## JOINT COMMITTEE

1. A Joint Committee shall be established as the
means for consultation between the Government of the
United States and the Government of the Republic of
Korea on all matters requiring mutual consultation
regarding the implementation of this Agreement except
where otherwise provided. In particular, the Joint
Committee shall serve as the means for consultation
in determining the facilities and areas in the Republic
of Korea which are required for the use of the United
States in carrying out the purpose of this Agreement.

2. The Joint Committee shall be composed of a
representative of the Government of the United States
and a representative of the Government of the Republic
of Korea, each of whom shall have one or more deputies
and a staff. The Joint Committee shall determine its
own procedures, and arrange for such auxiliary organs
and administrative services as may be required. The
Joint Committee shall be so organized that it may meet
immediately at any time at the request of the representative of either the Government of the United States
or the Government of the Republic of Korea.

3. If the Joint Committee is unable to resolve any
matter, it shall refer that matter to the respective
Government for further consideration through appropriate
channels.

## A AGREED MINUTE

"The exception provided for in the first sentence of paragraph 1 is relevent only to paragraph 2, subparagraphs (b) and (c) of Article _____"

0082

The text of Enrollment and Training of Reservists Article
as agreed upon during the 15th session of the SOFA
negotiation held on February 25, 1963:


Enrollment and Training of Reservists

The United States may enroll in its reserve forces
and train, in Korea, eligible United States citizens
who are in the Republic of Korea.

0083

<u>The text of Definitions Article and an Agreed Minute</u>
<u>thereto as finally agreed upon during the 17th Session</u>
<u>of the SOFA negotiation held on March 19, 1963:</u>

### Definitions

In this Agreement the expression

(a) "members of the United States armed forces"
means the personnel on active duty belonging to the
land, sea or air armed services of the United States
of America when in the territory of the Republic of
Korea except for personnel of the U.S. armed forces
attached to the U.S. Embassy and personnel for whom
status has been provided in the Military Advisory
Group Agreement of January 26, 1950, as amended.

(b) "civilian component" means the civilian
persons of the U.S. nationality who are in the employ,
serving with, or accompanying the United States armed
forces in the Republic of Korea, but excludes persons
who are ordinarily resident in the Republic of Korea
or who are mentioned in paragraph     of Article.

For the purposes of the Agreement only, dual nationals,
i.e. persons having both United States and Korean nationality, who are brought into the Republic of Korea by the
United States shall be considered as United States
nationals.

(c) "dependents" means

    (1) Spouse and children under 21;

    (2) Parents, and children over 21, or other
        relatives dependent for over half their
        support upon a member of the United States
        armed forces or civilian component.

0084

## Agreed Minute

With regard to subparagraph (b), it is recognized that persons possessing certain skills, not available from United States or Korean sources, who are nationals of third states may be brought into Korea by the United States armed forces solely for employment by the United States armed forces. Such persons, and third state nationals who are employed by, serving with, or accompanying the United States armed forces in Korea when this agreement becomes effective, shall be considered as members of the civilian component.

0085

The text of Meteorological Services Article as agreed
upon during the 20th session of the SOFA Negotiation
held on April 24, 1963:

## Meteorological Services Article

The Government of the Republic of Korea undertakes
to furnish the United States armed forces with the
following meteorological services in accordance with
arrangements between the appropriate authorities of
the two Governments:

(a) Meteorological observations from land and
ocean areas including observations from ships;

(b) Climatological information including
periodic summaries and historical data wherever
available;

(c) Telecommunications service to disseminate
meteorological information;

(d) Seismographic data.

0086

The Text of Respect for Local Law Article as agreed
upon during the 24th session of the SOFA negotiation
held on June 12th, 1963:

Respect for Local Law Article

It is the duty of members of the United States
Armed Forces, the civilian component, the persons
who are present in the Republic of Korea pursuant
to Article _____, and their dependents, to respect
the law of Korea and to abstain from any activity
inconsistent with the spirit of this Agreement, and,
in particular, from any political activity in Korea.

0087

The Text of Health and Sanitation Article as agreed
upon at the 27th session of the SOFA negotiation
held on July 25th, 1963:

Health and Sanitation Article

Consistent with the right of the United States
to furnish medical support for its armed forces,
civilian component and their dependents, matters of
mutual concern pertaining to the control and prevention of diseases and the corrdination of other public
health, medical, sanitation, and veterinary services
shall be resolved by the authorities of the two
Governments in the Joint Committee established under
Article _____.

0088

<u>The Text of Vehicle and Drivers License Article as</u>
<u>agreed upon at the 29th session of the SOFA negotiation</u>
<u>held on August 22, 1963:</u>

<u>Vehicle and Drivers license Article</u>

   1. Korea shall accept as valid, without a driving
test or fee, the driving permit or license or military
driving permit issued by the United States, or political
subdivision thereof, to a member of the United States
armed forces, the civilian component, and their dependents.

   2. Official vehicles of the United States armed
forces and the civilian component shall carry distinctive
numbered plates or individual markings which will readily
identify them.

   3. The Government of the Republic of Korea will
license and register those vehicles privately owned by
members of the United States armed forces, the civilian
component, or dependents. The names of the owners of such
vehicles and such other pertinent information as is required by Korean law to effect the licensing and registration of such vehicles, shall be furnished to the Government of the Republic of Korea by officials of the United
States Government through the Joint Committee. Except
for the actual cost of the issuance of license plates,
members of the United States armed forces, the civilian
component, and their dependents shall be exempt from the
payment of all fees and charges relating to the licensing,
registration, or operation of vehicles in the Republic of
Korea and, in accordance with the provisions of Article ___,
from the payment of all taxes relating thereto.

0089

The Text of Taxation Article as agreed upon
at 33rd session of the SOFA negotiation held
on October 18, 1963:

## Taxation Article

1. The United States armed forces shall not be
subject to taxes or similar charges on property held,
used or transferred by such forces in Korea.

2. Members of the United States armed forces, the
civilian component, and their dependents shall not be
liable to pay any Korean taxes to the Government of
Korea or to any other taxing agency in Korea on income
received as a result of their service with or employment
by the United States armed forces, including their organizations provided for in Article _____. Persons in Korea
solely by reason of being members of the United States
armed forces, the civilian component, or their dependents
shall not be liable to pay any Korean taxes to the
Government of Korea or to any taxing agency in Korea on
income derived from sources outside of Korea, nor shall
periods during which such persons are in Korea be considered as periods of residence or domicile in Korea
for the purpose of Korean taxation. The provisions of
this Article do not exempt such persons from payment of
Korean taxes on income derived from Korean sources, other
than those sources referred to in the first sentence of
this paragraph, nor do they exempt United States citizens
who claim Korean residence for United States incoem tax
purposes from payment of Korean taxes on income.

3. Members of the United States armed forces, the
civilian component, and their dependents shall be exempt

0090

from taxation in Korea on the holding, use, transfer
_inter se_, or transfer by death of movable property,
tangible or intangible, the presence of which in Korea
is due solely to the temporary presence of these persons
in Korea, provided that such exemption shall not apply
to property held for the purpose of investment or the
conduct of business in Korea or to any intangible
property registered in Korea.

0091

The Text of Air Traffic Control and Navigational
Aids Article as agreed upon at the 34th session
of the SOFA negotiation held on October 30, 1963:

### Air Traffic Control and Navigational Aids Article

1. All civil and military air traffic control shall
be developed in close coordination and shall be integrated
to the extent necessary for the operation of this Agreement.
Procedures, and any subsequent changes thereto, necessary
to effect this coordination and integration will be
established by arrangement between the appropriate
authorities of the two Governments.

2. The United States is authorized to establish,
construct and maintain aids to navigation for vessels and
aircraft, both visual and electronic as required, throughout the Republic of Korea and in the territorial waters
thereof. Such navigation aids shall conform generally to
the system in use in Korea. The United States and Korean
authorities which have established navigation aids shall
duly notify each other of their positions and characteristics and shall give advance notification where
practicable before making any changes in them or
establishing additional navigation aids.

### Agreed Minute

Installation by the United States Armed Forces of
permanent navigational aids for vessels and aircraft
outside of areas and facilities in use by the United
States Armed Forces will be effected in accordance with
the procedures established under paragraph 1 of Article___.

0092

The Text of Revision of the Agreement Article
as agreed upon at the 36th session of the
SOFA negotiation held on December 5, 1963:

Revision of the Agreement Article

Either Government may at any time request the
revision of any Article of this Agreement, in which
case the two Governments shall enter into negotiations
through appropriate channels.

0093

<u>The Text of Military Post Offices Article</u>
<u>as agreed upon at the 40th session of the</u>
<u>SOFA negotiation held on January 24, 1964:</u>

<u>Military Post Offices Article</u>

The United States may establish and operate, within
the facilities and areas in use by the U.S. Armed Forces,
United States military post offices for the use of
members of the United States armed forces, the civilian
component, and their dependents, for the transmission
of mail between United States military post offices
in Korea and between such military post offices and
other United States post offices.

<u>Agreed Minute</u>

United States military post offices may be used
by other officers and personnel of the United States
Government, and their dependents, ordinarily accorded
such privileges abroad.

0094

<u>The Text of Utilities and Services Article</u>
<u>as agreed upon at the 45th session of the</u>
<u>SOFA negotiation held on March 6, 1964:</u>

<u>Utilities and Services Article</u>

1. The United States armed forces shall have the use of all utilities and services which are owned, controlled or regulated by the Government of the Republic of Korea or local administrative subdivisions thereof. The term "utilities and services" shall include, but not be limited to, transportation and communications facilities and systems, electricity, gas, water, steam, heat, light, power, and sewage disposal. The use of utilities and services as provided herein shall not prejudice the right of the United States to operate military transportation, communication, power and such other utilities and services deemed necessary for the operations of the United States armed forces. This right shall not be exercised in a manner inconsistent with the operation by the Government of the Republic of Korea of its utilities and services.

2. The use of such utilities and services by the United States shall be in accordance with priorities, conditions, and rates or tariffs no less favorable than those accorded any other user.

<u>Agreed Minutes</u>

1. It is understood that any changes determined by the Korean authorities in priorities, conditions, and rates or tariffs, applicable to the United States armed forces shall be the subject of consultation in the Joint Committee prior to their effective date.

0095

2. Paragraph 3 of Article _____ will not be
construed as in any way abrogating the Utilities and
Claims Settlement Agreement of December 18, 1958, which
continues in full force and effect unless otherwise
agreed by the two governments.

3. In an emergency the Republic of Korea agrees
to take appropriate measures to assure provision of
utilities and services necessary to meet the needs of
the United States armed forces.

0096

<u>The Text of Accounting Procedures Article</u>
<u>as agreed upon at the 46th session of the</u>
<u>SOFA negotiation held on March 13, 1964</u>

<u>Accounting Procedures Article</u>

It is agreed that arrangements will be effected between the Governments of the United States and the Republic of Korea for accounting applicable to financial transactions arising out of this Agreement.

0097

<u>The text of Local Procurement Article as</u>
<u>Agreed upon at the 53rd Session of the</u>
<u>SOFA negotiation held on May 28, 1964:</u>

<u>Local Procurement Article</u>

1. The United States may contract for any materials, supplies, equipment and services (including construction work) to be furnished or undertaken in the Republic of Korea for purposes of, or authorized by, this Agreement, without restriction as to choice of contractor, supplier or person who provides such services. Such materials, supplies, equipment and services may, upon agreement between the appropriate authorities of the two Governments, also be procured through the Government of the Republic of Korea.

2. Materials, supplies, equipment and services which are required from local sources for the maintenance of the United States armed forces and the procurement of which may have an adverse effect on the economy of the Republic of Korea shall be procured in coordination with, and, when desirable, through or with the assistance of, the competent authorities of the Republic of Korea.

3. Materials, supplies, equipment and services procured for official purposes in the Republic of Korea by the United States armed forces, including their authorized procurement agencies, or procured for ultimate use by the United States armed forces shall be exempt from the following Korean taxes upon appropriate certification in advance by the United States armed forces:

0098

(a) Commodity tax;

(b) Traffic tax;

(c) Petroleum tax;

(d) Electricity and gas tax;

(e) Business tax;

With respect to any present or future Korean taxes not specifically referred to in this Article which might be found to constitute a significant and readily identifiable part of the gross purchase price of materials, supplies, equipment and services procured by the United States armed forces, or for ultimate use by such forces, the two Governments will agree upon a procedure for granting such exemption or relief therefrom as is consistent with the purpose of the Article.

4. Neither members of the United States armed forces, civilian component, nor their dependents, shall by reason of this Article enjoy any exemption from taxes or similar charges relating to personal purchases of goods and services in the Republic of Korea chargeable under Korean legislation.

5. Except as such disposal may be authorized by the United States and Korean authorities in accordance with mutually agreed conditions, goods purchased in the Republic of Korea exempt from the taxes referred to in paragraph 3, shall not be disposed of in the Republic of Korea to persons not entitled to purchase such goods exempt from such tax.

Agreed Minute

1. The United States armed forces will furnish the Korean authorities with appropriate information as far in

0099

advance as practicable on anticipated major changes in their procurement program in the Republic of Korea.

2. The problem of a satisfactory settlement of difficulties with respect to procurement contracts arising out of differences between Korean and United States economic laws and business practices will be studied by the Joint Committee or other appropriate representatives.

3. The procedures for securing exemptions from taxation on purchases of goods for ultimate use by the United States armed forces will be as follows:

(a) Upon appropriate certification by the United States armed forces that materials, supplies and equipment consigned to or destined for such forces, are to be used, or wholly or partially used up, under the supervision of such forces, exclusively in the execution of contracts for the construction, maintenance or operation of the facilities and areas referred to in Article       or for the support of the forces therein, or are ultimately to be incorporated into article or facilities used by such forces, an authorized representative of such forces shall take delivery of such materials, supplies and equipment directly from manufacturers thereof. In such circumstances the collection of taxes referred to in Article       paragraph 3, shall be held in abeyance.

(b) The receipt of such materials, supplies and equipment in the facilities and areas shall be confirmed by an authorized representative of the United States armed forces to the Korean authorities.

(c) Collection of the taxes on such materials, supplies and equipment shall be held in abeyance until:

0100

(1) The United States armed forces confirm
and certify the quantity or degree of consumption
of the above referred to materials, supplies and
equipment, or

(2) The United States armed forces confirm and
certify the amount of the above referred to materials,
supplies, aid equipment which have been incorporated
into articles or facilities used by the United States
armed forces.

(d) Materials, supplies, and equipment certified
under (e) (1) or (2) shall be exempt from taxes referred
to in Article _____, paragraph 3, insofar as the price
thereof is paid out of United States Government
appropriations or out of funds contributed by the Government of the Republic of Korea for idsbursement by the
United States.

4. Regarding paragraph 3, it is understood that
"materials, supplies, equipment and services procured
for official purposes" refers to direct procurement by
the United States armed forces or its authorized
procurement agencies from Korean suppliers. "Materials,
supplies, equipment and services procured for ultimate
use" refers to procurement by contractors of the United
States armed forces from Korean suppliers of itmes to
be incorporated into or necessary for the production of
the end product of their contracts with the United States
Armed Forces."

한·미국 간의 상호방위조약 제4조에 의한 시설과 구역 및 한국에서의 미국군대의 지위에 관한 협정(SOFA)
전59권. 1966.7.9 서울에서 서명 : 1967.2.9 발효(조약 232호) (V.48 의제 및 초안) 389

2. 초안

0102

• 合意事項 17
◦ 討議事項 10
未討議事項 2

① 協定의 批准, 效數 및 施行事項.
② 協定 有效期間 및 終了事項.

보통문서로 재분류 (1986.12.31)

0103

검토필 (196  .  .  )

Whereas the United States of America has disposed its armed forces in and about the territory of the Republic of Korea pursuant to the resolutions of the United Nations Security Council of June 25, 1950, June 27, 1950, and July 7, 1950, and pursuant to Article IV of the Mutual Defense Treaty between the United States of America and the Republic of Korea signed on October 1, 1953.

Therefore, the United States of America and the Republic of Korea, in order to strengthen the close bonds of mutual interest between their two countries, have entered into this Agreement regarding facilities and areas and the status of United States armed forces in the Republic of Korea in terms as set forth below:

- 1 -

0104

## Definitions Article

In this Agreement the expression

(a) "members of the United States armed forces" means the personnel on active duty belonging to the land, sea or air armed services of the United States of America when in the territory of the Republic of Korea except for personnel of the U.S. armed forces attached to the U.S. Embassy and personnel for whom status has been provided in the Military Advisory Group Agreement of January 26, 1950, as amended.

(b) "civilian component" means the civilian persons of the U.S. nationality who are in the employ, serving with, or accompanying the United States armed forces in the Republic of Korea, but excludes persons who are ordinarily resident in the Republic of Korea or who are mentioned in paragraph     of Article.

For the purposes of the Agreement only, dual nationals, i.e. persons having both United States and Korean nationality, who are brought into the Republic of Korea by the United States shall be considered as United States nationals.

(c) "dependents" means

(1) Spouse and children under 21;

(2) Parents, and children over 21, or other relatives dependent for over half their support upon a member of the United States armed forces or civilian component.

## Agreed Minute

With regard to subparagraph (b), it is recognized that persons possessing certain skills, not available from United States or Korean sources, who are nationals of third states may be brought into Korea by the United States armed forces solely for employment

한·미국 간의 상호방위조약 제4조에 의한 시설과 구역 및 한국에서의 미국군대의 지위에 관한 협정(SOFA)
전59권. 1966.7.9 서울에서 서명 : 1967.2.9 발효(조약 232호) (V.48 의제 및 초안)    393

by the United States armed forces. Such persons, and third state nationals who are employed by, serving with, or accompanying the United States armed forces in Korea when this agreement becomes effective, shall be considered as members of the civilian component.

0106

1. The United States may bring into the Republic of Korea persons who are members of the United States armed forces, the civilian component, and their dependents, subject to the provisions of this Article. The Government of the Republic of Korea will be notified at regular intervals, in accordance with procedures to be agreed between the two Governments, of numbers and categories of persons entering and departing.

2. Members of the United States armed forces shall be exempt from Korean passport and visa laws and regulations. Members of the United States armed forces, the civilian component, and their dependents shall be exempt from Korean laws and regulations on the registration and control of aliens, but shall not be considered as acquiring any right to permanent residence or domicile in the territory of the Republic of Korea.

3. Upon entry into or departure from the Republic of Korea members of the United States armed forces shall be in possession of the following documents:

(a) personal identity card showing name, date of birth, rank and service number, service, and photograph; and

(b) individual or collective travel order certifying to the status of the individual or group as a member or members of the United States armed forces and to the travel ordered.

For purposes of their identification while in the Republic of Korea, members of the United States armed forces shall be in possession of the foregoing personal identity card which must be presented on request to the appropriate Korean authorities.

4. Members of the civilian component, their dependents, and

- 4 -

한·미국 간의 상호방위조약 제4조에 의한 시설과 구역 및 한국에서의 미국군대의 지위에 관한 협정(SOFA)
전59권. 1966.7.9 서울에서 서명 : 1967.2.9 발효(조약 232호) (V.48 의제 및 초안)   395

the dependents of members of the United States armed forces shall be in possession of appropriate documentation issued by the United States authorities so that their status may be verified by Korean authorities upon their entry into or departure from the Republic of Korea, or while in the Republic of Korea.

5. If the status of any person brought into the Republic of Korea under paragraph 1 of this Article is altered so that he would no longer be entitled to such admission, the United States authorities shall notify the Korean authorities and shall, if such person be required by the Korean authorities to leave the Republic of Korea, assure that transportation from the Republic of Korea will be provided within a reasonable time at no cost to the Government of the Republic of Korea.

6. If the Government of the Republic of Korea has requested the removal from its Territory of a member of the United States armed forces or civilian component or has made an expulsion order against an ex-member of the United States armed forces or the civilian component or against a dependent of a member or an ex-member, the authorities of the United States shall be responsible for receiving the person concerned into its own territory or otherwise disposing of him outside the Republic of Korea. This paragraph shall apply only to persons who are not nationals of the Republic of Korea and have entered the Republic of Korea as members of the United States armed forces or civilian component or for the purpose of becoming such members, and to the dependents of such persons.

## Agreed Minutes

1. With regard to Paragraph 3(a), United States Armed Forces law enforcement personnel (such as MP, SP, AP, CID and CIC), who engage in military police activities in the Republic of Korea, will carry a

- 5 -

0108

bilingual identity card containing the bearer's name, position, and the fact that he is a member of a law enforcement agency. This card will be shown upon request to persons concerned when the bearer is in the performance of duty.

2. The United States Armed Forces will furnish, upon request, to Korean authorities the form of the identification cards of the members of the United States Armed Forces, the civilian component, and their dependents and descriptions of the various uniforms of the United States Armed Forces in the Republic of Korea.

3. The final sentence of Paragraph 3 means that members of the United States Armed Forces will display their identity cards upon request but will not be required to surrender them to Korean authorities.

4. Following a change of status pursuant to Paragraph 5, the responsibilities of the United States authorities under Paragraph 6 shall arise only if the expulsion order is issued within a reasonable time after the notice under Paragraph 5 has been communicated to the Korean authorities.

한·미국 간의 상호방위조약 제4조에 의한 시설과 구역 및 한국에서의 미국군대의 지위에 관한 협정(SOFA)
전59권. 1966.7.9 서울에서 서명 : 1967.2.9 발효(조약 232호) (V.48 의제 및 초안) 397

## Health and Sanitation Article

Consistent with the right of the United States to furnish medical support for its armed forces, civilian component and their dependents, matters of mutual concern pertaining to the control and prevention of diseases and the coordination of other public health medical, sanitation, and veterinary services shall be resolved by the authorities of the two Governments in the Joint Committee established under Article _____.

## Taxation Article

1. The United States armed forces shall not be subject to taxes or similar charges on property held, used or transferred by such forces in Korea.

2. Members of the United States armed forces, the civilian component, and their dependents shall not be liable to pay any Korean taxes to the Government of Korea or to any other taxing agency in Korea on income received as a result of their service with or employment by the United States armed forces, including their activities provided for in Article ___. Persons in Korea solely by reason of being members of the United States armed forces, the civilian components, or their dependents shall not be liable to pay any Korean taxes to the Government of Korea or to any taxing agency in Korea on income derived from sources outside of Korea, nor shall periods during which such persons are in Korea be considered as periods of residence or domicile in Korea for the purpose of Korean taxation. The provisions of this Article do not exempt such persons from payment of Korean taxes on income derived from Korean sources, other than those sources referred to in the first sentence of this paragraph, nor do they exempt United States citizens who claim Korean residence for United States income tax purposes from payment of Korean taxes on income.

3. Members of the United States armed forces, the civilian component, and their dependents shall be exempt from taxation in Korea on the holding, use, transfer inter se, or transfer by death of movable property, tangible or intangible, the presence of which in Korea is due solely to the temporary presence of these persons in Korea, provided that such exemption shall not apply to property held for the purpose of investment or the conduct of business in Korea or to any intangible property registered in Korea.

- 8 -

0111

# Joint Committee Article

1. A Joint Committee shall be established as the means for consultation between the Government of the United States and the Government of the Republic of Korea on all matters requiring mutual consultation regarding the implementation of this Agreement except where otherwise provided. In particular, the Joint Committee shall serve as the means for consultation in determining the facilities and areas in the Republic of Korea which are required for the use of the United States in carrying out the purpose of this Agreement.

2. The Joint Committee shall be composed of a representative of the Government of the United States and a representative of the Government of the Republic of Korea, each of whom shall have one or more deputies and a staff. The Joint Committee shall determine its own procedures, and arrange for such auxiliary organs and administrative services as may be required. The Joint Committee shall be so organized that it may meet immediately at any time at the request of the representative of either the Government of the United States or the Government of the Republic of Korea.

3. If the Joint Committee is unable to resolve any matter, it shall refer that matter to the respective Government for further consideration through appropriate channels.

## Agreed Minute

"The exception provided for in the first sentence of paragraph 1 is relevent only to paragraph 2, subparagraphs (b) and (c) of Article

0112

The United States may enroll in its reserve forces and train, in Korea, eligible United States citizens who are in the Republic of Korea.

0113

한·미국 간의 상호방위조약 제4조에 의한 시설과 구역 및 한국에서의 미국군대의 지위에 관한 협정(SOFA)
전59권. 1966.7.9 서울에서 서명 : 1967.2.9 발효(조약 232호) (V.48 의제 및 초안)　401

## Meteorological Services Article

The Government of the Republic of Korea undertakes to furnish the United States armed forces with the following meteorological services in accordance with arrangements between the appropriate authorities of the two Governments:

(a) Meteorological observations from land and ocean areas includ observations from ships;

(b) Climatological information including periodic summaries and historical data wherever available;

(c) Telecommunications service to disseminate meteorological information;

(d) Seismographic data.

- 11 -

0114

## Respect for Local Law Article

It is the duty of members of the United States Armed Forces, the civilian component, the persons who are present in the Republic of Korea pursuant to Article _____, and their dependents, to respect the law of Korea and to abstain from any activity inconsistent with the spirit of this Agreement, and, in particular, from any political activity in Korea.

- 12 -

0115

## Vehicle and Drivers License Article

1. Korea shall accept as valid, without a driving test or fee, the driving permit or license or military driving permit issued by the United States, or political subdivision thereof, to a member of the United States armed forces, the civilian component, and their dependents.

2. Official vehicles of the United States armed forces and the civilian component shall carry distinctive numbered plates or individual markings which will readily identify them.

3. The Government of the Republic of Korea will license and register those vehicles privately owned by members of the United States armed forces, the civilian component, or dependents. The names of the owners of such vehicles and such other pertinent information as is required by Korean law to effect the licensing and registration of such vehicles, shall be furnished to the Government of the Republic of Korea by officials of the United States Government through the Joint Committee. Except for the actual cost of the issuance of license plates, members of the United States armed forces, the civilian component, and their dependents shall be exempt from the payment of all fees and charges relating to the licensing, registration, or operation of vehicles in the Republic of Korea and, in accordance with the provisions of Article _____, from the payment of all taxes relating thereto.

- 13 -

0116

## Access by Vessels and Aircraft Article

1. United States and foreign vessels and aircraft operated by, for, or under the control of the United States for official purposes shall be accorded access to any port or airport of Korea free from toll or landing charges. When cargo or passengers not accorded the exemptions of this Agreement are carried on such vessels and aircraft, notification shall be given to the appropriate Korean authorities, and their entry into and departure from Korea shall be according to the laws and regulations of Korea.

2. The vessels and aircraft mentioned in paragraph 1, United States Government-owned vehicles including armor, and members of the United States armed forces, the civilian component, and their dependents shall be accorded to and movement between facilities and areas in use by the United States armed forces and between such facilities and areas and the ports or airports of Korea. Such access to and movement between facilities and areas by United States military vehicles shall be free from toll and other charges.

3. When the vessels mentioned in paragraph 1 enter Korean ports, appropriate notification shall, under normal conditions, be made to the proper Korean authorities. Such vessels shall have freedom from compulsory pilotage, but if a pilot is taken pilotage shall be paid for at appropriate rates.

### Agreed Minutes

1. "United States and foreign vessels ... operated by, for, or under the control of the United States for official purposes" mean United States public vessels and chartered vessels (bare boat charter, voyage charter and time charter). Space charter is not inc

0117

Commercial cargo and private passengers are carried by them only in exceptional cases.

2. The Korean ports mentioned herein will ordinarily mean "open ports".

3. An exception from making the "appropriate notification" referred to in paragraph 3 will apply only in unusual cases where such is required for security of the United States armed forces or similar reasons.

4. The laws and regulations of Korea will be applicable except as specifically provided otherwise in this Article.

0118

## Air Traffic Control and Navigational Aids Article

1. All civil and military air traffic control shall be develo[
in close coordination and shall be integrated to the extent necessa[
for the operation of this Agreement. Procedures, and any subseques[
changes thereto, necessary to effect this coordination and integrat[
will be established by arrangement between the appropriate authorit[
of the two Governments.

2. The United States is authorized to establish, construct an[
maintain aids to navigation for vessels and aircraft, both visual a[
electronic as required, throughout the Republic of Korea and in th[
territorial waters thereof. Such navigation aids shall conform
generally to the system in use in Korea. The United States and Ko[
authorities which have established navigation aids shall duly noti[
each other of their positions and characteristics and shall give
advance notification where practicable before making any changes
in them or establishing additional navigation aids.

### Agreed Minute

Installation by the United States Armed Forces of permanent
navigational aids for vessels and aircraft outside of areas and
facilities in use by the United States Armed Forces will be effect[
in accordance with the procedures established under paragraph 1 o[
Article._____ .

<u>Revision of the Agreement Article</u>

Either Government may at any time request the revision of any Article of this Agreement, in which case the two Governments shall enter into negotiations through appropriate channels.

0120

408  주한미군지위협정(SOFA) 서명 및 발효 18

## Military Post Offices Article

The United States may establish and operate, within the facilit
and areas in use by the U.S. armed forces, United States military po
offices for the use of members of the United States armed forces, th
civilian component, and their dependents, for the transmission of ma
between United States military post offices in Korea and between suc
military post offices and other United States post offices.

## Agreed Minute

United States military post offices may be used by other office
and personnel of the United States Government, and their dependents,
ordinarily accorded such privileges abroad.

## ARTICLE

1. The Government of the Republic of Korea grants, under Article IV of the Mutual Defense Treaty between the Republic of Korea and the United States of America, to the United States the use of the facilities and areas in the Republic of Korea as provided for in this Agreement. Arrangements as to the specific facilities and areas shall be made by the two Governments through the Joint Committee.

2. Facilities and areas referred to in this Agreement include existing furnishings, equipment and fixtures necessary to the operation of such facilities and areas.

3. The facilities and areas of which the United States has the use at the time of entry into force of this Agreement, shall be regarded, for the purpose of this Agreement, as facilities and areas granted to the United States under this Agreement. For the purpose of this paragraph, all facilities and areas of which the United States has the use at the time of entry into force of this Agreement shall be surveyed and determined by the two Governments through the Joint Committee.

## ARTICLE

Art. A-1. (a) The United States is granted, under Article IV of the Mutual Defense Treaty, the use of facilities and areas in the Republic of Korea. Agreements as to specific facilities and areas shall be concluded by the two Governments through the Joint Committee provided for in Article        of this Agreement. "Facilities and Areas" include existing furnishings, equipment and fixtures, wherever located, used in the operation of such facilities and areas.

(b) The facilities and areas of which the United States has the use at the effective date of this Agreement shall be considered as facilities and areas agreed upon between the two Governments in accordance with sub-paragraph (a) above.

4. With regard to the private property used as facilities and areas by the United States armed forces under this Agreement, the United States shall make reasonable compensation through the Government of the Republic of Korea to the owners of such facilities and areas with a view to alleviating their losses. Detailed arrangements, including the amounts of compensation, shall be made between the two Government through the Joint Committee.

5. The Governments of the United States bears without cost to the Republic of Korea all expenditures incident to the maintenance of the facilities and areas granted under this Agreement.

6. At the request of either Government, the Government of the Republic of Korea and the Government of the United States shall review such arrangements referred to in paragraph 1 and may agree that such facilities and areas shall be returned to the Republic of Korea or that additional facilities and areas may be provided.

Art. D-1. It is agreed that the United States will bear for the duration of the Agreement without cost to the Republic of Korea all expenditures incident to the maintenance of the United States armed forces in the Republic of Korea, except those to be borne by the Republic of Korea as provided in paragraph 2.

2. At the request of either Government, the Governments of the United States and the Republic of Korea shall review such arrangements and may agree that such facilities and areas or portions thereof shall be returned to the Republic of Korea or that additional facilities and areas may be provided.

7. The facilities and areas used by the United States shall be promptly returned to the Government of the Republic of Korea whenever they are no longer needed for the purpose of this Agreement, and the Government of the United States agrees to keep the needs for facilities and areas under continual observation with a view toward such return.

8. When facilities and areas are temporarily not being used by the United States, interim use by the authorities of the Republic of Korea or nationals may be arranged through the Joint Committee.

9. With respect to facilities and areas which are to be used by the United States for limited period of time, the Joint Committee shall specify in the agreements covering such facilities and areas the extent to which the provisions of this Agreement shall apply.

3. The facilities and areas used by the United States shall be returned to the Republic of Korea under such conditions as may be agreed through the Joint Committee whenever they are no longer needed for the purposes of this Agreement and the United States agrees to keep the needs for facilities and areas under continual observation with a view toward such return.

4. (a) When facilities and areas are temporarily not being used and the Government of the Republic of Korea is so advised, the Government of the Republic of Korea may make, or permit Korean nationals to make, interim use of such facilities and areas provided that it is agreed between the two Governments through the Joint Committee that such use would not be harmful to the purposes for which the facilities and areas are normally used by the United States armed forces.

(b) With respect to facilities and areas which are to be used by United States armed forces for limited periods of time, the Joint Committee shall specify in the agreements covering such facilities and areas the extent to which the provisions of this Agreement shall apply.

10. Within the facilities and areas, the Government of the United States may take all the measures necessary for their establishment, operation, safeguarding and control. In order to provide access for the United States forces to the facilities and areas for their support, safeguarding and control, the Government of the Republic of Korea shall, at the request of the Government of the United States and upon consultation between the two Governments within the scope of applicable laws and regulations over land, territorial waters and airspace adjacent to, or in the vicinities of the facilities and areas. The Government of the United States may also take necessary measures for such purposes upon consultation between the two Governments through the Joint Committee.

11. The Government of the United States agrees not to take the measures referred to in paragraph 1 in such a manner as to interfere unnecessarily with navigation, aviation, communication, or land travel to or from or within the territories of the Republic of Korea.

Art. B-1. Within the facilities and areas, the United States may take all the measures necessary for their establishment, operation, safeguarding and control. In an emergency, measures necessary for their safeguarding and control may also be taken in the vicinity thereof. In order to provide access for the United States armed forces to the facilities and areas for their support, safeguarding and control, the Government of the Republic of Korea shall, at the request of the United States armed forces and upon consultation between the two Governments through the Joint Committee, take necessary measures within the scope of applicable laws and regulations over land, territory waters and airspace adjacent to, or in the vicinities of the facilities and areas. The United States may also take necessary measures for such purposes upon consultation between the two Governments through the Joint Committee.

2. (a) The United States agrees not to take the measures referred to in paragraph 1 in such a manner as to interfere unnecessarily with navigation, aviation, communication, or land travel to or from or within the territories of the Republic of Korea.

- 22 -

한·미국 간의 상호방위조약 제4조에 의한 시설과 구역 및 한국에서의 미국군대의 지위에 관한 협정(SOFA)
전59권. 1966.7.9 서울에서 서명 : 1967.2.9 발효(조약 232호) (V.48 의제 및 초안)　413

All questions relating to frequencies, power and like matters used by apparatus employed by the Government of the United States designed to emit electric radiation shall be settled by arrangement between the appropriate authorities of the two Governments.

12. Operations in the facilities and areas in use by the Government of the United States shall be carried on with due regard to the public safety.

13. The Government of the United States is not obliged, when it returns facilities and areas to the Government of the Republic of Korea on the expiration of this Agreement or at an earlier date, to restore the facilities and areas to the conditions in which they were at the time they became available to the United

(b) All questions relating to telecommunications including radio frequencies for electromagnetic radiating devices, or like matters, shall continue to be resolved expeditiously in the utmost spirit of coordination and cooperation by arrangement between the designated military communications authorities of the two Governments.

3. Operations in the facilities and areas in use by the United States armed forces shall be carried on with due regard for the public safety.

Art. B-2 (c) The Government of the Republic of Korea shall, within the scope of applicable laws, regulations and agreements, take all reasonable measures to avoid or eliminate interference with electromagnetic radiation sensitive devices, telecommunications devices, or other apparatus required by the United States armed forces.

Art. C-1. The United States is not obliged, when it returns facilities and areas to the Republic of Korea on the expiration of this Agreement or at an earlier date, to restore the facilities and areas to the condition in which they were at the time they became available to the United States armed

States, or to compensate the Government of the Republic of Korea in lieu of such restoration. However, in case of private property extremely demolished by the use of the United States, the Government of the United States shall, upon the request of the Government of the Republic of Korea, pay due consideration to its restoration or compensation in lieu thereof.

14. The Government of the Republic of Korea is not obliged to make any compensation to the Government of the United States for any improvements made in the facilities and areas or for the buildings, structures, supply or any other materials left thereon on the expiration of this Agreement or the earlier return of the facilities and areas.

forces, or to compensate the Republic of Korea in lieu of such restoration.

2. The Republic of Korea is not obligated to compensate the United States for improvements made in United States facilities and areas or for the buildings or structures remaining thereon upon the return of the facilities and areas.

3. All removable facilities erected or constructed by or on behalf of the United States at its expense and all equipment, materials and supplies brought into or procured in the Republic of Korea by or on behalf of the United States in connection with the construction, development, operation, maintenance, safeguarding and control of the facilities and areas will remain the property of the United States Government and may be

- 24 -

0127

removed from the Republic of Korea.

4. The foregoing provisions shall
not apply to any construction which the
Government of the United States may
undertake under special arrangements with
the Government of the Republic of Korea.

Art. D-2. It is agreed that the
Republic of Korea will furnish for the
duration of this Agreement without cost
to the United States and make compensatic
where appropriate to the owners and
suppliers thereof all facilities and
areas and rights of way, including
facilities and areas jointly used such
as those at airfields and ports as
provided in Articles II and III. The
Government of the Republic of Korea
assures the use of such facilities and
areas to the United States Government and
will hold the United States Government
as well as its agencies and employees
harmless from any third party claims
which may be advanced in connection with
such use.

Revised Draft

1. ......

(b) The facilities and areas
of which the United States armed forces
have the use at the effective date of
this agreement together with those areas

and facilities which the United States
armed forces have returned to the Republ
of Korea with the reserved right of re-
entry, when these facilities and areas
have been re-entered by U.S. forces,
shall be considered as the facilities
and areas agreed upon between the two
Governments in accordance with subparagraph (a) above. Records of
facilities and areas of which the
United States armed forces have the
use or right of re-entry shall be
maintained through the Joint Committee
after this Agreement comes into force.

## AGREED MINUTE

It is agreed that in the event of
an emergency, the United States armed
forces shall be authorized to take such
measures in the vicinity of the areas
and facilities as may be necessary to
provide for their safeguarding and
control.

한·미국 간의 상호방위조약 제4조에 의한 시설과 구역 및 한국에서의 미국군대의 지위에 관한 협정(SOFA)
전59권. 1966.7.9 서울에서 서명 : 1967.2.9 발효(조약 232호) (V.48 의제 및 초안)   417

Customs Duties

1. Except as provided expressly to the contrary in this Agreement, members of the United States forces, the civilian component, and their dependents shall be subject to the laws and regulations administered by the customs authorities of the Republic of Korea. In particular the customs authorities of the Republic of Korea shall have the right, under the general conditions laid down by the laws and regulations of the Republic of Korea, to search members of the United States forces, the civilian component and their dependents and to examine their luggage, and to seize articles pursuant to such laws and regulations.

2. All materials, supplies and equipment imported by the United States forces or by the organizations provided for in Article ____ exclusively for the official use of the United States forces or those organizations or for the use of members of the United States forces, the civilian component and their dependents shall be permitted entry into Korea free from customs duties and other such charges. When such materials, supplies and equipment are imported, a certificate issued by the authorities of the United States forces

ARTICLE (Customs)

1. Save as provided in this Agreement, members of the United States armed forces, the civilian component and their dependents shall be subject the laws and regulations administered by the customs authorities of the Republic of Korea.

2. All materials, supplies and equipment imported by the United States armed forces, including their authorized procurement agencies and their non-appropriated fund organizations provided for in Article , for the official use of the United States armed forces or for the use of the members of the United States armed forces, the civilian component, and their dependents, and materials, supplies and equipment which are to be used exclusively by the United States armed forces or are ultimately

- 27 -

0130

in the form to be determined by the Joint Committee shall be submitted to the customs authorities of the Republic of Korea.

to be incorporated into articles or facilities used by such forces, shall be permitted entry into the Republic of Korea; such entry shall be free from customs duties and other such charges. Appropriate certification shall be made that such materials, supplies and equipment are being imported by the United States armed forces, including their authorized procurement agencies and their non-appropriated fund organations provided for in Article        , or, in the case of materials, supplies and equipment to be used exclusively by the United States armed forces or ultimately to be incorporated into articles or facilities used by such forces, that delivery thereof is to be taken by the United States armed forces for the purposes specified above. The exemptions provided in this paragraph shall extend to materials, supplies and equipment imported by the United States armed forces for the use of other armed forces in Korea which receive logistical support from the United States armed forces.

3. Property consigned to and for the personal use of members of the United States forces, the civilian component and

3. Property consigned to and for the personal use of members of the United States armed forces, the civilian

their dependents, shall be subject to customs duties, except that no such duties or charges shall be paid with respect to:

(a) Furniture, household goods and other personal effects for their private use imported by the members of the United States forces, the civilian component and their dependents at time of their first arrival in Korea.

(b) Reasonable quantities of clothing and household goods which are mailed into the Republic of Korea through the United States military post offices.

(c) Vehicles and parts imported by members of the U.S. armed forces or civilian component within two months after their first arrival in Korea for the private use of themselves or their dependents.

4. The exemption granted in paragraph 2 and 3 shall apply only to cases of importation of goods and shall not be

component, and their dependents, shall be subject to customs duties and other such charges, except that no duties or charges shall be paid with respect to:

(a) Furniture, household goods, and personal effects for their private use imported by the members of the United States armed forces or civilian component when they first arrive to serve in the Republic of Korea or by their dependents when they first arrive for reunion with members of such forces or civilian component;

(b) Vehicles and parts imported by members of the United States armed forces or civilian component for the private use of themselves or their dependents;

(c) Reasonable quantities of personal effects and household goods of a type which would ordinarily be purchased in the United States for the private use of members of the United States armed forces, civilian component, and their dependents, which are mailed into the Republic of Korea through United States military post offices.

4. The exemptions granted in paragraph 2 and 3 shall apply only to cases of importation of goods and shall

- 29 -

0132

interpreted as refunding customs duties and domestic excises collected by the customs authorities at the time of entry in cases of purchases of goods on which such duties and excises have already been collected.

5. Customs examination shall be exempted only in the following cases:

(a) Units of the United States forces under orders entering or leaving the Republic of Korea;

(b) Official documents under official seal;

(c) Official mail in United States military postal channels;

(d) Military cargo shipped on a United States Government bill of lading.

6. Goods imported free from customs duties and other such charges pursuant to paragraphs 2 and 3 above:

(a) May be re-exported free from customs duties and other such charges;

(b) shall not be disposed of in the Republic of Korea, by way of either sale or gift, to person not entitled to import such goods free from duty, except as such disposal may be authorized on conditions

not be interpreted as refunding customs duties and domestic excises collected by the customs authorities at the time of entry in cases of purchase of goods on which such duties and excises have already been collected.

5. Customs examination shall not be made in the following cases:

(a) Members of the United States armed forces under orders entering or leaving the Republic of Korea;

(b) Official documents under official seal and mail in United States military postal channels;

(c) Military cargo consigned to the United States armed forces, including their authorized procurement agencies and their non-appropriated fund organizations provided for in Article.

6. Except as such disposal may be authorized by the United States and Korean authorities in accordance with mutually agreed conditions, goods imported into the Republic of Korea free of duty shall not be disposed of in the Republic of Korea to persons not entitled to import such goods free of duty.

7. Goods imported into the Republic of Korea free from customs

한·미국 간의 상호방위조약 제4조에 의한 시설과 구역 및 한국에서의 미국군대의 지위에 관한 협정(SOFA)
전59권. 1966.7.9 서울에서 서명 : 1967.2.9 발효(조약 232호) (V.48 의제 및 초안)   421

agreed between the authorities of the Republic of Korea and the United States.

7. (a) The authorities of the United States forces, in cooperation with the authorities of the Republic of Korea, shall take such steps as are necessary to prevent abuse of the privileges granted to the United States forces, members of such forces, the civilian component, and their dependents in accordance with this Article.

(b) In order to prevent offenses against customs and fiscal laws and regulations, the authorities of the Republic of Korea and of the United States forces shall assist each other in the conduct of inquiries and the collection of evidence.

(c) The authorities of the United States forces shall render all assistance within their power to ensure that articles liable to seizure by, or on behalf of, the customs authorities of the Republic of Korea are handed to those authorities.

duties and other such charges pursuant to paragraphs 2 and 3, may be re-exported free from customs duties and other such charges.

8. The United States armed forces, in cooperation with Korean authorities, shall take such steps as are necessary to prevent abuse of privileges granted to the United States armed forces, members of such forces, the civilian component, and their dependents in accordance with this Article.

9. (a) In order to prevent offenses against laws and regulations administered by the customs authorities of the Government of the Republic of Korea, the Korean authorities and the United States armed forces shall assi each other in the conduct of inquirie and the collection of evidence.

(b) The United States armed forces shall render all assistance with their power to ensure that articles lia to seizure by, or on behalf of, the customs authorities of the Government of the Republic of Korea are handed those authorities.

- 31 -

(d) The authorities of the United States forces shall render all assistance within their power to ensure the payment of duties, taxes and penalities payable by members of the United States forces or the civilian component, or their dependents.

(e) The authorities of the United States forces shall provide all practicable assistance to the customs officials dispatched to military controlled piers and airports for the purpose of customs inspection.

8. Vehicles and articles belonging to the United States armed forces seized by the customs authorities of the Government of the Republic of Korea in connection with an offense against its customs or fiscal laws or regulations shall be handed over to appropriate authorities of the force concerned.

Agreed Minute

The Korean authorities may request the United States military authorities whatever information they deem necessary pertaining to all cargo consigned to the non-appropriated fund organizations and the United States military authorities shall promptly provide such information in the manner as is specified by the

(c) The United States armed forces shall render all assistance within their power to ensure the payment of duties, taxes, and penalities payable by members of such forces or of the civilian component, or their dependents.

(d) Vehicles and articles belonging to the United States armed forces seized by the customs authorities of the Government of the Republic of Korea in connection with an offense against its customs or fiscal laws or regulations shall be handed over to the appropriate authorities of the forces concerned.

Agreed Minutes

1. The quantity of goods imported under paragraph 2 by non-appropriated fund organizations of the United States armed forces for the use of the members of the United States armed forces, the civilian component, and their dependents shall be limited to the extent reasonably required for such use.

- 32 -

0135

Korean authorities.

2. Paragraph 3(a) does not require
concurrent shipment of goods with travel
of owner nor does it require single
loading or shipment. In this connection,
members of the United States armed forces
or civilian component and their dependents
may import free of duty their personal
and household effects during a period of
six months from the date of their first
arrival.

3. The term "military cargo" as
used in paragraph 5(c) is not confined
to arms and equipment but refers to all
cargo consigned to the United States
armed forces, including their
authorized procurement agencies and their
non-appropriated fund organizations
provided for in Article .

4. The United States armed forces
will take every practicable measure to
ensure that goods will not be imported
into the Republic of Korea by or for
the members of the United States armed
forces, the civilian component, or their
dependents, the entry of which would be
in violation of Korean customs laws and
regulations. The United States armed
forces will promptly notify the Korean

- 33 -

0136

customs authorities whenever the entry
of such goods in discovered.

5. The Korean customs authorities m
may, if they consider that there has been
an abuse or infringement in connection
with the entry of goods under Article   ,
take up the matter with the appropriate
authorities of the United States armed
forces.

6. The words "The United States
armed forces shall render all assistance
within their power," etc., in paragraph 9
(b) and (c) refer to reasonable and
practicable measures by the United States
armed forces authorized by United States
law and service regulations.

7. It is understood that the duty
free treatment provided in paragraph 2
shall apply to materials, supplies, and
equipment imported for sale through
commissaries and non-appropriated fund
organizations, under such regulations
as the United States armed forces may
promulgate, to those individuals and
organizations referred to in Article____
and its Agreed Minute.

Proposed additional sentence, Agreed
Minute #3:

"Pertinent information on cargo
consigned to non-appropriated fund

- 34 -

한·미국 간의 상호방위조약 제4조에 의한 시설과 구역 및 한국에서의 미국군대의 지위에 관한 협정(SOFA)
전59권. 1966.7.9 서울에서 서명 : 1967.2.9 발효(조약 232호) (V.48 의제 및 초안)   425

organizations will be furnished authorities
of the Republic of Korea upon request
through the Joint Committee."

- 35 -

ARTICLE

1. (a) Navy exchanges, post exchanges, messes, commissaries, social clubs, theaters and other non-appropriated fund organizations authorized and regulated by the authorities of the United States armed forces may be established within the facilities and areas in use by the United States armed forces for the exclusive use of the members of such forces, the civilian component, and their dependents. Except as otherwise provided in this Agreement, such organizations shall not be subject to Korean regulations, license, fees, taxes or similar controls.

(b) When a newspaper authorized and regulated by the authorities of the United States armed forces is sold to the general public, it shall be subject to Korean regulations, license, fees, taxes or similar controls so far as such circulation is concerned.

2. No Korean tax shall be imposed on sales of merchandise and services by such organizations, except as provided in paragraph 1(b) but purchase within the Republic of Korea of merchandise and supplies by such organizations shall be subject to Korean taxes unless otherwise agreed between the two Governments.

ARTICLE

1. (a) Military exchanges, messes, social clubs, theaters, newspapers and other non-appropriated fund activities authorized and regulated by the United States military authorities may be established by the United States armed forces for the use of members of such forces, the civilian component, and their dependents. Except as otherwise provided in this Agreement, such activities shall not be subject to Korean regulations, licenses, fees, taxes, or similar controls.

(b) When a newspaper authorized and regulated by the United States military authorities is sold to the general public, it shall be subject to Korean regulations, licenses, fees, taxes or similar controls so far as such circulation is concerned.

2. No Korean tax shall be imposed on sales of merchandise and services by such organizations, except as provided in paragraph 1(b) of this Article. Purchases within the Republic of Korea of merchandise and supplies by such organizations shall be subject to the Korean taxes to which other purchasers

- 36 -

0139

한·미국 간의 상호방위조약 제4조에 의한 시설과 구역 및 한국에서의 미국군대의 지위에 관한 협정(SOFA)
전59권. 1966.7.9 서울에서 서명 : 1967.2.9 발효(조약 232호) (V.48 의제 및 초안) 427

of such merchandise and supplies are subject unless otherwise agreed between the two Governments.

3. Goods which are sold by such organizations shall not be disposed of in the Republic of Korea to persons not authorized to make purchases from such organizations. Administrative measures shall be taken by the authorities of the United States to prevent such disposition.

4. The quantity of goods imported by such organizations for use of the members of the United States armed forces, the civilian component, and their dependents shall be limited to the extent reasonably required for such use.

5. The organizations referred to in this Article shall provide such information to the authorities of the Republic of Korea as is required by Korean legislations.

3. Except as such disposal may be permitted by the United States and Korean authorities in accordance with mutually agreed conditions, goods which are sold by such activities shall not be disposed of in Korea to persons not authorized to make purchases from such activities.

4. The activities referred to in this Article shall, after consultation between the representatives of the two governments in the Joint Committee, provide such information to the Republic of Korea tax authorities as is required by Korean tax legislation.

<u>Agreed Minute</u>

The activities referred to in paragraph 1 may be used by other officers or personnel of the United States Government ordinarily accorded such

- 37 -

privileges, by non-Korean persons
whose presence in Korea is solely for
the purpose of providing contract
services financed by the United States
Government, by the dependents of the
foregoing, by organizations which are
present in the Republic of Korea
primarily for the benefit and service of
the United States armed forces personnel,
such as the American Red Cross and the
United Service Organizations, and by
the non-Korean personnel of such
organizations and their dependents.

Revised Draft of the Agreed Minute

The United States Armed Forces may
grant the use of the organizations
referred to in paragraph 1 of Article___
to: (a) other officers or personnel of
the United States Government ordinarily
accorded such privileges; (b) those
other non-Korean Armed Forces in Korea
under the Unified Command which receive
logistical support from the United
States Armed Forces, and their members;
(c) those non-Korean persons whose
presence in the Republic of Korea is solely
for the purpose of providing contract
services financed by the United States
Government; (d) those organizations which
are present in the Republic of Korea

- 38 -

0141

primarily for the benefit and service
of the United States Armed Forces, such
as the American Red Cross and the United
Service Organizations, and their non-
Korean personnel; (e) dependents of the
foreoging; and (f) other persons and
organizations with the express consent
of the Government of the Republic of
Korea.

1. The United States armed forces shall have the use of all public utilities and services belonging to or controlled or regulated by the Government of the Republic of Korea. The term "utilities and services" shall include, but not be limited to, transportation and communications facilities and systems, electricity, gas, water, steam, heat, light, power, and sewage disposal. In the use of such utilities and services the United States armed forces shall enjoy priorities under conditions no less favorable that those that may be applicable from time to time to the ministries and agencies of the Government of the Republic of Korea.

3. (a) The United States armed forces shall have the use of all utilities and services, whether publicly or privately owned, which are controlled or regulated by the Government of the Republic of Korea or political subdivisions thereof. The term "utilities and services" shall include, but not be limited to, transportation and communications facilities and systems, electricity, gas, water, steam, heat, light, power, however, produced, and sewage disposal. The use of utilities and services as provided herein shall not prejudice the right of the United States to operate military transportation, communication, power and such other services and facilities deemed necessary for the operations of the United States armed forces.

(b) The use of such utilities and services by the United States shall be in accordance with priorities, conditions, and rates or tariffs no less favorable than those accorded any other user, governmental or private. The Republic of Korea shall insure that by reason of legislation of otherwise, there shall be no discrimination again

한·미국 간의 상호방위조약 제4조에 의한 시설과 구역 및 한국에서의 미국군대의 지위에 관한 협정(SOFA)
전59권. 1966.7.9 서울에서 서명 : 1967.2.9 발효(조약 232호) (V.48 의제 및 초안)   431

the United States armed forces in the procurement of such utilities and services. Should the emergency operating needs of the United States armed forces so require, the Republic of Korea shall, upon notification thereon, take all measures to assure provision of utilities and services necessary to meet these needs.

2. (a) Specific arrangements as to the use of such public utilities and services by the United States armed forces and the payment therefor shall be made between the appropriate authorities of the two Governments or their agencies.

(b) The existing arrangements concerning the use of such public utilities and services by the United States armed forces at the effective date of this Agreement shall be regarded as the arrangements referred to in the foregoing paragraph.

Revised Draft

3. (a) The United States armed forces shall have the use of all utilities and services which are owned, controlled ore regulated by the Government of the Republic of Korea or local administrative subdivisions thereof. The term "utilities and services" shall include, but not be limited to, transportation and communications facilities and systems, electricity, gas, water, steam, heat, light, power,

4. It is agreed that arrangements will be effected between the Governments of the United States and the Republic of Korea for accounting applicable to financial transactions arising out of this Agreement.

Revised Draft of third and fourth sentences, paragraph 3(a)

The use of utilities and services as provided herein shall not prejudice the right of the United States to operate military transportation, communication, power and such other utilities and services deemed necessary for the operations of the United States armed forces. This right shall not be exercised in a manner inconsistent with the operation by the Government of the Republic of

- 4 -

and sewage disposal. The use of utilities and services as provided herein shall not prejudice the right of the United States to operate military transportation, communication, power and such other utilities and services deemed necessary for the operations of the United States armed forces. This right shall not be exercised in a manner inconsistent with the operation by the Government of the Republic of Korea of its utilities and services.

(b) The use of such utilities and services by the United States shall be in accordance with priorities, conditions, and rates or tariffs no less favorable than those accorded any other user.

(4. Removed from this article; to be placed elsewhere in SOFA.)

### Agreed Minute

1. The Joint Committee shall be given the opportunity of discussing any changes determined by the Korean authorities of priority or rates applicable to the United States armed forces prior to their effective date.

2. Paragraph 3 of Article ____ will not be construed as in any way abrogating the Utilities and Claims

Korea of its utilities and services.

### Agreed Minute

1. It is understood that any change in priority or increase in utility or service rates applicable to the United States armed forces shall be the subject of prior consultation in the Joint Committee.

2. Paragraph 3 of Article ____ will not be construed as in any way abrogating the Utilities and Claims

한·미국 간의 상호방위조약 제4조에 의한 시설과 구역 및 한국에서의 미국군대의 지위에 관한 협정(SOFA)
전59권. 1966.7.9 서울에서 서명 : 1967.2.9 발효(조약 232호) (V.48 의제 및 초안) 433

Settlement Agreement of December 18, 1958, which continues in full force and effect unless otherwise agreed by the two governments.

Settlement Agreement of December 18, 1958 which continues in full force and effect.

3.   Should the emergency operating needs of the United States armed forces so require, the Republic of Korea shall, after consultation thereon, take appropriate measures to assure provision of utilities and services necessary to meet these needs.

- 43 -

0146

ARTICLE

1. The United States may contract for any supplies or construction work to be furnished or undertaken in the Republic of Korea for purposes of, or authorized by, this Agreement, without restriction as to choice of supplier or persons who does the construction work. Such supplies or construction work may, upon agreement between the appropriate authorities of the two Governments, also be procured through the Government of the Republic of Korea.

2. Materials, supplies, equipment and services which are required from local sources for the maintenance of the United States armed forces and the procurement of which may have an adverse effect on the economy of the Republic of Korea shall be procured in coordination with, and, when desirable, through or with the assistance of, the competent authorities of the Republic of Korea.

3. Materials, supplies, equipment and services procured for official purposes in the Republic of Korea by the United States armed forces, or by authorized procurement agencies of the United

ARTICLE

1. The United States may contract for any supplier or construction work to be furnished or undertaken in the Republic of Korea for purposes of, or authorized by, this Agreement, without restriction as to choice of supplier or persons who does the construction work. Such supplier or construction work may, upon agreement between the appropriate authorities of the two Governments, also be procured through the Government of the Republic of Korea.

2. Materials, supplies, equipment and services which are required from local sources for the maintenance of the United States armed forces and the procurement of which any have an adverse effect on the economy of the Republic of Korea shall be procured in coordination with, and, when desirable, through or with the assistance of, the competent authorities of the Republic of Korea.

3. Materials, supplies, equipment and services procured for official purposes in the Republic of Korea by the United States armed forces, including their authorized procurement agencies,

0147

한·미국 간의 상호방위조약 제4조에 의한 시설과 구역 및 한국에서의 미국군대의 지위에 관한 협정(SOFA)
전59권. 1966.7.9 서울에서 서명 : 1967.2.9 발효(조약 232호) (V.48 의제 및 초안) 435

States armed forces upon appropriate certification shall be exempt from the following Korean taxes:

    (a) Commodity tax

    (b) Gasoline tax

    (c) Electricity and gas tax

Materials, supplies, equipment and services procured for ultimate use by the United States armed forces shall be exempt from commodity and gasoline taxes upon appropriate certification by the United States armed forces. With respect to any present or future Korean taxes not specifically referred to in this Article which might be found to constitute a significant and readily identifiable part of the gross purchase price of materials, supplies, equipment and services procured by the United States armed forces, the two Governments will agree upon a procedure for granting such exemption or relief therefrom as is consistent with the purpose of this Article.

4. Neither members of the United States armed forces, civilian component, nor their dependents, shall by reason of this Article enjoy any exemption from taxes or similar charges relating to personal purchases of goods and

or procured for ultimate use by the United States armed forces shall be exempted from the following Korean taxes upon appropriate certification by the United States armed forces:

    (a) commodity tax

    (b) Traffic tax

    (c) Petroleum tax

    (d) Electricity and gas tax

    (e) Business tax

With respect to any present and future Korean taxes not specifically referred to in this Article which might be found to constitute a significant and readily identifiable part of the gross purchase price of materials, supplies, equipment and services procured by the United States armed forces, or for ultimate use by such forces, the two Governments will agree upon a procedure for granting such exemption or relief therefrom as is consistent with the prupose of this Article.

4. Neither members of the United States armed forces, civilian component, nor their dependents, shall by reason of this Article enjoy any exemption from taxes or similar charges relating to personal purchases of goods and

services in the Republic of Korea
chargeable under Korean legislation.

5.    Except as such disposal may be
authorized by the Korean and United
States authorities in accordance with
mutually agreed conditions, goods
purchased in the Republic of Korea
exempt from the taxes referred to in
paragraph 3, shall not be disposed of
in the Republic of Korea to persons not
entitled to purchase such goods exempt
from such tax.

services in the Republic of Korea
chargeable under Korean legislation.

5.    Except as such disposal may
be authorized by the United States and
Korean authorities in accordance
with mutually agreed conditions, goods
purchased in the Republic of Korea
exempt from taxes referred to in paragraph 3, shall not be disposed of in
the Republic of Korea to persons not
entitled to purchase such goods
exempt from such tax.

### Agreed Minute

1.    The United States armed forces
will furnish the Korean authorities
with appropriate information as far in
advance as practicable on anticipated
major changes in their procurement
program in the Republic of Korea.

2.    The problem of a satisfactory
settlement of difficulties with respect
to procurement contracts arising out of
differences between Korea and United
States economic laws and business
practices will be studied by the Joint
Committee or other appropriate persons.

3.    The procedures for securing
exemptions from taxation on purchases
of goods for ultimate use by the United
States armed forces will be as follows:

- 46 -

0149

(a) Upon appropriate certification by the United States armed forces that materials, supplies and equipment consigned to or destined for such forces, are to be used, or wholly or partially used up, under the supervision of such forces, exclusively in the execution of contracts for the construction, maintenance or operation of the facilities and areas referred to in Article    or for the support of the forces therein, or are ultimately to be incorporated into articles or facilities used by such forces, an authorized representative of such forces shall take delivery of such materials, supplies and equipment directly from manufacturers thereof. In such circumstances the collection of taxes referred to in Article    , paragraph 3, shall be held in abeyances.

(b) The receipt of such materials, supplies and equipment in the facilities and areas shall be confirmed by an authorized agent of the United States armed forces to the Korean authorities.

(c) Collection of the taxes on such materials, supplies and equipment shall be held in abeyance until

- 47-

(1) The United States
armed forces confirm and certify the
quantity or degree of consumption of
the above referred to materials,
supplies and equipment, or

(2) The United States
armed forces confirm and certify the
amount of the above referred to
materials, supplies, and equipment
which have been ~~incorporated~~ into
articles or facilities used by the
United States armed forces.

(d) Materials, supplies, and
equipment certified under (e) (1) or
(2) shall be exempt from ~~taxes~~ referred
to in Article     , paragraph 3,
insofar as the price thereof is paid
out of United States Government
appropriations or out of funds contributed by the Government of the Republic
of Korea for disbursement by the United
States.

## ARTICLE

1. Persons, including corporations organized under the laws of the United States, and their employees who are ordinarily resident in the United States and whose presence in the Republic of Korea is solely for the purpose of executing contracts with the United States, for the benefit of the United States armed forces, and who are designated by the Government of the United States in accordance with the provisions of the paragraph 2 below, shall, except as provided in this Article, be subject to the laws and regulations of the Republic of Korea.

2. The designation referred to in paragraph 1 above shall be made upon consultation with the Government of the Republic of Korea and shall be restricted to cases where open competitive bidding is not practicable due to security considerations, to the technical qualifications of the contractors involved, to the unavailability of materials or services required by United States standards, or to the limitations of United States law. The designation shall be withdrawn by the Government of the United States:

## ARTICLE

1. Persons, including corporations, their employees, and the dependents of such persons, present in Korea solely for the purpose of executing contracts with the United States for the benefit of the United States armed forces or other armed forces in Korea under the Unified Command receiving logistical support from the United States armed forces, who are designated by the Government of the United States in accordance with the provisions of paragraph 2 below, shall, except as provided in this Article, be subject to the laws and regulations of Korea.

2. The designation referred to in paragraph 1 above shall be made upon consultation with the Government of Korea and shall be restricted to cases where open competitive bidding is not practicable due to security considerations, to the technical qualifications of the contractors involved, to the unavailability of materials or services required by United States standards, or to limitations of United States law. The designation shall be withdrawn by the Government of the United States:

(a) upon completion of contracts with the United States for the United States armed forces;

(b) upon proof that such persons are engaged in business activities in the Republic of Korea other than those pertaining to the United States armed forces; or

(c) when such persons are engaged in practices illegal in the Republic of Korea.

3. Upon certification by the appropriate authorities of the United States as to their identity, such persons and their employees shall be accorded the following benefits of this Agreement:

(a) Entry into the Republic of Korea in accordance with the provisions of Article ____;

(b) The exemption from customs duties and other such charges provided

(a) upon completion of contracts with the United States for the United States armed forces or other armed forces in Korea under the Unified command receiving logistical support from the United States armed forces;

(b) Upon proof that such persons are engaged in business activities in Korea other than those pertaining to the United States States armed forces or other armed forces in Korea under the Unified Command receiving logistical support from the United States armed forces;

(c) Upon proof that such persons are engaged in practices illegal in Korea.

3. Upon certification by appropriate United States authorities as to their identity, such persons shall be accorded the following benefits of this Agreement:

(a) Rights of accession and movement, as provided for Article , paragraph 2;

(b) Entry into Korea in accordance with the provisions of Article ____;

(c) The exemption from customs duties, and other such charges provided

- 50 -

한·미국 간의 상호방위조약 제4조에 의한 시설과 구역 및 한국에서의 미국군대의 지위에 관한 협정(SOFA) 전59권. 1966.7.9 서울에서 서명 : 1967.2.9 발효(조약 232호) (V.48 의제 및 초안) 441

for in Article _____, paragraph 3 for members of the United States forces, the civilian component, and their dependents;

(c) If authorized by the Government of the United States, the right to use the services of the organizations provided for in Article _____;

(d) Those provided for in Article _____, paragraph 2, for members of the United States armed forces, the civilian component, and their dependents;

(e) If authorized by the Government of the United States, the right to use military payment certificates, as provided for in Article _____;

(f) The use of postal facilities provided for in Article _____;

for in Article _____, paragraph 3, for members of the United States armed forces, the civilian component, and their dependents;

(d) If authorized by the Government of the United States, the right to use the services of the activities provided for in Article _____;

(e) Those rights provided in Article _____, paragraph 2, for members of the United States armed forces, the civilian component, and their dependents;

(f) If authorized by the Government of the United States, the right to use military payment certificates, as provided for in Article _____;

(g) The use of postal facilities provided for in Article _____;

(h) Those rights accorded the United States armed forces by Article ___, paragraph 3, relating to utilities and services;

(i) Those rights provided to members of the United States armed forces, the civilian component, and their dependents by Article ___ , relating to driving permits and registration of vehicles;

(g) Exemption from the laws and regulations of the Republic of Korea with respect to terms and conditions of employment.

4. Such persons and their employees shall be subject to the Korean passport and visa regulations and shall possess passports with their status described therein. Their arrival, departure and their residence while in the Republic of Korea shall be notified by the United States to the Government of the Republic of Korea.

5. Upon certification by an authorized officer of the United States armed forces, such contractors and their employees shall be exempt from taxation in the Republic of Korea on the holding, use, transfer by death, or transfer to persons or agencies entitled to tax

(j) Exemption from the laws and regulations of Korea with respect to terms and conditions of employment, and licensing and registration of business and corporations.

4. The arrival, departure, and place of residence in Korea of such persons shall from time to time be notified by the United States armed forces to the Korean authorities.

5. Upon certification by an authorized representative of the United States armed forces, depreciable assets, except hourse, held, used or transferred by such persons exclusively for the execution of contracts referred to in paragraph 1 shall not be subject to taxes or similar charges of Korea.

6. Upon certification by an authorized representative of the United States armed forces, such persons shall be exempt from taxation in Korea on the holding, use, transfer by death, or transfer to persons or agencies entitled to tax exemption under this

- 52 -

한·미국 간의 상호방위조약 제4조에 의한 시설과 구역 및 한국에서의 미국군대의 지위에 관한 협정(SOFA) 전59권. 1966.7.9 서울에서 서명 : 1967.2.9 발효(조약 232호) (V.48 의제 및 초안) 443

exemption under this Agreement, of any movable property, the presence of which in the Republic of Korea is due solely to the temporary presence of these persons in the Republic of Korea, provided that such exemption shall not apply to property held for the purpose of investment those executing contracts as described in paragraph 1 of this Article in the Republic of Korea.

6. The persons and their employees referred to in paragraph 1 shall not be liable to pay income tax to the Government of the Republic of Korea or to any other taxing agency in the Republic of Korea on any income derived under a contract made in the United States with the Government of the United States in connection with the construction, maintenance or operation of any of the facilities or areas covered by this Agreement. The provisions of this paragraph do not exempt such persons from payment of income or corporation taxed on income derived from other engagement than those mentioned in this paragraph.

Agreement, of movable property, tangible or intangible, the presence of which in Korea is due solely to the temporary presence of these persons in Korea, provided that such exemption shall not apply to property held for the purpose of investment or the conduct of other business in Korea or to any intangible property registered in Korea.

7. The persons referred to in paragraph 1 shall not be liable to pay income or corporation taxes to the Government of Korea or to any other taxing agency in Korea on any income derived under a contract with the Government of the United States in connection with the construction, maintenance or operation of any of the facilities or areas covered by this Agreement. Persons in Korea in connection with the execution of such a contract with the United States shall not be liable to pay any Korean taxes to the Government of Korea or to any taxing agency in Korea on income derived from sources outside of Korea nor shall periods during which such persons are in Korea be considered periods of

0156

residence or domicile in Korea for the purposes of Korean taxation. The provisions of this paragraph do not exempt such persons from payment of income or corporation taxes on income derived from Korean sources, other than those sources referred to in the first sentence of this paragraph, nor do they exempt such persons who claim Korean residence for United States income tax purposes from payment of Korean taxes on income.

7. The Korean authorities shall have the primary right to exercise jurisdiction over the contractors and their employees referred to in paragraph 1 of this Article in relation to offenses committed in the Republic of Korea and punishable by the law of the Republic of Korea. In those cases, in which the Korean authorities decide not to exercise such jurisdiction they shall notify the military authorities of the United States as soon as possible. Upon such notification they military authorities of the United States shall have the right to exercise such jurisdiction over the persons referred to as is conferred on them by the law of the United States.

한·미국 간의 상호방위조약 제4조에 의한 시설과 구역 및 한국에서의 미국군대의 지위에 관한 협정(SOFA)
전59권. 1966.7.9 서울에서 서명 : 1967.2.9 발효(조약 232호) (V.48 의제 및 초안)    445

6. The persons referred to in paragraph 1 shall not be liable to pay income or corporation taxes to the Government of the Republic of Korea or to any other taxing agency in Korea on any income derived under a contract with the Government of the United States in connection with the construction, maintenance or operation of any of the facilities or areas covered by this Agreement. The provisions of this paragraph do not exempt such persons from payment of income or corporation taxes on income derived from Korean sources, other than those sources referred to in the first such persons who claim Korean residence for United States income tax purposes from payment of Korean taxes on income. Periods during which such persons are in Korea solely in connection with the execution of a contract with the Government of the United States shall not be considered periods of residence or domicile in Korea for the purpose of such taxation.

3. Upon certification by appropriate United States authorities as to their identity, such persons shall be accorded the following benefits of this Agreement:

(a) Accession and movement, as provided for in Article ___, paragraph 2;

(b) Entry into Korea in accordance with the provisions of Article ___;

(c) The exemption from customs duties and other such charges provided for in Article ___, paragraph 3, for members of the United States armed forces, the civilian component, and their dependents;

(d) If authorized by the Government of the United States, the use of the services of the activities provided for in Article ___;

(e) Those provided in Article ___, paragraph 2, for members of the United States armed forces, the civilian component, and their dependents;

(f) If authorized by the Government of the United States, the use of military payment certificates, as provided in Article ___;

- 5 -

0158

(g) The use of postal facilities provided for in Article ____;

(h) The use of utilities and services in accordance with those priorities, conditions, rates, or tariffs accorded the United States armed forces by Article ____, paragraph 3, relating to utilities and services;

(i) Those provided to members of the United States armed forces, the civilian component, and their dependents by Article ____, relating to driving permits and registration of vehicles;

(j) Exemption from the laws and regulations of Korea with respect to terms and conditions of employment, and registration of businesses and corporations.

Agreed Minute

The execution of contracts with the United States in addition to those specified in paragraph 1 of Article ____ shall not exclude the persons provided for in Article ____ from the application of that Article.

0159

ARTICLE

The Republic of Korea and the
United States will cooperate in taking
such steps as may from time to time be
necessary to ensure the security of the
United States armed forces, the members
thereof, the civilian component, their
dependents, and their property. The
Government of the Republic of Korea agrees
to seek such legislation and to take such
other action as may be necessary to ensure
the adequate security and protection within
its territory of installations, equipment,
property, records and official information
of the United States, and for the punishment of offenders under the applicable
laws of the Republic of Korea.

ARTICLE

The United States and the Republic
of Korea will cooperate in taking such
steps as may from time to time be
necessary to ensure the security of the
United States armed forces, the members
thereof, the civilian component, the
persons who are present in the
Republic of Korea pursuant to Article       ,
their dependents and their property.
The Government of the Republic of Korea
agrees to seek such legislation and
to take such other action as may be
necessary to ensure the adequate
security and protection within its
territory of installations, equipment,
property, records, and official information of the United States, of the
persons referred to in this paragraph,
and their property and, consistent with
Article      , to ensure the punishment
of offenders under the applicable laws
of the Republic of Korea.

ARTICLE

ARTICLE

1. Members of the United States armed forces, the civilian component, and their dependents shall be subject to the foreign exchange controls of the Government of the Republic of Korea.

2. The preceding paragraph shall not be construed to preclude the transmission into or outside of the Republic of Korea of the United States dollars or dollar instruments representing the official funds of the United States or realized as a result of service or employment in connection with this Agreement by members of the United States armed forces and the civilian component, or realized by such persons and their dependents from sources outside of the Republic of Korea.

3. The United States authorities shall take suitable measures to preclude the abuse of the privileges stipulated in the preceding paragraphs or circumvention of the Korean foreign exchange controls.

Agreed Minute

Payment in Korea by the United States armed forces and by those organizations provided in Article ____ to persons

1. Members of the United States armed forces, the civilian component, and their dependents, shall be subject to the foreign exchange controls of the Government of the Republic of Korea.

2. The preceding paragraph shall not be construed to preclude the transmission into or out of Korea of United States dollars or dollar instruments representing the official funds of the United States or realized as a result of service or employment in connection with this Agreement by members of the United States armed forces and the civilian component, or realized by such persons and their dependents from sources outside Korea.

3. The United States authorities shall take suitable measures to preclude the abuse of the privileges stipulated in the preceding paragraphs or circumvention of the Korean foreign exchange controls.

Agreed Minute

Payment in Korea by the United States armed forces including those activities provided in Article ____, to persons other than members of the United States armed forces, civilian component, their dependents and those persons referred to in Article ___ shall be effected in accordance with the Korean Foreign Exchange Control Law and regulations. In these transactions the basic rate of exchange shall be used.

other than members of the United States armed forces, civilian component, the dependents and those persons referred in Article ___ shall be effected in accordance with the Korean Foreign Exchange Control Law and regulations. The funds to be used for these transactions shall be convertible into currency of the Republic of Korea at the highest rate in terms of the number of Korean Won per United State dollar which, at the time the convers is made, is not unlawful in the Repub of Korea.

ARTICLE

1. (a) United States military payment certificates denominated in dollars
may be used by persons authorized by
the United States for internal trans-
action within the facilities and areas
in use by the United States forces.

(b) The United States Government
will take appropriate action to ensure
that authorized personnel are prohibited
from engaging in transactions involving
military payment certificates except
as authorized by United States regulations.

(c) The Government of the Republic
of Korea will take necessary action to
prohibit unauthorized person from engaging in transactions involving military
payment certificates and with the aid of
United States authorities will undertake
to apprehend and punish any person or
persons under its jurisdiction involved
in the counterfeiting or uttering of
counterfeit military payment certificates.

(d) It is agreed that the United
States authorities will apprehend and
punish members of the United States
forces, the civilian component, or their
dependents, who tender military payment
certificates to unauthorized persons and

ARTICLE

1. (a) United States military
payment certificates denominated in dolla:
may be used by persons authorized by
the United States for internal transactions. The Government of the United
States will take appropriate action to
ensure that authorized personnel are
prohibited from engaging in transactions
involving military payment certificates
except as authorized by United States
regulations.

(b) The Government of Korea
will take necessary action to prohibit
unauthorized persons from engaging in
transactions involving military payment
certificates and with the aid of United
States authorities will undertake to
apprehend and punish any person or persons
under its jurisdiction involved in the
counterfeiting or uttering of counterfeit
military payment certificates.

(b) It is agreed that the United
States authorities will to the extent
authorized by United States law, apprehend and punish members of the United
States armed forces, the civilian
component, or their dependents, who

- 60 -

0163

that no obligation will, after the date
of coming into force of this Agreement,
be due to such unauthorized persons or
to the Government of the Republic of
Korea or its agencies from the United
States or any of its agencies as a
result of any unauthorized use of military
payment certificates within the Republic
of Korea.

    2. (a) In order to exercise control
of military payment certificates the
United States may designate certain
American financial institutions to
maintain and operate, under United States
supervision, facilities for the use of
persons authorized by the United States
to use military payment certificates.

    (b) Institutions authorized to
maintain military banking facilities
will establish and maintain such facilities physically separated from their
Korean commercial banking business,
with personnel whose sole duty is to
maintain and operate such facilities.
Such facilities shall be permitted to
maintain United States currency bank
accounts and to perform all financial
transactions in connection therewith
including receipt and remission of funds
to the extent provided by Article ___,

tender military payment certificates
to unauthorized persons and that no
obligation will be due to such unauthorized persons or to the Government of
Korea or its agencies from the United
States or any of its agencies as a
result of any unauthorized use of
military payment certificates within
Korea.

    2. In order to exercise control
of military payment certificates the
United States may designate certain
American financial institutions to
maintain and operate, under United
States supervision, facilities for the
use of persons authorized by the United
States to use military payments certificates. Institutions authorized to
maintain military banking facilities
will establish and maintain such
facilities physically separated from
their Korean commercial banking
business, with personnel whose sole
duty is to maintain and operate such
facilities. Such facilities shall be
permitted to maintain United States
currency bank accounts and to perform
all financial transactions in connection therewith including receipt and
remission of funds to the extent

- 61 -

0164

paragraph 2, of this Agreement.

<u>Agreed Minute</u>

United States military payment certificates under custody of the Government of the Republic of Korea at the time of entry into force of this Agreement shall be disposed in accordance with the agreement between the two Government

provided by Article , paragraph 2, of this Agreement.

<u>Agreed Minute</u>

Inasmuch as United States military Payment Certificates are property of the United States Government, any Military Payment Certificates which are in, or come into, the possession of the Government of the Republic of Korea shall be returned without compensation to the authorities of the United States armed forces as expeditiously as practicable.

- 62 -

0165

ARTICLE

1. Each Party waives all its claims against the other Party for damage to any property owned by it and used by its armed services, if such damage --

(a) was caused by a member or an employee of the armed services of the other Party, in execution of his official duties; or

(b) arose from the use of any vehicle, vessel or aircraft owned by the other Party and used by its armed services, provided either that the vehicle, vessel or aircraft causing the damage was being used in the execution of its official duty or that the damage was caused to property being so used.

Claims for maritime salvage by one Party against the other Party shall be waived, provided that the vessel or cargo salved was owned by the other Party and being used by its armed services for official purposes.

2. (a) In the case of damage caused or arising as stated in paragraph 1 to other property owned by either Party and located in the Republic of Korea, the issue of liability of the other Party shall be determined and the amount of

ARTICLE

1. Each Party waives all its claims against the other Party for damage to any property owned by it and used by its land, sea or air armed forces, if such damage:

(a) was caused by a member or an employee of the armed forces of the other Party in the performance of his official duties; or

(b) arose from the use of any vehicle, vessel or aircraft owned by the other Party and used by its armed forces, provided either that the vehicle, vessel or aircraft causing the damage was being used for official purposes, or that the damage was caused to property being so used.

Claims by one Party against the other Party for maritime salvage shall be waived provided that the vessel, or cargo salvaged was owned by a Party and being used by its armed forces for official purposes.

2. In the case of damage caused or arising as stated in paragraph 1 to other property owned by a Party:

(a) each Party waives its claim up to the amount of $1400 or its equivalent in Korean currency at the rate

- 63 -

454 주한미군지위협정(SOFA) 서명 및 발효 18

damage shall be assessed, unless the
two Governments agree otherwise, by a
sole arbitrator selected in accordance
with subparagraph (b) of this paragraph.
The arbitrator shall also decide any
counter-measures arising out of the
same incidents.

(b) The arbitrator referred to
in subparagraph (a) above shall be
selected by agreement between the two
Governments from amongst the nationals
of the Republic of Korea who hold or
have held high judicial office.

(c) Any decision taken by the
arbitrator shall be binding and conclusive upon the Parties.

(d) The amount of any compensation
awarded by the arbitrator shall be
distributed in accordance with the
provisions of paragraph 5(e) (i), (ii)
and (iii) of this Article.

(e) The compensation of the
arbitrator shall be fixed by agreement
between the two Governments and shall,
together with the necessary expenses
incidental to the performance of his
duties, be defrayed in equal proportions
by them.

(f) Each Party waives its claim
in any such case up to the amount equivalent

of exchange provided for in the Agreed
Minute to Article ____ at the time the
claim is filed.

(b) Claims in excess of the
amount stated in subparagraph (a)
shall be settled by the Party against
which the claim is made in accordance
with its domestic law.

한·미국 간의 상호방위조약 제4조에 의한 시설과 구역 및 한국에서의 미국군대의 지위에 관한 협정(SOFA)
전59권. 1966.7.9 서울에서 서명 : 1967.2.9 발효(조약 232호) (V.48 의제 및 초안)     455

to 800 United States dollars or 104,000 won. In the case of considerable variation in the rate of exchange between these currencies the two Governments shall agree on the appropriate adjustments of these amounts.

3. For the purpose of paragraph 1 and 2 of this Article the expression "owned by a Party" in the case of a vessel includes a vessel on bare boat charter to that Party or requisitioned by it on bare boat terms or seized by it in prize (except to the extent that the risk of loss or liability is borne by some person other than such Party).

4. Each Party waives all its claims against the other Party for injury or death suffered by any member of its armed services while such member was engaged in the performance of his official duties.

5. Claims (other than contractual claims and those to which paragraph 6 or 7 of this Article apply) arising out of acts or omissions of members or employees of the United States armed forces, including those employees who are nationals of or ordinarily resident in the Republic of Korea, done in the performance of

3. For the purpose of paragraph 1 and 2 of this Article, the expression "owned by a Party" in the case of a vessel includes a vessel on bare boat charter to that Party or requisitioned by it on bare boat charter terms or seized by it in prize (except to the extent that the risk of loss or liability is borne by some other person than such Party).

4. Each Party waives all its claim against the other Party for injury or death suffered by any member of its armed forces while such member was engaged in the performance of his official duties.

5. Claims (other than contractual claims) arising out of acts or omissions of members or employees of the United States armed forces done in the performance of official duty, or out of any other act, omission or occurrence for which the United States armed forces are legally responsible, and causing damage

- 65 -

official duty, or out of any other act, omission or occurrence for which the United States armed forces are legally responsible, and causing damage in the Republic of Korea to third Parties, other than the Government of the Republic of Korea, shall be dealt with by the Republic of Korea in accordance with the following provisions:

(a) Claims shall be filed, considered and settled or adjudicated in accordance with the laws and regulations of the Republic of Korea with respect to the claims arising from the activities of its own armed forces.

(b) The Republic of Korea may settle any such claims, and payment of the amount agreed upon or determined by adjudication shall be made by the Republic of Korea in won.

(c) Such payment, whether made pursuant to a settlement or to adjudication of the case by a competent tribunal of the Republic of Korea, or the final adjudication by such a tribunal denying payment, shall be binding and conclusive upon the Parties.

(d) Every claim paid by the Republic of Korea shall be communicated to the appropriate United States authorities

in the Republic of Korea to third parties other than the two Governments shall be processed and settled in accordance with the applicable provisions of United States law. The United States Government shall entertain other non-contractual claims against members of the United States armed forces or of the civilian component and may offer an _ex gratia_ payment in such cases and in such amount as is determined by the appropriate United States authorities.

- 44 -

한·미국 간의 상호방위조약 제4조에 의한 시설과 구역 및 한국에서의 미국군대의 지위에 관한 협정(SOFA)
전59권. 1966.7.9 서울에서 서명 : 1967.2.9 발효(조약 232호) (V.48 의제 및 초안) 457

together with full particulars and a
proposed distribution in conformity
with subparagraph (e) (i) and (ii) below.

In default of a reply within two
months, the proposed distribution shall be
regarded as accepted.

(e) The cost incurred in satisfying claims pursuant to the preceding
subparagraph and paragraph 2 of this Article
shall be distributed between the Parties
as follows:

(i) Where the United States
alone is responsible, the amount awarded or
adjudged shall be distributed in the
proportion of 15 per cent chargeable to
the Republic of Korea and 85 per cent
chargeable to the United States.

(ii) Where the Republic of Korea
and the United States are responsible for the
damage, the amount awarded or adjudged
shall be distributed equally between them.
Where the damage was caused by the armed forces
of the Republic of Korea and the United
States and it is not possible to attribute
it specifically to one or both of those
armed services, the amount awarded or
adjudged shall be distributed equally
between the Republic of Korea and the
United States.

(iii) Every half-year, a statement of the sums paid by the Republic of
Korea in the course of the half-yearly
period in respect of every case regarding
which the proposed distribution on a
percentage basis has been accepted, shall
be sent to the appropriate authorities of
the United States, together with a request
for reimbursement.  Such reimbursement
shall be made, in won, within the
shortest possible time.

(f) Members or employees of
the United States armed forces, excluding
those employees who are nationals of or
ordinarily resident in the Republic of
Korea, shall not be subject to any proceedings for the enforcement of any judgement
given against them in the Republic of
Korea in a matter arising from the
performance of their official duties.

(g) Except in so far as subparagraph (e) of this paragraph applies
to claims covered by paragraph 2 of this
Article, the provisions of this paragraph
shall not apply to any claims arising out
of or in connection with the navigation
or operation of a ship or the loading,
carriage, or discharge of a cargo, other
than claims for death or personal injury
to which paragraph 4 of this Article does

- 69 -

0171

6.  Claims against members or employees of the United States armed forces (except employees who are nationals of or ordinarily resident in the Republic of Korea) arising out of tortious acts or omissions in the Republic of Korea not done in the performance of official duty shall be dealt with in the following manner:

(a) The authorities of the Republic of Korea shall consider the claim and access compensation to the claimant in a fair and just manner, taking into account all the circumstances of the case, including the conduct of the injured persons, and shall prepare a report on the matter.

(b) The report shall be delivered to the appropriate United States authorities, who shall then decide without delay whether they will offer an ex gratia payment, and if so, of what amount.

(c) If an offer of ex gratia payment is made, and accepted by the claimant in full satisfaction of his claim, the United States authorities shall make the payment themselves and inform the authorities of the Republic of Korea of their decision and of the sums paid.

- 69 -

0172

(d) Nothing in this paragraph shall affect the jurisdiction of the courts of the Republic of Korea to entertain an action against a member or an employee of the United States armed forces unless and until there has been payment in full satisfaction of the claim.

7. Claims arising out of the unauthorized use of any vehicle of the United States forces shall be dealt with in accordance with paragraph 6 of this Article, except in so far as the United States forces are legally responsible.

8. If a dispute arises as to whether a tortious act or omission of a member or an employee of the United States armed forces was done in the performance of official duty or as to whether the use of any vehicle of the United States armed forces was unauthorized, the question shall be submitted to an arbitrator appointed in accordance with paragraph 2(b) of this Article, whose decision on this point shall be final and conclusive.

9. (a) The United States shall not claim immunity from the jurisdiction of the courts of the Republic of Korea for

9. For the purposes of this Article, each Party shall have the r: to determine whether a member or employee of its armed forces was eng: in the performance of official duties and whether property owned by it was being used by its armed forces for official purposes.

6. (a) A member or employee of the United States armed forces shall not be afforded immunity from the

- 70 -

0173

members or employees of the United States armed forces in respect of the civil jurisdiction of the courts of the Republic of Korea except to the extent provided in paragraph 5(f) of this Article.

(b) In case any private movable property, excluding that in use by the United States armed forces, which is subject to compulsory execution under the Korean law, is within the facilities and areas in use by the United States armed forces, the United States authorities shall, upon the request of the courts of the Republic of Korea, possess and turn over such property to the authorities of the Republic of Korea.

(c) The authorities of the Republic of Korea and the United States shall cooperate in the procurement of evidence for a fair hearing and disposal of claims under this Article.

10. Disputes arising out of contracts concerning the procurement of materials, supplies, equipment, services by or for the United States armed forces, which are not resolved by the Parties to

jurisdiction of the civil courts of Korea except: (1) in a matter arising out of acts or omissions done in the performance of official duty; or (2) in respect to any claim where there has been payment in full satisfaction of the claimant.

(b) In the case of any private movable property, excluding that in use by the United States armed forces, which is subject to compulsory execution under Korean law, and is within the facilities and areas in use by the United States armed forces, the United States authorities shall, upon the request of the Korean courts, render all assistance within their power to see that such property is turned over to the Korean authorities.

7. The authorities of the United States and Korea shall cooperate in the procurement of evidence for a fair disposition of claims under this Article.

the contract concerned, may be submitted to the Joint Committee for conciliation, provided that the provisions of this paragraph shall not prejudice any right, which Parties to the contract may have, to file a civil suit.

11. Paragraphs 2 and 5 of this Article shall apply only to claims arising incident to non-combat activities.

9. Paragraphs 2 and 5 of this Article shall apply only to claims arising incident to noncombat activity.

10. For the purposes of this Article, members of the Korean augmentation to the United States Army (KATUSA) shall be considered as member of the United States armed forces, and members of the Korean Service Corps (KSC) shall be considered as employees of the armed forces of the Republic of Korea.

11. The provisions of this Article shall not apply to any claims which arose before the entry into force of this Agreement.

한·미국 간의 상호방위조약 제4조에 의한 시설과 구역 및 한국에서의 미국군대의 지위에 관한 협정(SOFA)
전59권. 1966.7.9 서울에서 서명 : 1967.2.9 발효(조약 232호) (V.48 의제 및 초안)   463

ARTICLE

1. The United States armed forces
and the organizations provided for in
Article ___ may employ civilian personnel
under this Agreement. Such civilian
personnel shall be nationals of the
Republic of Korea.

2. Local labour requirements of the
United States armed forces and of the
said organizations shall be satisfied with
the assistance of the Korean authorities.
The obligations for the withholding and
payment of income tax and social security
contributions, and, unless otherwise agreed
upon in this article, the conditions of
employment and work, such as those relating
to wages and supplementary payments, the
conditions for the protection of workers,
and the rights of workers concerning
labour relations shall be those laid down
by the legislation of the Republic of Korea.

ARTICLE

1. In this Article the expression

   (a) "employer" refers to the
United States armed forces (including
non-appropriated fund activities) and
the persons referred to in the first
paragraph of Article ____ .

   (b) "employee" refers to any
civilian (other than a member of the
civilian component) employed by an
employer, except (1) a member of the
Korean Service Corps, who is an employe
of the Government of Korea, and (2) a
domestic employed by an individual memb
of the United States armed forces,
civilian component or dependent thereof.

2. Employers may accomplish the
recruitment, employment and management
of employees directly.

3. The condition of employment,
the compensation, and the labor-
management practices shall be established by the United States armed forces
for their employees in general conformi
with the labor laws, customs and
practices of the Republic of Korea;
provided however, that an employer may
terminate employment whenever the
continuation of such employment would
materially impair the accomplishment of

- 73 -

0176

the mission of the United States armed forces.

4.  (a) An employee shall have the same right to strike as an employee in a comparable position in the employment of the armed forces of the Republic of Korea.  Such an employee may voluntarily organize and join a union or other employ group whose objectives are not inimical to the interests of the United States. Membership or nonmembership in such groups shall not be a cause for discharg or non-employment.

(b) Employers will maintain procedures designed to assure the just and timely resolution of employee grievances.

3.  Should the United States armed forces dismiss a worker and a decision of a court or a Labour Commission of the Republic of Korea to the effect that the contract of employment has not terminated become final, the following procedures shall apply:

(a) The United States armed forces shall be informed by the Government of the Republic of Korea of the decision of the court or Commission;

(b) Should the United States armed forces not desire to return the

- 74 -

worker to duty, they shall so notify the
Government of the Republic of Korea
within ten days after being informed by the
latter of the decision of the court or
Commission, and may temporarily withhold
the worker from duty;

      (c) Upon such notification, the
Government of the Republic of Korea and
the United States armed forces shall
consult together without delay with a
view to finding a practical solution of
the case;

      (d) Should such a solution not
be reached within a period of thirty days
from the date of commencement of the
consultations under (c) above, the worker
will not be entitled to return to duty.
In such case, the Government of the United
States shall pay to the Government of the
Republic of Korea an amount equal to the
cost of employment of the worker for a
period of time to be agreed between the
two Governments through the Joint Committee.

    5.  (a) Should the Republic of
Korea adopt measures allocating labor,
the United States armed forces shall be
accorded employment privileges no less
favorable than those enjoyed by the
armed forces of the Republic of Korea.

- 75 -

0178

(b) In the event of a national emergency, employees who have acquired skills essential to the mission of the United States armed forces shall be exempt from Republic of Korea military service or other compulsory service. The United States armed forces shall furnish to the Republic of Korea lists of those employees deemed essential.

4. The United States Government shall ensure that the contractors referred to in Article ____ employ the Korean personnel to the maximum extent practicable in connection with their activities under this Agreement. The provisions of paragraph 2 of this Article shall be applied to the employment by the contractors of the said Korean personnel.

6. Members of the civilian component shall not be subject to Korean laws or regulations with respect to their terms and conditions of employment.

Agreed Minutes

1. It is understood that the Government of the Republic of Korea shall be reimbursed for costs incurred under relevant contracts between appropriate authorities of the Korean Government and the United States armed forces or the

Agreed Minutes

1. The Republic of Korea will make available, at designated induction points qualified personnel for Korean Service Corps units in numbers sufficient to meet the requirements of United States armed forces. The employment of a

- 76 -

organizations provided for in Article ___ in connection with the employment of workers to be provided for the United States armed forces or such organizations.

2. It is understood that the term "the legislation of the Republic of Korea" mentioned in Paragraph 2, Article ___ includes decisions of the courts and the Labor Commissions of the Republic of Korea, subject to the provisions of Paragraph 3, Article ___.

3. It is understood that the provisions of Article ___, paragraph 3 shall only apply to discharges for security reasons including disturbing the maintenance of military discipline within the facilities and areas used by the United States armed forces.

domestic by an individual member of the United States armed forces, civilian component or dependent thereof shall be governed by applicable Korean law and in addition by wage scales and control measures promulgated by the United States armed forces.

2. The undertaking of the United States Government to conform to Korean labor laws, customs, and practices, does not imply any waiver by the United States Government of its immunities under international law.

- 77 -

韓고(안) 美(안)

ARTICLE

ARTICLE

1. Subject to the provisions of this Article:

    (a) the military authorities of the United States shall have the right to exercise within the Republic of Korea criminal and disciplinary jurisdiction conferred on them by the law of the United States over the members of the United States armed forces and the civilian components.

    (b) the authorities of the Republic of Korea shall have jurisdiction over the members of the United States armed forces, the civilian component, and their dependents with respect to offenses committed within the territory of the Republic of Korea and punishable by the law of the Republic of Korea.

2. (a) The military authorities of the United States shall have the right to exercise exclusive jurisdiction over members of the United States armed forces and the civilian components with respect to offenses, including offenses relating to its security, punishable by the law of the United States, but not by the law of the Republic of Korea.

1. Subject to the provisions of this Article,

    (a) the authorities of the United States shall have the right to exercise within the Republic of Korea all criminal and disciplinary jurisdiction conferred on them by the law of the United States over members of the United States armed forces or civilian component, and their dependents.

    (b) the civil authorities of the Republic of Korea shall have the right to exercise jurisdiction over the members of the United States armed forces or civilian component, and their dependents, with respect to offenses committed within the territory of the Republic of Korea and punishable by the law of the Republic of Korea.

2. (a) The authorities of the United States shall have the right to exercise exclusive jurisdiction over members of the United States armed forces or civilian component, and their dependents, with respect to offenses, including offenses relating to its security, punishable by the law of the United States, but not by the law of the Republic of Korea.

한·미국 간의 상호방위조약 제4조에 의한 시설과 구역 및 한국에서의 미국군대의 지위에 관한 협정(SOFA)
전59권. 1966.7.9 서울에서 서명 : 1967.2.9 발효(조약 232호) (V.48 의제 및 초안) 469

(b) The authorities of the Republic of Korea have the right to exercise exclusive jurisdiction over members of the United States armed forces, the civilian component, and their dependents with respect to offenses, including offenses relating to the security of the Republic of Korea, punishable by its law but not by the law of the United States.

(c) For the purpose of this paragraph and of paragraph 3 of this Article a security offense against a State shall include:

(i) treason against the State;

(ii) sabotage, espionage or violation of any law relating to official secrets of that State, or secrets relating to the national defense of that State.

3. In cases where the right to exercise jurisdiction is concurrent the following rules shall apply:

(a) The <u>military</u> authorities of the United States shall have the primary right to exercise jurisdiction over members of the United States armed forces or the civilian component in relation to:

(b) The authorities of the Republic of Korea shall have the right to exercise exclusive jurisdiction over members of the United States armed forces or civilian component, and their dependents, with respect to offenses, including offenses relating to the security of the Republic of Korea, punishable by its law but not by the law of the United States.

(c) For the purpose of this paragraph and of paragraph 3 of this Article, a security offense against a State shall include:

(i) treason against the State;

(ii) sabotage, espionage or violation of any law relating to official secrets of that State, or secrets relating to the national defense of that State.

3. In case where the right to exercise jurisdiction is concurrent the following rules shall apply:

(a) The authorities of the United States shall have the primary right to exercise jurisdiction over members of the United States armed for or civilian component, and <u>their depen-dents,</u> in relating to:

- 79 -

0182

(i) offenses solely against
the property or security of the United
States, or offenses solely against the
person or property of another member of
the United States armed forces or the
civilian component or of a dependent;

(ii) offenses arising out
of any act or omission done in the performance of official duty provided that
such act or omission is directly related
to the duty. The question as to whether
offenses were committed in the performance
of official duty shall be decided by a
competent district public prosecutor
of the Republic of Korea.
In case the offender's commanding officer
finds otherwise, he may appeal from the
prosecutor's decision to the Minister
of Justice within ten days from the
receipt of the decision of the prosecutor,
and the decision of the Minister of
Justice shall be final.

(b) In the case of any other
offenses the authorities of the Republic
of Korea shall have the primary right to
exercise jurisdiction.

(c) If the State having the
primary right decides not to exercise
jurisdiction, it shall notify the
authorities of the other State as soon

'(i) offenses solely again
the property or security of the United
States, or offenses solely against the
person or property of another member of
the United States armed forces or
civilian component or of a dependent;

(ii) offenses arising out
of any act of omission done in the
performance of official duty;

(b) In the case of any other
offense, the authorities of the Republic
of Korea shall have the primary right
to exercise jurisdiction.

(c) If the State having the
primary right decides not to exercise
jurisdiction, it shall notify the
authorities of the other State as soon

- 80 -

as practicable. The authorities of the State having the primary right shall give sympathetic consideration to a request from the authorities of the other State for a waiver of its right in cases where that other State considers such waiver to be of particular importance.

4. The foregoing provisions of this Article shall not imply any right for the military authorities of the United States to exercise jurisdiction over persons who are nationals of or ordinarily resident in the Republic of Korea, unless they are members of the United States forces.

5. (a) The military authorities of the United States and the authorities of the Republic of Korea shall assist each other in the arrest of members of the United States armed forces, the civilian component, or their dependents in the territory of the Republic of Korea and in handing them over to the authorities which is to exercise jurisdiction in accordance with the above provisions.

(b) The authorities of the Republic of Korea shall notify the military authorities of the United States of the arrest of any member of the United States armed forces, the civilian

as practicable. The authorities of the State having the primary right shall give sympathetic consideration to a request from the authorities of the other State for a waiver of its right in cases where that other State considers such waiver to be of particular importance.

4. The foregoing provisions of this Article shall not imply any right for the authorities of the United States to exercise jurisdiction over persons who are nationals of or ordinary resident in the Republic of Korea, unless they are members of the United States armed forces.

5. (a) The authorities of the United States and the authorities of the Republic of Korea shall assist each other in the arrest of members of the United States armed forces, the civilian component, or their dependents in the territory of the Republic of Korea and in handing them over to the authority which is to have custody in accordance with the following provisions.

(b) The authorities of the Republic of Korea shall notify promptly the authorities of the United States of the arrest of any member of the United States armed forces, or civilian component, or their dependents.

(c) The military authority of the United States shall immediately notify the authority of the Republic of Korea of the arrest of a member of the United States armed forces, the civilian component, or a dependent, unless the United States authority has the right to exercise exclusive jurisdiction over such a person.

(d) An accused member of the United States armed for the civilian component or a dependent over whom the Republic of Korea is to exercise jurisdiction over whom the Republic of Korea is to shall, if he is in the hand of the United States, be under the custody of the United States upon presentation of a warrant issued by a judge of the Republic of Korea he shall be handed over immediately to the Korean Authorities.

component, or a dependent:

(c) The custody of an accused member of the United States armed forces or civilian component, or of a dependent, over whom the Republic of Korea is to exercise jurisdiction shall, if he is in the hands of the United States, remain with the United States pending the conclusion of all judicial proceedings and until custody is requested by the authorities of the Republic of Korea. If he is in the hands of the Republic of Korea, he shall be promptly handed over to the authorities of the United States and remain in their custody pending completion of all judicial proceedings and until custody is requested by the authorities of the Republic of Korea. The United States authorities will make any such accused available to the authorities of the Republic of Korea

- 82 -

6. (a) The authorities of the
Republic of Korea and the military
authorities of the United States shall
assist each other in the carrying out
of all necessary investigations into
offenses, and in the collection and
production of evidence including the
seizure and, in proper case, the handing
over of objects connected with an
offense. The handing over of such
objects may, however, be made subject
to their return within the time specified
by the authority delivering them.

(b) The authorities of the
Republic of Korea and the military
authorities of the United States shall
notify each other of the disposition
of all cases in which there are concurrent
rights to exercise jurisdiction.

7. (a) A death sentence shall not
be carried out in the Republic of Korea

upon their request for purposes of investigation and trial. The authorities
of the Republic of Korea shall give
sympathetic consideration to a request
from the authorities of the United
States for assistance in maintaining
custody of an accused member of the
United States armed forces, the civilian
component, or a dependent.

6. (a) The authorities of the
United States and the authorities of the
Republic of Korea shall assist each other
in the carrying out of all necessary
investigations into offenses, and in
the collection and production of evidence
including the seizure and, in proper
cases, the handing over of objects
connected with an offense. The handing
over of such objects may, however, be
made subject to their return within
the time specified by the authority
delivering them.

(b) The authorities of the
United States and the authorities of
the Republic of Korea shall notify each
other of the disposition of all cases
in which there are concurrent rights
to exercise jurisdiction.

7. (a) A death sentence shall not
be carried out in the Republic of Korea

- 83 -

by the military authorities of the United
States if the legislation of the Republic
of Korea does not provide for such
punishment in a similar case.

(b) The authorities of the
Republic of Korea shall give sympathetic
consideration to a request from the
military authorities of the United States
for assistance in carrying out a sentence
of imprisonment pronounced by the military
authorities of the United States under
the provisions of this Article within
the territory of the Republic of Korea.

by the authorities of the United States
if the legislation of the Republic of
Korea does not provide for such punishment in a similar case.

(b) The authorities of the
Republic of Korea shall give sympathetic
consideration to a request from the
authorities of the United States for
assistance in carrying out a sentence
of imprisonment pronounced by the
authorities of the United States under
the provisions of this Article within
the territory of the Republic of Korea.
The authorities of the Republic of Korea
shall also give sympathetic consideration
to a request from the authorities of the
United States for the custody of any
member of the United States armed forces
or civilian component or a dependent,
who is serving a sentence of confinement
imposed by a court of the Republic of
Korea. If such custody is released to
the authorities of the United States,
the United States shall be obligated to
continue the confinement of the individua
in an appropriate confinement facility
of the United States until the sentence
to confinement shall have been served
in full or until release from such

8. Where an accused has been tried in accordance with the provisions of this Article either by the authorities of the Republic of Korea or the military authorities of the United States and has been acquitted, or has been convicted and is serving, or has served, his sentence or has been pardoned, he may not be tried again for the same offense within the territory of the Republic of Korea by the authorities of the other State. However, nothing in this paragraph shall prevent the military authorities of the United States from trying a member of its forces for any violation of rules of discipline arising from an act or omission which constituted an offense for which he was tried by the authorities of the Republic of Korea.

9. Whenever a member of the United States armed forces, the civilian component or a dependent is prosecuted under the jurisdiction of the Republic of Korea he shall be entitled:

(a) to a prompt and speedy trial;

8. Where an accused has been tried in accordance with the provisions of this Article either by the authorities of the United States or the authorities of the Republic of Korea and has been acquitted, or has been convicted and is serving, or has served, his sentence, or his sentence has been remitted or suspended or he has been pardoned, he may not be tried again for the same offense within the territory of the Republic of Korea by the authorities of the other State. However, nothing in this paragraph shall prevent the authorities of the United States from trying a member of its armed forces for any violation of rules of discipline arising from an act or omission which constituted an offense for which he was tried by the authorities of the Republic of Korea.

9. Whenever a member of the United States armed forces or civilian component or a dependent is prosecuted under the jurisdiction of the Republic of Korea he shall be entitled:

(a) to a prompt and speedy trial

0188

(b) to be informed, in advance of trial, of the specific charge or charges made against him;

(c) to be confronted with the witnesses against him;

(d) to have compulsory process for obtaining witnesses in his favor, if they are within the jurisdiction of the Republic of Korea;

(e) to have legal representation of his own choice for his defense or to have free or assisted legal representation under the conditions prevailing in the Republic of Korea;

(f) If he considers it necessary, to be provided with the services of a competent interpreter; and

(g) to communicate with a representative of the Government of the United States and to have such a representative present at his trial.

10. (a) Regularly constituted military units or formation of the United States armed forces shall have the right to police any facilities or areas which they use under Article I7 of this Agreement. The military police of such forces may take all appropriate measures to ensure the maintenance of order and security within such facilities and areas.

(b) to be informed, in advance of trial, of the specific charge or charges made against him;

(c) to be confronted with the witnesses against him;

(d) to have compulsory process for obtaining witnesses in his favor, if they are within the jurisdiction of the Republic of Korea;

(e) to have legal representation of his own choice for his defense or to have free or assisted legal representation under the conditions prevailing for the time being in the Republic of Korea;

(f) if he considers it necessary, to have the services of a competent interpreter; and

(g) to communicate with a representative of the Government of the United States and to have such a representative present at his trial.

10. (a) Regularly constituted military units or formations of the United States armed forces shall have the right to police any facilities or areas which they use under Article ____ of this Agreement. The military police of such forces may take all appropriate measures to ensure the maintenance of order and security within such facilities and areas.

0189

한·미국 간의 상호방위조약 제4조에 의한 시설과 구역 및 한국에서의 미국군대의 지위에 관한 협정(SOFA)
전59권. 1966.7.9 서울에서 서명 : 1967.2.9 발효(조약 232호) (V.48 의제 및 초안)    477

(b) Outside these facilities and areas such military police shall be employed only subject to arrangements with the authorities of the Republic of Korea and in liaison with those authorities and in so far as such employment is necessary to maintain discipline and order among the members of the United States armed forces.

(b) Outside these facilities and areas, such military police shall be employed only subject to arrangements with the authorities of the Republic of Korea and in liaison with those authorities and in so far as such employment is necessary to maintain discipline and order among the members of the United States armed forces, or ensure their security.

11. In the event of hostilities to which the provisions of Article II of the Treaty of Mutual Defense apply, the provisions of this Agreement pertaining to criminal jurisdiction shall be immediately suspended and the authorities of the United States shall have the right to exercise exclusive jurisdiction over members of the United States armed forces, the civilian component, and their dependents.

12. The provisions of this Article shall not apply to any offenses committed before the entry into force of this Agreement. Such cases shall be governed by the provisions of the Agreement between the United States of America and the Republic of Korea effected by an exchange of notes at Taejon, Korea on July 12, 1950.

0190

The provisions of this Article shall
not affect existing agreements, arrangements, or practices, relating to the
exercise of jurisdiction over personnel
of the United Nations forces present in
Korea other than forces of the United
States.

RE Paragraph 1(b)

1. The authorities of the United
States shall have the right to exercise
exclusive jurisdiction over members of
the United States armed forces or civilian
component, and their dependents, if any,
in the combat zone. The extent of the
combat zone shall be defined by the
Joint Committee and shall include the
area from the demilitarization zone to
the rear boundaries of the United
States corps (group) and the Republic of
Korea army-size unit deployed in that
zone.

2. In the event that martial law
is declared by the Republic of Korea,
the provisions of this Article shall be
immediately suspended in the part of the
Republic of Korea under martial law,
and the authorities of the United States
shall have the right to exercise exclusive

0191

- 88 -

jurisdiction over members of the United States armed forces or civilian component and their dependents, in such part until martial law is ended.

3. The jurisdiction of the authorities of the Republic of Korea over members of the United States armed forces or civilian component, and their dependent shall not extend to any offenses committed outside the Republic of Korea.

RE Paragraph 2

The Republic of Korea, recognizing the effectiveness in appropriate cases of the administrative and disciplinary sanctions which may be imposed by the United States authorities over members of the United States armed forces or civilian component, and their dependents, will give sympathetic consideration in such cases to requests in the Joint Committee for waivers of its right to exercise jurisdiction under paragraph 2.

RE Paragraph 2(c)

Both Governments shall inform each other of the details of all the security offenses mentioned in this subparagraph and the provisions governing such offenses in the existing laws of their respective countries.

RE Paragraph 2(c)

Each Government shall inform the other of the details of all security offenses mentioned in this subparagraph, and of the provisions regarding such offenses in its legislation.

- 89 -

0192

<u>RE Paragraph 3</u>

The Republic of Korea, recognizing that it is the primary responsibility of the United States authorities to maintain good order and discipline (among the members of the United States Armed Forces and civilian component), and their dependents,) waives the right of the authorities of the Republic of Korea to exercise jurisdiction under paragraph 3. The United States authorities shall notify the competent authorities of the Republic of Korea of individual cases falling under the waiver thus provided. If, by reason of special circumstances in a specific case, the authorities of the Republic of Korea consider that it is of particular importance that jurisdiction be exercised by the Republic of Korea in that case, they shall, within 15 days of receipt of the notification envisaged above, seek agreement of the Joint Committee to recall the waiver for that particular case.

Subject to the foregoing, the waiver granted by the Republic of Korea shall be unconditional and final for all purposes and shall bar both the authorities

- 90 -

0193

한·미국 간의 상호방위조약 제4조에 의한 시설과 구역 및 한국에서의 미국군대의 지위에 관한 협정(SOFA)
전59권. 1966.7.9 서울에서 서명 : 1967.2.9 발효(조약 232호) (V.48 의제 및 초안) 481

and the nationals of the Republic of Korea from instituting criminal proceedings.

To facilitate the expeditious disposal of offenses of minor importance, arrangements may be made between United States authorities and the competent authorities of the Republic of Korea to dispense with notification.

RE Paragraph 3(a)

1. The authorities of the United States shall have the primary right to exercise jurisdiction over members of the United States armed forces in relation to offenses which, if committed by a member of the armed forces of the Republic of Korea, would be tried by court-martial rather than by a civilian court.

2. Where a member of the United States armed forces or civilian component is charged with an offense, a certificate issued by or on behalf of his commanding officer stating that the alleged offense, if committed by him, arose out of an act or omission done in the performance of official duty, shall be conclusive for the purpose of determining primary jurisdiction.

RE Paragraph 3(a)(ii)

The term "official duty" is not meant to include all acts by members of the United States armed forces or the civilian component during periods while they are on duty. Any departure from acts which are duly required to be done as a normal function of a particular duty shall be deemed as an act outside of his "official duty."

RE Paragraph 3(c)

Mutual procedures relating to waivers of the primary right to exercise jurisdiction shall be determined by the Joint Committee.

② Trials of cases in which the authorities of the Republic of Korea waived the primary right to exercise jurisdiction, and trials of cases involving offenses described in paragraph 3(a)(ii) committed against the State or nationals

- 91 -

0194

of the Republic of Korea shall be held
promptly in the Republic of Korea within
a reasonable distance from the places
where the offenses are alleged to have
taken place unless other arrangements
are mutually agreed upon. Representatives
of the authorities of the Republic of
Korea may be present at such trials.

RE Paragraph 4

Dual nationals, the Republic of
Korea and United States, who are the
members of the United States armed forces
or the civilian component and are brought
to the Republic of Korea shall not be
considered as nationals of the Republic
of Korea, but shall be considered as
United States nationals for the purposes
of this paragraph.

RE Paragraph 5(b)

In case the authorities of the
Republic of Korea have arrested an
offender who is a member of the United
States armed forces, the civilian component
or a dependent with respect to a case over
which the Republic of Korea has the
primary right to exercise jurisdiction,
the authorities of the Republic of Korea
will, unless they deem that there is adequate
cause and necessity to retain such
offender, release him to the custody of

0195

The United States military authorities
provided that he shall, on request, be made
available to the authorities of the
Republic of Korea, if such be the
condition of his release. The United
States authorities shall, on request,
transfer his custody to the authorities
of the Republic of Korea at the time he
is indicted by the latter.

RE Paragraph 6

1. A member of the United States
armed forces or the civilian component
shall, if summoned by the authorities of
the Republic of Korea as a witness in the
course of investigations and trials, make
himself available to the authorities of
the Republic of Korea.

2. If any person summoned as witness
did not make himself available to the
authorities of the Republic of Korea,
they may take necessary measures in
accordance with the provisions of the
law of the Republic of Korea. Subject
to the foregoing, the military authorities
of the United States shall, upon presentation of a warrant issued by a judge
of the Republic of Korea, immediately
take all appropriate measures to ensure
the execution of the warrant by the
authorities of the Republic of Korea.

RE Paragraph 6

1. The authorities of the United
States and the authorities of the Republic
of Korea shall assist each other in
obtaining the appearance of witnesses
necessary for the proceedings conducted
by such authorities within the Republic
of Korea.

When a member of the United States
armed forces in Korea is summoned to appear
before a Korean court, as a witness or as
a defendant, United States authorities
shall unless military exigency requires
otherwise, secure his attendance provides
such attendance is compulsory under
Korean law. If military exigency
prevents such attendance, the authorities
on the United States shall furnish a
certificate stating the estimated
duration of such disability.

Service of process upon a member
of the United States armed forces or
civilian component, or a dependent
required as a witness or a defendant must

0196

be personal service in the English language. Where the service of process is to be effected by a Korean process server upon any person who is inside a military installation or area, the authorities of the United States shall take all measures necessary to enable the Korean process server to effect such service.

In addition, the Korean authorities shall promptly give copies of all criminal writs (including warrants, summonses, indictments, and subpoenas) to an agent designated by the United States authorities to receive them in all cases of Korean criminal proceedings involving a member of the United States armed forces or civilian component, or a dependent.

When citizens or residents of the Republic of Korea are required as witnesses or experts by the authorities of the United States, the courts and authorities of the Republic of Korea shall, in accordance with Korean law, secure the attendance of such persons. In these cases the authorities of the United States shall act through the Attorney General of the Republic of Korea, or such other agency as is designated by the authorities of the Republic of Korea.

Fees and other payments for witnesses shall be determined by the Joint Committee established under Article ____.

2. The privileges and immunities of witnesses shall be those accorded by

- 94 -

한·미국 간의 상호방위조약 제4조에 의한 시설과 구역 및 한국에서의 미국군대의 지위에 관한 협정(SOFA) 전59권. 1966.7.9 서울에서 서명 : 1967.2.9 발효(조약 232호) (V.48 의제 및 초안) 485

the law of the court, tribunal or authority before which they appear. In no event shall a witness be required to provide testimony which may tend to incriminate him.

3. If, in the course of criminal proceedings before authorities of the United States or the Republic of Korea, the disclosure of an official secret of either of these States or the disclosure of any information which may prejudice the security of either appears necessary for the just disposition of the proceedings, the authorities concerned shall seek written permission to make such disclosure from the appropriate authority of the State concerned.

RE Paragraph 9(a)

The right to a prompt and speedy trial by the courts of the Republic of Korea shall include public trial by an impartial tribunal composed exclusively of judges who have completed their probationary period. A member of the United States armed forces or civilian component, or a dependent, shall not be tried by a military tribunal of the Republic of Korea.

RE Paragraph 9(b)

A member of the United States armed forces or civilian component, or a dependent, shall not be arrested or detained by the authorities of the Republic of Korea without adequate cause, and he

- 95 -

0198

shall be entitled to an immediate hearing
at which such cause must be shown in open
court in his presence and the presence
of his counsel. His immediate release
shall be ordered if adequate cause is
not shown. Immediately upon arrest or
detention he shall be informed of the
charges against him in a language which
he understands.

He shall also be informed a reasonable
time prior to trial of the nature of the
evidence that is to be used against him.
Counsel for the accused shall, upon
request, be afforded the opportunity
before trial to examine and copy the
statements of witnesses obtained by
authorities of the Republic of Korea
which are included in the file forwarded
to the court of the Republic of Korea
scheduled to try the case.

RE Paragraph 9(c) and (d)

A member of the United States armed
forces or civilian component, or a dependent, who is prosecuted by the authorities
of the Republic of Korea shall have the
right to be present throughout the
testimony of all witnesses, for and
against him, in all judicial examinations,
pretrial hearings, the trial itself, and
subsequent proceedings, and shall be

- 96 -

permitted full opportunity to examine
the witnesses.

RE Paragraph 9(e)

The right to legal representation
shall exist from the moment of arrest
or detention and shall include the right
to have counsel present, and to consult
confidentially with such counsel, at all
preliminary investigations, examinations,
pretrial hearings, the trial itself,
and subsequent proceedings, at which the
accused is present.

RE Paragraph 9(f)

The right to have the services of a
competent interpreter shall exist from
the moment of arrest or detention.

RE Paragraph 9(g)

The right to communicate with a
representative of the Government of the
United States shall exist from the moment
of arrest or detention, and no statement
of the accused taken in the absence of
such a representative shall be admissible
as evidence in support of the guilt of
the accused. Such representative shall
be entitled to be present at all preliminary investigations, examinations,
pretrial hearings, the trial itself,
and subsequent proceedings, at which the
accused is present.

2. Nothing in the provisions of
paragraph 9(g) concerning the presence of
a representative of the United States
Government at the trial of a member of
the United States armed forces, the
civilian component or a dependent prosecuted under the jurisdiction of the
Republic of Korea, shall be so construed
as to prejudice the provisions of the
Constitution of the Republic of Korea
with respect to public trials.

- 97 -

0200

<u>RE Paragraph 9</u>

A member of the United States armed forces or civilian component, or a dependent, tried by the authorities of the Republic of Korea shall be accorded every procedural and substantive right granted by law to the citizens of the Republic of Korea. If it should appear that an accused has been, or is likely to be, denied any procedural or substantive right granted by law to the citizens of the Republic of Korea, representatives of the two Governments shall consult in the Joint Committee on the measures necessary to prevent or cure such denial of rights.

In addition to the rights enumerated in items (a) through (g) of paragraph 9 of this Article, a member of the United States armed forces or civilian component, or a dependent, who is prosecuted by the authorities of the Republic of Korea:

(a) shall be furnished a verbatim record of his trial in English;

(b) shall have the right to appeal a conviction or sentence; in addition, he shall be informed by the court at the time of conviction or sentencing of his right to appeal and of the time limit within which that right must

<u>RE Paragraph 9</u>

1. The rights enumerated in this paragraph are guaranteed to all persons on trial in the Korean courts by the provisions of the Constitution of the Republic of Korea. In addition to these rights, a member of the United States armed forces, the civilian component or a dependent who is prosecuted under the jurisdiction of the Republic of Korea shall have such other rights as are guaranteed under the Constitution and laws of the Republic of Korea to all persons on trial in the Korean courts.

- 98 -

한·미국 간의 상호방위조약 제4조에 의한 시설과 구역 및 한국에서의 미국군대의 지위에 관한 협정(SOFA) 전59권. 1966.7.9 서울에서 서명 : 1967.2.9 발효(조약 232호) (V.48 의제 및 초안) 489

be exercised;

(c) shall have credited to any sentence of confinement his period of pretrial confinement in a United States or Korean confinement facility;

(d) shall not be held guilty of a criminal offense on account of any act or omission which did not constitute a criminal offense under the law of the Republic of Korea at the time it was committed;

(e) shall not be subject to a heavier penalty than the one that was applicable at the time the alleged criminal offense was committed or was adjudged by the court of first instance as the original sentence;

(f) shall not be held guilty of an offense on the basis of rules of evidence or requirements of proof which have been altered to his prejudice since the date of the commission of the offense.

(g) shall not be compelled to testify against or otherwise incriminate himself;

(h) shall not be subject to cruel or unusual punishment;

(i) shall not be subject to prosecution or punishment by legislative or executive act;

(j) shall not be prosecuted or punished more than once for the same offense.

(k) shall not be required to stand trial if he is physically or mentally unfit to stand trial and participate in his defense;

(l) shall not be subjected to trial except under conditions consonant with the dignity of the United States armed forces, including appearing in appropriate military or civilian attire and unmanacled.

No confession, admission, or other statement, or real evidence, obtained by illegal or improper means will be considered by courts of the Republic of Korea in prosecutions under this Article.

In any case prosecuted by the authorities of the Republic of Korea under this Article no appeal will be taken by the prosecution from a judgment of not guilty or an acquittal nor will an appeal be taken by the prosecution from any judgment which the accused does not appeal, except upon grounds of errors of law.

The authorities of the United States shall have the right to inspect any

- 100 -

한·미국 간의 상호방위조약 제4조에 의한 시설과 구역 및 한국에서의 미국군대의 지위에 관한 협정(SOFA)
전59권. 1966.7.9 서울에서 서명 : 1967.2.9 발효(조약 232호) (V.48 의제 및 초안)   491

Korean confinement facility in which a member of the United States armed forces, civilian component, or dependent is confined, or in which it is proposed to confine such an individual.

In the event of hostilities, the Republic of Korea will take all possible measures to safeguard members of the United States armed forces, members of the civilian component, and their dependents who are confined in Korean confinement facilities, whether awaiting trial or serving a sentence imposed by the courts of the Republic of Korea. The Republic of Korea shall give sympathetic consideration to request for release of these persons to the custody of responsible United States authorities. Necessary implementing provisions shall be agreed upon between the two governments through the Joint Committee.

Facilities utilized for the execution of a sentence to death or a period of confinement, imprisonment, or penal servitude, or for the detention of members of the United States armed forces or civilian component or dependents, will meet minimum standards as agreed by the Joint Committee. The United States authorities shall have the right upon request to have access at any time to members of the United States armed forces, the civilian component, or their dependents who are confined or detained by authorities of the Republic of Korea. During the visit of these persons at Korean confinement facilities, United States authorities shall be authorized to provide supplementary care and provisions for such persons, such as clothing, food, bedding, and medical and dental treatment.

## RE Paragraph 10(a) and 10(b)

1. The United States military authorities will normally make arrests of the members of the United States armed forces and the civilian component within facilities and areas in use by and guarded under the authority of the United States armed forces. The authorities of the Republic of Korea may arrest all persons who are subject to the jurisdiction of the Republic of Korea within facilities and areas in cases where the authorities of the United States armed forces have given consent, or in cases of pursuit of a flagrant offender who has committed a serious crime.

## RE Paragraph 10(a) and 10(b)

The United States authorities will normally make all arrests within facilities and areas in use by the United States armed forces. The Korean authorities will normally not exercise the right of search, seizure, or inspection with respect to any person or property within facilities and areas in use by the authorities of the United States or with respect to property of the United States wherever situated, except in cases where the competent authorities of the United States consent to such search, seizure, or inspection by the Korean authorities of such persons or property.

한·미국 간의 상호방위조약 제4조에 의한 시설과 구역 및 한국에서의 미국군대의 지위에 관한 협정(SOFA)
전59권. 1966.7.9 서울에서 서명 : 1967.2.9 발효(조약 232호) (V.48 의제 및 초안)    493

Where persons whose arrest is desired by the authorities of the Republic of Korea and who are not subject to the jurisdiction of the United States armed forces are within facilities and areas in use by the United States armed forces, the United States military authorities shall, upon request, promptly arrest such persons. All persons arrested by the United States military authorities, who are not subject to the jurisdiction of the United States armed forces, shall immediately be turned over to the authorities of the Republic of Korea.

2. The authorities of the Republic of Korea will normally not exercise the right of seizure, search, or inspection with respect to any person or property within facilities and areas in use by and guarded under the authorities of the United States armed forces or with respect to property of the United States armed forces wherever situated except in cases where the authorities of the United States armed forces consent to such seizure, search, or inspection by the authorities of the Republic of Korea of such persons or property.

Where search, seizure, or inspection with respect to persons or property within facilities and areas in use by the United States or with respect to property of the United States in Korea is desired by the Korean authorities, the United States authorities will undertake, upon request, to make such search, seizure, or inspection. In the event of a judgment concerning such property, except property owned or utilized by the United States Government or its instrumentalities, the United States will in accordance with its laws turn over such property to the Korean authorities for disposition in accordance with the judgment.

The United States authorities may arrest or detain in the vicinity of a facility or area any person in the commission or attempted commission of an offense against the security of that facility or area. Any such person who is not a member of the United States armed forces or civilian component or a dependent shall immediately be turned over to the Korean authorities.

Where seizure, search, or inspection
with respect to persons or property within
facilities and areas in use by the United
States armed forces or with respect to
property of the United States armed forces
in the Republic of Korea is desired by
the authorities of the Republic of Korea,
the United States military authorities
shall, upon request, make such seizure,
search, or inspection.   In the event of
a judgement concerning such property,
except property owned or utilized by the
United States Government or its instrumentalities, the United States shall
turn over such property to the authorities
of the Republic of Korea for disposition
in accordance with the judgement.

   The United States military authorities
under due process of law, arrest within
the vicinity of a facility or area
any person in the commission of an offense
against the security of that facility or
area.   Any such person not subject to the
jurisdiction of the United States armed
forces shall immediately be turned over
to the authorities of the Republic of Korea.

104

0207

한미 양측 SOFA 초안

1965. 11. 30.

0208

ARTICLES IN US-ROK STATUS OF FORCES AGREEMENT

(Article numbers are tentatively assigned for
mutual convenience and are subject to change)

0209

Whereas the United States of America has disposed its
armed forces in and about the territory of the Republic of Korea
pursuant to the resolutions of the United Nations Security Council
of June 25, 1950, June 27, 1950, and July 7, 1950, and pursuant to
Article IV of the Mutual Defense Treaty between the United States
of America and the Republic of Korea signed on October 1, 1953;

Therefore, the United States of America and the Republic
of Korea, in order to strengthen the close bonds of mutual interest
between their two countries, have entered into this Agreement
regarding facilities and areas and the status of United States
armed forces in the Republic of Korea in terms as set forth below:

0210

# ARTICLE I

## Definitions

In this Agreement the expression—

(a)  "members of the United States armed forces"
means the personnel on active duty belonging to the land,
sea, or air armed services of the United States of America
when in the territory of the Republic of Korea except for
personnel of the United States armed forces attached to
the United States Embassy and personnel for whom status
has been provided in the Mutual Defense Assistance Agreement
*Military advisory Group*
of January 26, 1950, as amended;

(b)  "civilian component" means the civilian
persons of United States nationality who are in the employ
of, serving with, or accompanying the United States armed
forces in the Republic of Korea, but excludes persons who
are ordinarily resident in the Republic of Korea or who
are mentioned in paragraph 1 of Article XV.  For the purposes of the Agreement only, dual nationals, i.e., persons
*nationality of United States and of the Republic of Korea*
having both United States and Korean nationality, who are
brought into the Republic of Korea by the United States
shall be considered United States nationals.

(c)  "dependents" means

    (i)  Spouse and children under 21;

    (ii) Parents, children over 21, or other
        relatives dependent for over half their
        support upon a member of the United States
        armed forces or civilian component.

0211

<u>Agreed Minute</u>

   With regard to Subparagraph (b), it is recognized
that persons possessing certain skills, not available
from <u>United States or Korean sources</u>, who are nationals
of third states, may be brought into Korea by the United
States armed forces solely for employment by the United
States armed forces.  Such persons, and third state
nationals who are employed by, serving with, or accompanying the United States armed forces in Korea when this
agreement becomes effective, shall be considered as members
of the civilian component.

'0212

## ARTICLE II

### FACILITIES AND AREAS - GRANT OF AND RETURN

1. (a) The United States is granted, under Article IV of the Mutual Defense Treaty, the use of facilities and areas in the Republic of Korea. Agreements as to specific facilities and areas shall be concluded by the two Governments through the Joint Committee provided for in Article XXVIII of this Agreement. "Facilities and Areas" include existing furnishings, equipment, and fixtures, wherever located, used in the operation of such facilities and areas.

(b) The facilities and areas of which the United States armed forces have the use at the effective date of this Agreement together with those facilities and areas which the United States armed forces have returned to the Republic of Korea with the reserved right of re-entry, when these facilities and areas have been re-entered by the United States armed forces, shall be considered as the facilities and areas agreed upon between the two Governments in accordance with sub-paragraph (a) above. Records of facilities and areas of which the United States armed forces have the use or the right of re-entry shall be maintained through the Joint Committee after this Agreement comes into force.

2. At the request of either Government, the Governments of the United States and the Republic of Korea shall review such agreements and may agree that such facilities and areas or portions thereof shall be returned to the Republic of Korea or that additional facilities and areas may be provided.

0213

3. The facilities and areas used by the United States shall be returned to the Republic of Korea under such conditions as may be agreed through the Joint Committee whenever they are no longer needed for the purposes of this Agreement and the United States agrees to keep the needs for facilities and areas under continual observation with a view toward such return.

4. (a) When facilities and areas are temporarily not being used and the Government of the Republic of Korea is so advised, the Government of the Republic of Korea may make, or permit Korean nationals to make, interim use of such facilities and areas provided that it is agreed between the two Governments through the Joint Committee that such use would not be harmful to the purposes for which the facilities and areas are normally used by the United States armed forces.

(b) With respect to facilities and areas which are to be used by the United States armed forces for limited periods of time, the Joint Committee shall specify in the agreements covering such facilities and areas the extent to which the provisions of this Agreement shall not apply.

0214

# ARTICLE III

## FACILITIES AND AREAS - SECURITY MEASURES

1. Within the facilities and areas, the United States may take all the measures necessary for their establishment, operation, safeguarding and control. In order to provide access for the United States armed forces to the facilities and areas for their support, safeguarding, and control, the Government of the Republic of Korea shall, at the request of the United States armed forces and upon consultation between the two Governments through the Joint Committee, take necessary measures, within the scope of applicable laws and regulations, with respect to land, territorial waters and airspace adjacent to, or in the vicinities of the facilities and areas. The United States may also take necessary measures for such purposes upon consultation between the two Governments through the Joint Committee.

2. (a) The United States agrees not to take the measures referred to in paragraph 1 in such a manner as to interfere unnecessarily with navigation, aviation, communication, or land travel, to, or from, or within the territories of the Republic of Korea.

(b) All questions relating to telecommunications including radio frequencies for electromagnetic radiating devices, or like matters, shall continue to be resolved expeditiously in the utmost spirit of coordination and cooperation by arrangement between the designated communications authorities of the two Governments.

(c) The Government of the Republic of Korea shall, within the scope of applicable laws, regulations and agreements, take all

0215

reasonable measures to avoid or eliminate interference with electromagnetic radiation sensitive devices, telecommunications devices, or
other apparatus required by the United States armed forces.

3. Operations in the facilities and areas in use by ~~the Govern-~~
~~ment of the United States~~ shall be carried on with due regard to the
public safety. ( *by U.S. armed forces* )

<u>AGREED MINUTE</u>

It is agreed that in the event of an emergency, the United
States armed forces shall be authorized to take such measures in
the vicinity of the areas and facilities as may be necessary to
provide for their safeguarding and control.

0216

## ARTICLE IV

## FACILITIES AND AREAS - RETURN OF FACILITIES

1. The United States is not obliged, when it returns facilities and areas to the Republic of Korea on the expiration of this Agreement or at an earlier date, to restore the facilities and areas to the condition in which they were at the time they became available to the United States armed forces, or to compensate the Republic of Korea in lieu of such restoration.

2. The Government of the Republic of Korea is not obliged to make any compensation to the Government of the United States for any improvements made in facilities and areas or for the buildings and structures left thereon on the expiration of this Agreement or the earlier return of the facilities and areas.

3. The foregoing provisions shall not apply to any construction which the Government of the United States may undertake under special arrangements with the Government of the Republic of Korea.

## AGREED MINUTE

removable
1. All/~~xxxxxx~~ facilities erected or constructed by or on behalf of the United States at its expense and all equipment, material and supplies brought into or procured in the Republic of Korea by or on behalf of the United States in connection with the construction, development, operation, maintenance, safeguarding and control of the facilities and areas will remain the property of the United States Government and may be removed from the Republic of Korea.

0217

    removable
2.  All/xxxxxxx facilities, equipment and material or portions thereof provided by the Republic of Korea under this Agreement and located within the areas and facilities referred to in this Article shall be returned to the Republic of Korea whenever they are no longer needed for the purpose of this Agreement.

0218

## ARTICLE V

### FACILITIES AND AREAS - COST AND MAINTENANCE

1. It is agreed that the United States will bear for the duration of the Agreement *(this)* without cost to the Republic of Korea all expenditures incident to the maintenance of the United States armed forces in the Republic of Korea, except those to be borne by the Republic of Korea as provided in paragraph 2.

2. It is agreed that the Republic of Korea will furnish for the duration of this Agreement without cost to the United States and make compensation where appropriate to the owners and suppliers thereof all facilities and areas and rights of way, including facilities and areas jointly used such as those at airfields and ports as provided in Articles II and III. The Government of the Republic of Korea assures the use of such facilities and areas to the United States Government and will hold the United States Government as well as its agencies and employees harmless from any third party claims which may be advanced in connection with such use.

0219

# ARTICLE VI

## Utilities and Services

1. The United States armed forces shall have the use of all utilities and services which are owned, controlled or regulated by the Government of the Republic of Korea or local administrative subdivisions thereof. The term "utilities and services" shall include, but not be limited to, transportation and communications facilities and systems, electricity, gas, water, steam, heat, light, power, and sewage disposal. The use of utilities and services/~~xxx~~ as provided herein shall not prejudice the right of the United States to operate military transportation, communication, power and such other utilities and services deemed necessary for the operations of the United States armed forces. This right shall not be exercised in a manner inconsistent with the operation by the Government of the Republic of Korea of its utilities and services.

2. The use of such utilities and services by the United States shall be in accordance with priorities, conditions, and rates or tariffs no less favorable than those accorded any other user.

## Agreed Minutes

1. It is understood that any changes determined by the authorities of the Republic of Korea in priorities, conditions,

and rates or tariffs, applicable to the United States armed forces shall be the subject of consultation in the Joint Committee prior to their effective date.

2.  This Article will not be construed as in any way abrogating the Utilities and Claims Settlement Agreement of December 18, 1958, which continues in full force and effect unless otherwise agreed by the two governments.

3.  In an emergency the Republic of Korea agrees to take appropriate measures to assure provision of utilities and services necessary to meet the needs of the United States armed forces.

# ARTICLE VII

## Respect for Local Law

It is the duty of members of the United States armed forces, the civilian component, the persons who are present in the Republic of Korea pursuant to Article XV, and their dependents, to respect the law of/Korea and to abstain from any activity inconsistent with the spirit of this Agreement, and, in particular, from any political activity in Korea.

the Republic of

0222

## ARTICLE VIII

### Entry and Exit

1. The United States may bring into the Republic of Korea persons who are members of the United States armed forces, the civilian component, and their dependents, subject to the provisions of this Article. The Government of the Republic of Korea will be notified at regular intervals, in accordance with procedures to be agreed between the two Governments, of numbers and categories of persons entering and departing.

2. Members of the United States armed forces shall be exempt from (Korean) passport and visa laws and regulations. *of the Republic of Korea,* Members of the United States armed forces, the civilian component, and their dependents shall be exempt from (Korean) laws and regulations *of the Republic of Korea,* on the registration and control of aliens, but shall not be considered as acquiring any right to permanent residence or domicile in the territory of the Republic of Korea.

3. Upon entry into or departure from the Republic of Korea members of the United States armed forces shall be in possession of the following documents:

    (a) personal identity card showing name, date of birth, rank and service number, service, and photograph; and

    (b) individual or collective travel order certifying to the status of the individual or group as a member or members of the United States armed forces and to the travel ordered.

0223

For purposes of their identification while in the Republic of Korea, members of the United States armed forces shall be in possession of the foregoing personal identity card which must be presented on request to the appropriate [Korean] authorities.

4.   Members of the civilian component, their dependents, and the dependents of members of the United States armed forces shall be in possession of appropriate documentation issued by the United States authorities so that their status may be verified by [Korean] authorities upon their entry into or departure from the Republic of Korea, or while in the Republic of Korea.

5.   If the status of any person brought into the Republic of Korea under paragraph 1 of this Article is altered so that he would no longer be entitled to such admission, the authorities of the United States shall notify the authorities of the Republic of Korea and shall, if such person be required by the authorities of the Republic of Korea to leave the Republic of Korea, assure that transportation from the Republic of Korea will be provided within a reasonable time at no cost to the Government of the Republic of Korea.

6.   If the Government of the Republic of Korea has requested the removal from its territory of a member of the United States armed forces or civilian component or has made an expulsion order against an ex-member of the United States armed forces or the

0224

civilian component or against a dependent of a member or an ex-member, the authorities of the United States shall be responsible for receiving the person concerned into its own territory or otherwise disposing of him outside the Republic of Korea. This paragraph shall apply only to persons who are not nationals of the Republic of Korea and have entered the Republic of Korea as members of the United States armed forces or civilian component or for the purpose of becoming such members, and to the dependents of such persons.

<u>Agreed Minutes</u>

1. With regard to paragraph 3(a), United States armed forces law enforcement personnel (such as Military Police, Shore Patrol, Air Police, Criminal Investigation Division, and Counterintelligence Corps), who engage in military police activities in the Republic of Korea, will carry a bilingual identity card containing the bearer's name, position, and the fact that he is a member of a law enforcement agency. This card will be shown upon request to persons concerned when the bearer is in the performance of duty.

2. The United States armed forces will furnish, upon request, to the authorities of the Republic of Korea the form of the identification cards of the members of the United States armed forces, the civilian component, and their dependents and descriptions of the various uniforms of the United States armed forces in the Republic of Korea.

0225

3.    The final sentence of ~~Paragraph 3~~ ~~of this Article~~ means that members of
the United States armed forces will display their identity cards
upon request but will not be required to surrender them to the authorities of the Republic of Korea.

4.    Following a change of status pursuant to Paragraph 5,
the responsibilities of the United States authorities under Paragraph 6 shall arise only if the expulsion order is issued within
a reasonable time after the notice under Paragraph 5 has been
communicated to the authorities of the Republic of Korea.

## ARTICLE IX

### Customs and Duties

1.  Save as provided in this Agreement, members of the
United States armed forces, the civilian component, and their
dependents shall be subject to the laws and regulations
administered by the customs authorities of the Republic of
Korea.

2.  All materials, supplies and equipment imported by
the United States armed forces (including their authorized
procurement agencies and their non-appropriated fund organizations
provided for in Article XIII), for the official use of the United
States armed forces or for the use of the members of the United
States armed forces, the civilian component, and their dependents,
and materials, supplies and equipment which are to be used
exclusively by the United States armed forces or are ultimately
to be incorporated into articles or facilities used by such
forces, shall be permitted entry into the Republic of Korea;
such entry shall be free from customs duties and other such
charges. Appropriate certification shall be made that such
materials, supplies and equipment are being imported by the
United States armed forces (including their authorized procurement
agencies and their non-appropriated fund organizations provided
for in Article XIII), or, in the case of materials, supplies

0227

and equipment to be used exclusively by the United States
armed forces or ultimately to be incorporated into articles or
facilities used by such forces, that delivery thereof is to be
taken by the United States armed forces for the purposes specified
above. The exemptions provided in this paragraph shall extend
to materials, supplies and equipment imported by the United
States armed forces for the use of other armed forces in the Republic of Korea
under the Unified Command which receive logistical support
from the United States armed forces.

3. Property consigned to and for the personal use of members
of the United States armed forces, the civilian component, and
their dependents, shall be subject to customs duties and other
such charges, except that no duties or charges shall be paid
with respect to:

(a) furniture, household goods, and personal effects
for their private use imported by the members of the United
States armed forces or the civilian component when they first
arrive to serve in the Republic of Korea or by their
dependents when they first arrive for reunion with the members
of such forces or the civilian component;

(b) vehicles and parts imported by the members of the
United States armed forces or the civilian component for the
private use of themselves or their dependents;

0228

(c) reasonable quantities of personal effects and household goods of a type which would ordinarily be purchased in the United States for the private use of the members of the United States armed forces, the civilian component, and their dependents, which are mailed into the Republic of Korea through United States military post offices.

4. The exemptions granted in paragraphs 2 and 3 shall apply only to cases of importation of goods and shall not be interpreted as refunding customs duties and domestic excises collected by the customs authorities at the time of entry in cases of purchase of goods on which such duties and excises have already been collected.

5. Customs examination shall not be made in the following cases:

(a) members of the United States armed forces under orders, other than leave orders, entering or leaving the Republic of Korea;

(b) official documents under official seal and First Class letter mail in the United States military postal channels under official postal seal;

(c) military cargo consigned to the United States armed forces.

0229

6.    Except as such disposal may be authorized by the /
United States and authorities of the Republic of Korea in
accordance with mutually agreed conditions, goods imported into
the Republic of Korea free of duty shall not be disposed of in
the Republic of Korea to persons not entitled to import such
goods free of duty.

7.    Goods imported into the Republic of Korea free from
customs duties and other such charges pursuant to paragraphs 2
and 3, may be re-exported free from customs duties and other
such charges.

8.    The United States armed forces, in cooperation with the
authorities of the Republic of Korea, shall take such steps as
are necessary to prevent abuse of privileges granted to the
United States armed forces, members of such forces, the civilian
component, and their dependents in accordance with this Article.

9.    (a)  In order to prevent offenses against laws and
regulations administered by the customs authorities of the
Government of the Republic of Korea, the authorities of the
Republic of Korea and the United States armed forces shall
assist each other in the conduct of inquiries and the collection
of evidence.

        (b)  The United States armed forces shall render all
assistance within their power to ensure that articles liable

0230

to seizure by, or on behalf of, the customs authorities of
the Government of the Republic of Korea are handed/to those over
authorities.

(c) The United States armed forces shall render
all assistance within their power to ensure the payment of
duties, taxes, and penalties payable by members of such forces
or of the civilian component, or their dependents. and

(d) The authorities of the United States forces
shall provide all practicable assistance to the customs officials
dispatched to military controlled piers and airports for the
purpose of customs inspection.

(e) Vehicles and articles belonging to the United
States armed forces seized by the customs authorities of the
Government of the Republic of Korea in connection with an
offense against its customs or fiscal laws or regulations shall
be handed over to the appropriate authorities of/xxx forces. such

한·미국 간의 상호방위조약 제4조에 의한 시설과 구역 및 한국에서의 미국군대의 지위에 관한 협정(SOFA)
전59권. 1966.7.9 서울에서 서명 : 1967.2.9 발효(조약 232호) (V.48 의제 및 초안)

<u>Agreed Minutes</u>

1.   The quantity of goods imported under paragraph 2 by non-appropriated fund organizations of the United States armed forces for the use of persons authorized by Article XIII and its Agreed Minute shall be limited to the extent reasonably required for such use.

2.   Paragraph 3(a) does not require concurrent shipment of goods with travel of owner nor does it require single loading or shipment.  In this connection, members of the United States armed forces or civilian component and their dependents may import free of duty reasonable quantities of their furniture, household goods and personal effects during a period of six months from the date of their first arrival.

3.   The term "military cargo" as used in paragraph 5(c) is not confined to arms and equipment but refers to all cargo consigned to the United States armed forces (including their authorized procurement agencies and their non-appropriated fund organizations provided for in Article XIII).  Pertinent information on cargo consigned to non-appropriated fund organizations will be furnished on a routine basis to the authorities of the Republic of Korea.  The extent of the pertinent information will be determined by the Joint Committee.

4.   The United States armed forces will take every practicable measure to ensure that goods will not be imported into the

0232

Republic of Korea by or for the members of the United States armed forces, the civilian component, or their dependents, the entry of which would be in violation of Korean customs laws and regulations. The United States armed forces will promptly notify customs authorities of the Republic of Korea whenever the entry of such goods is discovered.

5. The customs authorities of the Republic of Korea may, if they consider that there has been/an abuse or infringement in connection with the entry of goods under Article IX, take up the matter with the appropriate authorities of the United States armed forces.

6. The words "The United States armed forces shall render all assistance within their power;" etc., in paragraph 9(b) and (c) refer to reasonable and practicable measures by the United States armed forces.

7. It is understood that the duty free treatment provided in paragraph 2 of this Article shall apply to materials, supplies and equipment imported for sale through commissaries and non-appropriated fund organizations, under such regulations as the United States armed forces may promulgate, to those individuals and organizations referred to in Article XIII and its Agreed Minute.

0233

## ARTICLE X

### Access of Vessels and Aircraft

1. United States and foreign vessels and aircraft operated by, for, or under the control of the United States for official purposes shall be accorded access to any port or airport of Korea free from toll or landing charges. When cargo or passengers not accorded the exemptions of this Agreement are carried on such vessels and aircraft, notification shall be given to the appropriate authorities of the Republic of Korea, and ~~their~~ the entry into and departure from Korea of such cargo and passengers shall be according to the laws and regulations of Korea.

2. The vessels and aircraft mentioned in paragraph 1, United States Government-owned vehicles including armor, and members of the United States Armed Forces, the civilian component, and their dependents shall be accorded access to and movement between facilities and areas in use by the United States Armed Forces and between such facilities and areas and the ports or airports of Korea. Such access to and movement between facilities and areas by United States military vehicles shall be free from toll and other charges.

0234

3.    When the vessels mentioned in paragraph 1 enter
Korean ports *in the Republic of Korea* appropriate notification shall, under normal
conditions, be made to the proper authorities of the
Republic of Korea.  Such vessels shall have freedom from
compulsory pilotage, but if a pilot is taken pilotage
shall be paid for at appropriate rates.

### Agreed Minutes

·1.    "United States and foreign vessels...operated
by, for, or under the control of the United States for·
official purposes" means ~~United States~~ public vessels and
chartered vessels (bare boat charter, voyage charter and·
time charter).  Space charter is not included.  Commercial
cargo and private passengers are carried by them only in
exceptional cases.   *of the Republic of Korea*

2.    The Korean ports *of the Republic of Korea* mentioned herein will ordinarily
mean "open ports".

3.    The exemption / ~~from exemption~~ from making the "appropriate noti-
*of this Article*
fication" referred to in paragraph 3/will apply only in
unusual cases where such is required for security of the
United States armed forces or similar reasons.

4.    The laws and regulations of the Republic of
Korea will be applicable except as specifically provided
otherwise in this Article.

0235

## ARTICLE XI

## Meteorological Services

The Government of the Republic of Korea undertakes to furnish the United States armed forces with the following meteorological services in accordance with arrangements between the appropriate authorities of the two Governments:

(a) meteorological observations from land and ocean areas including observations from ships;

(b) climatological information including periodic summaries and historical data wherever available;

(c) telecommunications service to disseminate meteorological information;

(d) seismographic data.

0236

# ARTICLE XII
## Air Traffic Control and Navigational Aids

1. All civil and military air traffic control shall
be developed in close coordination and shall be integrated
to the extent necessary for the operation of this Agreement.
Procedures, and any subsequent changes thereto, necessary
to effect this coordination and integration will be established by arrangement between the appropriate authorities
of the two Governments.

2. The United States is authorized to establish, construct and maintain aids to navigation for vessels and aircraft, both visual and electronic as required, throughout
the Republic of Korea and in the territorial waters thereof.
Such navigation aids shall conform generally to the system
in use in the Republic of Korea. The authorities of the
United States and the Republic of Korea which have established
navigation aids shall duly notify each other of their positions
and characteristics and shall give advance notification
where practicable before making any changes in them or establishing additional navigation aids.

0237

## Agreed Minute

Installation by the United States/~~armed forces~~ armed forces of permanent navigational aids for vessels and aircraft outside of areas and facilities in use by the United States armed forces will be effected in accordance with the procedures established under paragraph 1 of Article ~~XX~~ III.

0238

## ARTICLE XIII

## Non-appropriated Funds Organizations

1. (a) Military exchanges, messes, social clubs, theaters, newspapers and other non-appropriated fund organizations authorized and regulated by the United States military authorities may be established by the United States armed forces for the use of members of such forces, the civilian component, and their dependents. Except as otherwise provided in this Agreement such organizations shall not be subject to Korean regulations, licenses, fees, taxes, or similar controls of the Republic of Korea.

(b) When a newspaper authorized and regulated by the United States military authorities is sold to the general public, it shall be subject to Korean regulations, licenses, fees, taxes, or similar controls of the Republic of Korea so far as such circulation is concerned.

2. No Korean tax shall be imposed on sales of merchandise or services by such organizations, except as provided in paragraph 1 (b) of this Article. Purchases within the Republic of Korea of merchandise and supplies by such organizations shall be subject to the Korean taxes

한·미국 간의 상호방위조약 제4조에 의한 시설과 구역 및 한국에서의 미국군대의 지위에 관한 협정(SOFA) 전59권. 1966.7.9 서울에서 서명 : 1967.2.9 발효(조약 232호) (V.48 의제 및 초안) 527

to which other purchasers of such merchandise and supplies are subject unless otherwise agreed between the two Governments.

3. Except as such disposal may be permitted by the authorities of the United States and the Republic of Korea in accordance with mutually agreed conditions, goods which are sold by such organizations shall not be disposed of in the Republic of Korea to persons not authorized to make purchases from such organizations.

4. The organizations referred to in this Article shall, through consultation between the representatives of the two Governments in the Joint Committee, provide such information to the Republic of Korea tax authorities as is required by Korean tax legislation.

## Agreed Minute

The United States Armed Forces may grant the use of the organizations referred to in paragraph 1 of Article XIII to: (a) other officers or personnel of the Government of the United States ordinarily accorded such privileges; (b) those other non-Korean armed forces in the Republic of Korea under the Unified Command which receive logistical support from the United States armed forces, and their members; (c) those non-Korean persons whose presence in the Republic of Korea is solely for the purpose of providing contract services financed by the United States Government; (d) those

0240

organizations which are present in the Republic of Korea primarily for the benefit and service of the United States armed forces, such as the American Red Cross and the United Service Organizations, and their non-Korean personnel; (e) dependents of the foregoing; and (f) other persons and organizations with the express consent of the Government of the Republic of Korea.

ARTICLE XIV

Taxation

1.     The United States armed forces shall not be
subject to taxes or similar charges on property held,
used or transferred by such forces in the Republic of
Korea..

2.     Members of the United States armed forces, the
civilian component, and their dependents shall not be liable
to pay any Korean taxes to the Government of the Republic
of Korea or to any other taxing agency in the Republic of
Korea on income received as a result of their service with
or employment by the United States armed forces, including
the organizations provided for in Article XIII.  Persons
in the Republic of Korea solely by reason of being members
of the United States armed forces, the civilian component,
or their dependents shall not be liable to pay any Korean
taxes to the Government of the Republic of Korea or to any
taxing agency in the Republic of Korea on income derived
from sources outside of the Republic of Korea, nor shall
periods during which such persons are in the Republic of
Korea be considered as periods of residence or domicile in
the Republic of Korea for the purpose of Korean taxation of the Republic of Korea
The provisions of this Article do not exempt such persons
from payment of Korean taxes on income derived from Korean
sources of the Republic of Korea other than those sources referred to in the first
sentence of this paragraph, nor do they exempt United States

0242                    page 3

citizens who claim residence of the Republic of
Korea for United States income tax purposes from
payment of Korean taxes on income.

3. Members of the United States armed forces,
the civilian component, and their dependents shall
be exempt from taxation in the Republic of Korea
on the holding, use, transfer _inter se_, or transfer
by death of movable property, tangible or intangible,
the presence of which in the Republic of Korea
is due solely to the temporary presence of these
persons in the Republic of Korea, provided that such
exemption shall not apply to property held for the
purpose of investment or the conduct of business
in the Republic of Korea or to any intangible property
registered in the Republic of Korea.

0243

한·미국 간의 상호방위조약 제4조에 의한 시설과 구역 및 한국에서의 미국군대의 지위에 관한 협정(SOFA)
전59권. 1966.7.9 서울에서 서명 : 1967.2.9 발효(조약 232호) (V.48 의제 및 초안)  531

# ARTICLE XV

## Invited Contractors

(i) a
1.     Persons, including/corporations organized under the laws
(ii) b
of the United States,/their employees who are ordinarily resident
(iii) c                          the foregoing,
in the United States, and/the dependents of/such persons, present
in the Republic of Korea solely for the purpose of executing contracts with the United States for the benefit of the United States
armed forces or other armed forces in the Republic of Korea under
the Unified Command receiving logistical support from the United
States armed forces, who are designated by the Government of the
United States in accordance with the provisions of paragraph 2
below, shall, except as provided in this Article, be subject to
the laws and regulations of the Republic of Korea.

2.     The designation referred to in paragraph 1 above shall
be made upon consultation with the Government of the Republic of
Korea and shall be restricted to cases where open competitive
bidding is not practicable due to security considerations, to
the technical qualifications of the contractors involved, to the
unavailability of materials or services required by the United
States standards, or to limitations of United States law. The
designation shall be withdrawn by the Government of the United
States:

0244

(a)  upon completion of contracts with the United States armed forces or other armed forces in the Republic of Korea under the Unified Command receiving logistical support from the United States armed forces;

(b)  upon proof that such persons are engaged in business activities in the Republic of Korea other than those pertaining to the United States armed forces or other armed forces in the Republic of Korea under the Unified Command receiving logistical support from the United States armed forces;

(c)  upon proof that such persons are engaged in practices illegal in the Republic of Korea.

3.  Upon certification by appropriate United States authorities as to their identity, such persons shall be accorded the following benefits of this Agreement:

(a)  accession and movement, as provided for in Article X, Paragraph 2;

(b)  entry into the Republic of Korea in accordance with the provisions of Article VIII;

(c)  the exemption from customs duties, and other such charges provided for in Article IX, Paragraph 3, for members of the United States armed forces, the civilian component, and their dependents;

0245

(d)  if authorized by the Government of the United States, the use of the services of the organizations provided for in Article XIII;

(e)  those provided in Article XVII, paragraph 2, for members of the United States armed forces, the civilian component, and their dependents;

(f)  if authorized by the Government of the United States, the use of military payment certificates, as provided for in Article XIX;

(g)  the use of postal facilities provided for in Article XX;

(h)  the use of utilities and services in accordance with those priorities, conditions, rates or tariffs accorded the United States armed forces by Article VI relating to utilities and services;

(i)  exemption from the laws and regulations of the Republic of Korea with respect to terms and conditions of employment, and licensing and registration of businesses and corporations.

4.  The arrival, departure, and place of residence in the Republic of Korea of such persons shall from time to time be notified by the United States armed forces to the authorities of the Republic of Korea.

0246

5. Upon certification by an authorized representative of the United States armed forces, depreciable assets, except houses, held, used or transferred by such persons exclusively for the execution of contracts referred to in paragraph 1 shall not be subject to taxes or similar charges of the Republic of Korea.

6. Upon certification by an authorized representative of the United States armed forces, such persons shall be exempt from taxation in the Republic of Korea on the holding, use, transfer by death, or transfer to persons or agencies entitled to tax exemption under this Agreement, of movable property, tangible or intangible, the presence of which in the Republic of Korea is due solely to the temporary presence of these persons in the Republic of Korea, provided that such exemption shall not apply to property held for the purpose of investment or the conduct of other business in the Republic of Korea or to any intangible property registered in the Republic of Korea.

7. Such persons referred to in paragraph 1 shall not be liable to pay income or corporation taxes to the Government of the Republic of Korea or to any other taxing agency in the Republic of Korea on any income derived under a contract with the Government of the United States in connection with the construction, maintenance or operation of any of the facilities or areas covered by this Agreement. Such persons

0247

~~xxxxxxxxxxxxxxxxxxxxxxxxxxxxxxxxxxxxxxxxxxxxxxxxxxxxxxxxStates~~ shall

not be liable to pay any Korean taxes to the Government of the

Republic of Korea or to any taxing agency in the Republic of

Korea on income derived from sources outside of the Republic

of Korea nor shall periods during which such persons are in the

Republic of Korea be considered periods of residence or domicile

in the Republic of Korea for the purposes of ~~Korean~~ the taxation *of the Republic of Korea*.

The provisions of this paragraph do not exempt such persons from

payment of income or corporation taxes on income derived from

Korean *the Republic of Korea* sources, other than those sources referred to in the first

sentence of this paragraph, nor do they exempt such persons who

claim ~~Korean~~ residence *in the Republic of Korea* for United States income tax purposes from

payment of Korean taxes on income.

    8.    The authorities of the Republic of Korea shall have the

right to exercise jurisdiction over such persons ~~referred to in~~

~~paragraph 1 of this Article above~~ for offenses committed in the Republic

of Korea and punishable by the law of the Republic of Korea.  In

recognition of the role of such persons ~~personnel~~ in the defense of the

Republic of Korea, they ~~the persons referred to in paragraph~~ shall

be subject to the provisions of paragraphs 5, 7(b), and 9 and

its the related Agreed Minutes, of Article XXII. In those cases in which the ~~Korean~~ authorities decide not to exercise jurisdiction they shall notify

the military authorities of the United States as soon as possible.  Upon such

notification the military authorities of the United States shall have the

right to exercise such jurisdiction over the persons referred to as is con-

ferred on them by the law of the United States.

0249

Agreed Minutes

1.  The execution of contracts with the United States in
addition to those specified in paragraph 1 of Article XV shall
not exclude the persons provided for in Article XV from the application of that Article.

2.  Contractor employees who are present in the Republic
of Korea on the effective date of this Agreement and who would
qualify for the privileges contained in Article XV but for the
fact that they are not ordinarily resident in the United States
shall be entitled to enjoy such privileges so long as their
presence is for the purpose stated in paragraph 1 of Article XV. .

0250

# ARTICLE XVI

## Local Procurement

1.    The United States may contract for any materials, supplies, equipment and services (including construction work) to be furnished or undertaken in the Republic of Korea for purposes of, or authorized by, this Agreement, without restriction as to choice of contractor, supplier or person who provides such services. Such materials, supplies, equipment and services may, upon agreement between the appropriate authorities of the two Governments, also be procured through the Government of the Republic of Korea.

2.    Materials, supplies, equipment and services which are required from local sources for the maintenance of the United States armed forces and the procurement of which may have an adverse effect on the economy of the Republic of Korea shall be procured in coordination with, and, when desirable, through or with the assistance of, the competent authorities of the Republic of Korea.

3.    Materials, supplies, equipment and services procured for official purposes in the Republic of Korea by the United States armed forces, including their authorized procurement agencies, or procured for ultimate use by the United States armed forces shall be exempt from the following Korean taxes upon appropriate certification in advance by the United States armed forces:

0251

(a)  commodity tax;

(b)  traffic tax;

(c)  petroleum tax;

(d)  electricity and gas tax;

(e)  business tax.

With respect to any present or future Korean taxes not specifically referred to in this Article which might be found to constitute a significant and readily identifiable part of the gross purchase price of materials, supplies, equipment and services procured by the United States armed forces, or for ultimate use by such forces, the two Governments will agree upon a procedure for granting such exemption or relief therefrom as is consistent with the purpose of this Article.

4.  Neither members of the United States armed forces, the civilian component, nor their dependents, shall by reason of this Article enjoy any exemption from taxes or similar charges relating to personal purchases of goods and services in the Republic of Korea chargeable under Korean the legislation of the Republic of Korea

5.  Except as such disposal may be authorized by the authorities of the United States and the Republic of Korea in accordance with mutually agreed conditions, goods purchased in the Republic of Korea exempt from taxes referred to in paragraph 3, shall not be disposed of in the Republic of Korea to persons not entitled to purchase such goods exempt from such taxes.

0252

## Agreed Minutes

1. The United States armed forces will furnish authorities of the Republic of Korea with appropriate information as far in advance as practicable on anticipated major changes in their procurement program in the Republic of Korea.

2. The problem of a satisfactory settlement of difficulties with respect to procurement contracts arising out of differences between economic laws and business practices of the Republic of Korea and the United States will be studied by the Joint Committee or other appropriate representatives.

3. The procedures for securing exemptions from taxation on purchases of goods for ultimate use by the United States armed forces will be as follows:

   (a) Upon appropriate certification by the United States armed forces that materials, supplies and equipment consigned to or destined for such forces, are to be used, or wholly or partially used up, under the supervision of such forces, exclusively in the execution of contracts for the construction, maintenance or operation of the facilities and areas referred to in Article V or for the support of the forces therein, or are ultimately to be incorporated into articles or facilities used by such forces, an authorized representative of such forces shall take delivery of such materials, supplies and equipment directly from manufacturers thereof. In such circumstances the collection of taxes referred to in Article XIV, paragraph 3, shall be held in abeyance.

(b) The receipt of such materials, supplies and equipment in the facilities and areas shall be confirmed by an authorized representative of the United States armed forces to the authorities of the Republic of Korea.

(c) Collection of the taxes on such materials, supplies and equipment shall be held in abeyance until

(i) the United States armed forces confirm and certify the quantity or degree of consumption of the above referred to materials, supplies and equipment, or

(ii) the United States armed forces confirm and certify the amount of the above referred to materials, supplies, and equipment which have been incorporated into articles or facilities used by the United States armed forces.

(d) Materials, supplies and equipment certified under (c)(i) or (ii) shall be exempt from taxes referred to in Article XIV, paragraph 3, insofar as the price thereof is paid out of appropriations of the Government of the United States or out of funds contributed by the Government of the Republic of Korea for disbursement by the/Government of the United States.

0254

4. Regarding paragraph 3/ it is understood that "materials, supplies, equipment and services procured for official purposes" refers to direct procurement by the United States armed forces or their authorized procurement agencies from Korean suppliers. "Materials, supplies, equipment and services procured for ultimate use" refers to procurement by contractors of the United States armed forces from Korean suppliers of items to be incorporated into or necessary for the production of the end product of their contracts with the United States armed forces.

0255

# ARTICLE XVII

## Labor Article

1. In this Article the expression:

   (a) "employer" refers to the United States armed forces (including non-appropriated fund organizations) and the persons referred to in the first paragraph of Article XV;

   (b) "employee" refers to any civilian (other than a member of the civilian component or a contractor employee under Article XV) employed by an employer, except (1) a member of the Korean Service Corps and (2) a domestic employed by an individual member of the United States armed forces, the civilian component or dependent thereof. Such employees shall be nationals of the Republic of Korea.

2. Employers may recruit, employ and administer their personnel. Recruitment services of the Government of the Republic of Korea will be utilized insofar as is practicable. In case employers accomplish direct recruitment of employees, employers will provide such relevant information as may be required for labor administration to the Office of Labor Affairs of the Republic of Korea.

3. To the extent not inconsistent with the provisions of this Article or the military requirements of the United States armed forces, the conditions of employment, compensation, and labor-management relations established by the United States armed

0256

forces for their employees shall conform with provisions of labor legislation of the Republic of Korea.

4. (a) In consideration of provision for collective action in labor legislation of the Republic of Korea, any dispute between employers and employees or any recognized employee organization, which cannot be settled through grievance or labor relations procedures of the United States armed forces, shall be settled as follows:

(i) The dispute shall be referred to the Office of Labor Affairs of the Republic of Korea for conciliation.

(ii) In the event that the dispute is not settled by the procedure described in (i) above, the matter will be referred to the Joint Committee, which may refer the matter to a special committee designated by the Joint Committee for further conciliation efforts.

(iii) In the event that the dispute is not settled by the procedures outlined above, the Joint Committee will resolve the dispute, assuring that expeditious procedures are followed. The decisions of the Joint Committee shall be binding.

(iv) Failure of any recognized employee organization or employee to abide by the decision of the Joint Committee on any dispute, or engaging in practices disruptive of normal work requirements during settlement procedures, shall be considered

0257

just cause for the withdrawal of recognition of that organization and the discharge of that employee.

(v) Neither employee organizations nor employees shall engage in any practices disruptive of normal work requirements unless a period of at least 70 days has elapsed after the dispute is referred to the Joint Committee, as stipulated in Subparagraph (ii), above.

(b) The Joint Committee, taking into consideration the role of the employees of the United States armed forces in the defense of the Republic of Korea and pertinent provisions of legislation of the Republic of Korea, shall determine those categories of essential employees who shall not exercise the right of further collective action in the event a labor dispute is not resolved by the foregoing procedures. In the event an agreement cannot be reached on this question in the Joint Committee, it may be made the subject of review through discussions between appropriate officials of the Government of the Republic of Korea and the diplomatic mission of the United States of America.

(c) In the event of a national emergency, such as war, hostilities or situations where war or hostilities may be imminent, the application of this Article shall be limited in accordance with emergency measures taken by the Government of the Republic of Korea in consultation with the military authorities of the United States.

0258

5. (a) Should the Republic of Korea adopt measures allocating labor, the United States armed forces shall be accorded allocation privileges no less favorable than those enjoyed by the armed forces of the Republic of Korea.

(b) In the event of a national emergency, such as war, hostilities, or situations where war or hostilities may be imminent, employees who have acquired skills essential to the mission of the United States armed forces shall, upon request of the United States armed forces, be deferred through mutual consultation from Republic of Korea military service or other compulsory service. The United States armed forces shall furnish in advance to the Republic of Korea lists of those employees deemed essential.

6. Members of the civilian component shall not be subject to laws or regulations of the Republic of Korea with respect to their terms and condition of employment.

## Agreed Minutes

1. It is understood that the Government of the Republic of Korea shall be reimbursed for direct costs incurred in providing assistance requested pursuant to paragraph 2.

2. The undertaking of the Government of the United States to conform to the provisions of labor legislation of the Republic of Korea does not imply any waiver by the Government of the United States of its immunities under international law. The Government

0259

of the United States may terminate employment at any time the continuation of such employment is inconsistent with the military requirements of the United States armed forces.

3. Employers will withhold from the pay of their employees, and pay over to the Government of the Republic of Korea withholdings required by the income tax legislation of the Republic of Korea.

4. When employers cannot conform with provisions of labor legislation of the Government of the Republic of Korea applicable under this Article on account of the military requirements of the United States armed forces, the matter shall be referred in advance whenever possible, to the Joint Committee for consideration and appropriate action. In the event mutual agreement cannot be reached in the Joint Committee regarding appropriate action, the issue may be made the subject of review through discussions between appropriate officials of the Government of the Republic of Korea and the diplomatic mission of the United States of America.

5. A union or other employee group shall be recognized by the employers unless its objectives are inimical to the/interests of the United States and the Republic of Korea. Membership or non-membership in such groups shall not be a factor in employment or other actions affecting employees.

0260

## ARTICLE XVIII
### Foreign Exchange Controls

1. Members of the United States armed forces, the civilian component and their dependents, shall be subject to the foreign exchange controls of the Government of the Republic of Korea.

2. The preceding paragraph shall not be construed to preclude the transmission into or out of the Republic of Korea of United States dollars or dollar instruments representing the official funds of the United States or realized as a result of service or employment in connection with this Agreement by members of the United States armed forces and the civilian component, or realized by such persons and their dependents from sources outside of the Republic of Korea.

3. The United States authorities shall take suitable measures to preclude the abuse of the privileges stipulated in the preceding paragraph or circumvention of the Korean foreign exchange controls. *of the Republic of Korea*

### Agreed Minute

Payment in the Republic of Korea by the United States armed forces, including those organizations provided for in Article XIII, to persons other than members of the United States armed forces, civilian component, their dependents and those persons referred to in Article XV

0261

be effected in accordance with the Korean Foreign Exchange
Control Law and regulations. The funds to be used for
these transactions shall be convertible into currency of
the Republic of Korea at the highest rate in terms of the
number of Korean won per United States dollar which, at the
time the conversion is made, is not unlawful in the Republic
of Korea.

0262

## ARTICLE XIX

## Military Payment Certificates

1.    (a)  United States military payment certificates
denominated in dollars may be used by persons authorized
by the United States for internal transactions.  The Government of the United States will take appropriate action to
ensure that authorized personnel are prohibited from engaging
in transactions involving military payment certificates
except as authorized by United States regulations.  The
Government of the Republic of Korea will take necessary
action to prohibit unauthorized persons from engaging in
transactions involving military payment certificates and.
with the aid of United States authorities will undertake
to apprehend and punish any person or persons under its
jurisdiction involved in the counterfeiting or uttering of
counterfeit military payment certificates.

(b)  It is agreed that the United States autho-
rities of the United States will to the extent authorized by United States law,
apprehend and punish members of the United States armed
forces, the civilian component, or their dependents, who
tender military payment certificates to unauthorized persons
and that no obligation will be due to such unauthorized
persons or to the Government of the Republic of Korea or
its agencies from the United States or any of its agencies

0263

as a result of any unauthorized use of military payment certificates within the Republic of Korea.

2. In order to exercise control of military payment certificates the United States may designate certain American financial institutions to maintain and operate, under United States supervision, facilities for the use of persons authorized by the United States to use military payment certificates. Institutions authorized to maintain military banking facilities will establish and maintain such facilities physically separated from their Korean commercial banking business, with personnel whose sole duty is to maintain and operate such facilities. Such facilities shall be permitted to maintain United States currency bank accounts and to perform all financial transactions in connection therewith including receipt and remission of funds to the extent provided by Article XVIII, paragraph 2, of this Agreement.

## ARTICLE XX

### Military Post Offices

The United States may establish and operate, within the facilities and areas in use by the United States armed forces, United States military post offices for the use of members of the United States armed forces, the civilian component, and their dependents, for the transmission of mail between United States military post offices in the Republic of Korea and between such military post offices and other United States post offices.

### Agreed Minute

United States military post offices may be used by other officers and personnel of the Government of the United States, and their dependents, ordinarily accorded such privileges abroad.

0265

## ARTICLE XXI

### Accounting Procedures

It is agreed that arrangements will be effected between the Governments of the United States and the Republic of Korea for accounting applicable to financial transactions arising out of this Agreement.

## ARTICLE XXII

## Criminal Jurisdiction Article

1.     Subject to the provisions of this Article,

(a)  the military authorities of the United States shall have the right to exercise within the Republic of Korea all criminal and disciplinary jurisdiction conferred on them by the law of the United States over members of the United States armed forces or civilian component, and their dependents;

(b)  the authorities of the Republic of Korea shall have jurisdiction over the members of the United States armed forces or civilian component, and their dependents, with respect to offenses committed within the territory of the Republic of Korea and punishable by the law of the Republic of Korea.

2.     (a)  The military authorities of the United States shall have the right to exercise exclusive jurisdiction over members of the United States armed forces or civilian component, and their dependents, with respect to offenses, including offenses relating to its security, punishable by the law of the United States, but not by the law of the Republic of Korea.

(b)  The authorities of the Republic of Korea shall have the right to exercise exclusive jurisdiction over members of the United States armed forces or civilian component, and their dependents, with respect to offenses, including offenses relating to the security of the Republic of Korea, punishable by its law

0267

but not by the law of the United States.

(c) For the purpose of this paragraph and of paragraph 3 of this Article, a security offense against a State shall include:

(i) treason against the State;

(ii) sabotage, espionage or violation of any law relating to official secrets of that State, or secrets relating to the national defense of that State.

3. In cases where the right to exercise jurisdiction is concurrent the following rules shall apply:

(a) The military authorities of the United States shall have the primary right to exercise jurisdiction over members of the United States armed forces or civilian component, and their dependents, in relation to:

(i) offenses solely against the property or security of the United States, or offenses solely against the person or property of another member of the United States armed forces or civilian component or of a dependent;

(ii) offenses arising out of any act or omission done in the performance of official duty.

(b) In the case of any other offense, the authorities of the Republic of Korea shall have the primary right to exercise jurisdiction.

0268

(c)  If the State having the primary right decides not to exercise jurisdiction, it shall notify the authorities of the other State as soon as practicable.  The authorities of the State having the primary right shall give sympathetic consideration to a request from the authorities of the other State for a waiver of its right in cases where that other State considers such waiver to be of particular importance.

4.  The foregoing provisions of this Article shall not imply any right for the military authorities of the United States to exercise jurisdiction over persons who are nationals of or ordinarily resident in the Republic of Korea, unless they are members of the United States armed forces.

5.  (a)  The military authorities of the United States and the authorities of the Republic of Korea shall assist each other in the arrest of members of the United States armed forces, the civilian component, or their dependents in the territory of the Republic of Korea and in handing them over to the authority which is to have custody in accordance with the following provisions.

(b)  The authorities of the Republic of Korea shall notify promptly the military authorities of the United States of the arrest of any member of the United States armed forces, or civilian component, or a dependent.  The military authorities of the United States shall promptly notify the authorities of the Republic of Korea of the arrest of a member of the United States

0269

armed forces, the civilian component, or a dependent in any case in which the Republic of Korea has the primary right to exercise jurisdiction.

(c) The custody of an accused member of the United States armed forces or the civilian component, or of a dependent, over whom the Republic of Korea is to exercise jurisdiction shall, if he is in the hands of the military authorities of the United States, remain with the military authorities of the United States pending the conclusion of all judicial proceedings and until custody is requested by the authorities of the Republic of Korea. If he is in the hands of the Republic of Korea, he shall, on request, be handed over to the military authorities of the United States and remain in their custody pending completion of all judicial proceedings and until custody is requested by the authorities of the Republic of Korea. When an accused has been in the custody of the military authorities of the United States, the military authorities of the United States may transfer custody to the authorities of the Republic of Korea at any time, and shall give sympathetic consideration to any request for the transfer of custody which may be made by the authorities of the Republic of Korea in specific cases. The military authorities of the United States shall promptly make any such accused available to the authorities of the Republic of Korea upon their request for purposes of investigation and trial, and shall take all appropriate

0270

measures to that end and to prevent any prejudice to the course of justice. They shall take full account of any special request regarding custody made by the authorities of the Republic of Korea. The authorities of the Republic of Korea shall give sympathetic consideration to a request from the military authorities of the United States for assistance in maintaining custody of an accused member of the United States armed forces, the civilian component, or a dependent.

(d) In respect of offenses solely against the security of the Republic of Korea provided in paragraph 2(c), an accused shall be in the custody of the authorities of the Republic of Korea.

6. (a) The military authorities of the United States and the authorities of the Republic of Korea shall assist each other in the carrying out of all necessary investigations into offenses, and in the collection and production of evidence, including the seizure and, in proper cases, the handing over of objects connected with an offense. The handing over of such objects may, however, be made subject to their return within the time specified by the authority delivering them.

(b) The military authorities of the United States and the authorities of the Republic of Korea shall notify each other of the disposition of all cases in which there are concurrent rights to exercise jurisdiction.

0271

7.　(a)　A death sentence shall not be carried out in the
Republic of Korea by the military authorities of the United States
if the legislation of the Republic of Korea does not provide for
such punishment in a similar case.

　　　　(b)　The authorities of the Republic of Korea shall give
sympathetic consideration to a request from the military authorities of the United States for assistance in carrying out a sentence
of imprisonment pronounced by the military authorities of the
United States under the provisions of this Article within the
territory of the Republic of Korea.  The authorities of the
Republic of Korea shall also give sympathetic consideration to a
request from the authorities of the United States for the custody
of any member of the United States armed forces or the civilian component or a dependent, who is serving a sentence of confinement
imposed by a court of the Republic of Korea.  If such custody
is released to the military authorities of the United States, the
United States shall be obligated to continue the confinement of
the individual in an appropriate confinement facility of the
United States until the sentence to confinement shall have been
served in full or until release from such confinement shall be
approved by the competent authorities of the Republic of Korea.
In such cases, the authorities of the United States shall furnish
relevant information on a routine basis to the authorities of the

0272

Republic of Korea, and a representative of the Government of the Republic of Korea shall have the right to have access to a member of the United States armed forces, the civilian component, or a dependent who is serving a sentence imposed by a court of the Republic of Korea in confinement facilities of the United States.

8.    Where an accused has been tried in accordance with the provisions of this Article either by the military authorities of the United States or the authorities of the Republic of Korea and has been acquitted, or has been convicted and is serving, or has served, his sentence, or his sentence has been remitted or suspended, or he has been pardoned, he may not be tried again for the same offense within the territory of the Republic of Korea by the authorities of the other State. However, nothing in this paragraph shall prevent the military authorities of the United States from trying a member of its armed forces for any violation of rules of discipline arising from an act or omission which constituted an offense for which he was tried by the authorities of the Republic of Korea.

9.    Whenever a member of the United States armed forces or civilian component or a dependent is prosecuted under the jurisdiction of the Republic of Korea he shall be entitled:

한·미국 간의 상호방위조약 제4조에 의한 시설과 구역 및 한국에서의 미국군대의 지위에 관한 협정(SOFA)
전59권. 1966.7.9 서울에서 서명 : 1967.2.9 발효(조약 232호) (V.48 의제 및 초안)    561

(a)  to a prompt and speedy trial;

(b)  to be informed, in advance of trial, of the specific charge or charges made against him;

(c)  to be confronted with the witnesses against him;

(d)  to have compulsory process for obtaining witnesses in his favor, if they are within the jurisdiction of the Republic of Korea;

(e)  to have legal representation of his own choice for his defense or to have free or assisted legal representation under the conditions prevailing for the time being in the Republic of Korea;

(f)  if he considers it necessary, to have the services of a competent interpreter; and

(g)  to communicate with a representative of the Government of the United States and to have such a representative present at his trial.

10.  (a)  Regularly constituted military units or formations of the United States armed forces shall have the right to police any facilities or areas which they use under Article/II of this Agreement.  The military police of such forces may take all appropriate measures to ensure the maintenance of order and security within such facilities and areas.

0271

(b)  Outside these facilities and areas, such military
police shall be employed only subject to arrangements with the
authorities of the Republic of Korea and in liaison with those
authorities, and in so far as such employment is necessary to
maintain discipline and order among the members of the United
States armed forces, or ensure their security.

11.  In the event of hostilities to which the provisions of
Article II of the Treaty of Mutual Defense apply, the provisions
of this Agreement pertaining to criminal jurisdiction shall be
immediately suspended and the military authorities of the United
States shall have the right to exercise exclusive jurisdiction
over members of the United States armed forces, the civilian
component, and their dependents.

12.  The provisions of this Article shall not apply to any
offenses committed before the entry into force of this Agreement.
Such cases shall be governed by the provisions of the Agreement
between the United States of America and the Republic of Korea
effected by an exchange of notes at Taejon, Republic of Korea on July 12, 1950.

0275

## Agreed Minutes

The provisions of this Article shall not affect existing agreements, arrangements, or practices, relating to the exercise of jurisdiction over personnel of the United Nations forces present in the Republic of Korea other than forces of the United States.

RE Paragraph 1(b)

1. In the event that martial law is declared by the Republic of Korea, the provisions of this Article shall be immediately suspended in the part of the Republic of Korea under martial law, and the military authorities of the United States shall have the right to exercise exclusive jurisdiction over members of the United States armed forces or the civilian component, and their dependents, in such part until martial law is ended.

2. The jurisdiction of the authorities of the Republic of Korea over members of the United States armed forces or the civilian component, and their dependents, shall not extend to any offenses committed outside the Republic of Korea.

RE Paragraph 2

The Republic of Korea, recognizing the effectiveness in appropriate cases of the administrative and disciplinary sanctions which may be imposed by the United States authorities or the over members of the United States armed forces or the civilian component, and their dependents, will give sympathetic consideration in such cases to requests in the Joint Committee for waivers of its right to exercise jurisdiction under paragraph 2.

0276

<u>RE Paragraph 2(c)</u>

Each Government shall inform the other of the details of all security offenses mentioned in this Subparagraph, and of the provisions regarding such offenses in its legislation.

<u>RE Paragraph 3(a)</u>

1. Where a member of the United States armed forces or civilian component is charged with an offense, a certificate issued by competent military authorities of the United States forces stating that the alleged offense, if committed by him, arose out of an act or omission done in the performance of official duty shall be sufficient evidence of the fact for the purpose of determining primary jurisdiction. The term "official duty" as used in this Article and Agreed Minute is not meant to include all acts by members of the United States armed forces and the civilian component during periods when they are on duty, but is meant to apply only to acts which are required to be done as functions of those duties which the individuals are performing.

2. In those exceptional cases where the Chief Prosecutor for the Republic of Korea considers that there is proof contrary to a certificate of official duty, it shall be made the subject of review through discussions between appropriate officials of the Government of the Republic of Korea and the diplomatic mission of the United States in the Republic of Korea.

0277

RE Paragraph 3(b)

1. The Government of the Republic of Korea waives in favor of the United States the primary right granted to the authorities of the Republic of Korea under subparagraph (b) of paragraph 3 of this Article in cases of concurrent jurisdiction, in accordance with Paragraphs 2, 3, 4, 5, 6, and 7 of this Minute.

2. Subject to any particular arrangements which may be made under paragraph 7 of this Minute, the military authorities of the United States shall notify the competent authorities of the Republic of Korea of individual cases falling under the waiver provided in paragraph 1 of this Minute.

3. Where the competent authorities of the Republic of Korea hold the view that, by reason of special circumstances in a specific case, major interests of Korean administration of justice make imperative the exercise of ~~Korean~~ jurisdiction _of the Republic of Korea_ ~~they may recall the~~ waiver granted under paragraph 1 of this Minute by a statement to the competent military authorities of the United States within a period of twenty-one days after receipt of the notification envisaged in paragraph 2 of this Minute or any shorter period which may be provided in arrangements made under paragraph 7 of this Minute. The authorities of the Republic of Korea may also submit the statement prior to receipt of such notification.

0278.

(a) Subject to a careful examination of each specific case and to the results of such examination, major interests of Korean administration of justice within the meaning of paragraph 3 above may make imperative the exercise of ~~Korean~~ the jurisdiction [of the Republic of Korea] in particular, in the following cases:

(i) security offenses against the Republic of Korea;

(ii) offenses causing the death of a human being, robbery, and rape, except where the offenses are directed against a member of the United States armed forces or the civilian component, or a dependent; and

(iii) attempts to commit such offenses or participation therein.

(b) In respect of the offenses referred to in sub-paragraph (a) of this paragraph, the authorities concerned shall proceed in particularly close cooperation from the beginning of the preliminary investigation in order to provide the mutual assistance envisaged in paragraph 6 of this Article.

4. If, pursuant to paragraph 3 of this Minute, the competent Korean
of the Republic of Korea
authorities/have recalled the waiver in a specific case and in such case an understanding cannot be reached in discussions between the authorities concerned, the Government of the United States may make representations to the Government of the Republic of Korea through diplomatic channels. The Government of the Republic of Korea, giving due consideration to the

0279

interests of Korean administration of justice and to the interests
of the Government of the United States, shall resolve the disagreement
in the exercise of its authority in the field of foreign affairs.   In
case the Government of the Republic of Korea, in resolving (the)
disagreement in accordance with the foregoing provisions, determines
that it is imperative that jurisdiction be exercised by the authorities
of the Republic of Korea, the recall of waiver shall be final and
conclusive.

     5.  With the consent of the competent authorities of the Republic
of Korea, the military authorities of the United States may transfer
to the Korean courts or authorities of the Republic of Korea for
investigation, trial and decision, particular criminal cases in which
jurisdiction rests with the United States.

     With the consent of the military authorities of the United States,
the competent authorities of the Republic of Korea may transfer to the
military authorities of the United States for investigation, trial and
decision, particular criminal cases in which jurisdiction rests with
the Republic of Korea.

     6.  (a)  Where a member of the United States armed forces or
civilian component, or a dependent, is arraigned before a court of the
United States, for an offense committed in the Republic of Korea against
Korean interests, the trial shall be held within the Republic of Korea.

               (i)  except where the law of the United States requires
otherwise, or

(ii) except where, in cases of military exigency or in the interests of justice, the military authorities of the United States intend to hold the trial outside the Republic of Korea. In this event they shall afford the authorities of the Republic of Korea timely opportunity to comment on such intention and shall give due consideration to any comments the latter may make.

(b) Where the trial is held outside of the Republic of Korea the military authorities of the United States shall inform the authorities of the Republic of Korea of the place and date of the trial. A representative of the Government of the Republic of Korea shall be entitled to be present at the trial. The authorities of the United States shall inform the authorities of the Republic of Korea of the judgment and the final outcome of the proceedings.

7. In the implementation of the provisions of this Article and this Agreed Minute, and to facilitate the expeditious disposal of offenses of minor importance, arrangements may be made between the military authorities of the United States and the competent authorities of the Republic of Korea. These arrangements may also extend to dispensing with notification and to the period of time referred to in paragraph 3 of this Minute, within which the waiver may be recalled.

0281

<u>RE Paragraph 6</u>

    1. The military authorities of the United States and the authorities of the Republic of Korea shall assist each other in obtaining the appearance of witnesses necessary for the proceedings conducted by such authorities within the Republic of Korea.

    When a member of the United States armed forces in the Republic of Korea is summoned to appear before a ~~Korean~~ court of the Republic of Korea, as a witness or as a defendant, ~~United States~~ The military authorities of the United States shall, unless military exigency requires otherwise, secure his attendance provided such attendance is compulsory under the law of the Republic of Korea. If military exigency prevents such attendance, the military authorities of the United States shall furnish a certificate stating the estimated duration of such disability.

    Service of process upon a member of the United States armed forces or the civilian component, or a dependent required as a witness or a defendant must be personal service in the English language. Where the service of process is to be effected by a process server of the Republic of Korea upon any person who is inside a military installation or area, the military authorities of the United States shall take all measures necessary to enable the ~~Korean~~ of the Republic of Korea process server to effect such service.

    In addition, the authorities of the Republic of Korea shall promptly give copies of all criminal writs (including warrants, summonses, indictments, and subpoenas) to an agent designated by ~~the United States~~

)

0282

military authorities to receive them in all cases of Korean criminal
proceedings involving a member of the United States armed forces or
civilian component, or a dependent.

_[handwritten annotations: "of the United States", "the", "or the Republic of Korea", "A", "the"]_

When citizens or residents of the Republic of Korea are required
as witnesses or experts by the military authorities of the United
States, the courts and authorities of the Republic of Korea shall, in
accordance with the law of the Republic of Korea, secure the attendance
of such persons. In those cases the military authorities of the United
States shall act through the Attorney General of the Republic of Korea,
or such other agency as is designated by the authorities of the Republic
of Korea.

Fees and other payments for witnesses shall be determined by the
Joint Committee established under Article XXVIII.

2. The privileges and immunities of witnesses shall be those
accorded by the law of the court, tribunal or authority before which
they appear. In no event shall a witness be required to provide
testimony which may tend to incriminate him.

3. If, in the course of criminal proceedings before authorities
of the United States or the Republic of Korea, the disclosure of an
official secret of either of these States or the disclosure of any
information which may prejudice the security of either appears
necessary for the just disposition of the proceedings, the authorities
concerned shall seek written permission to make such disclosure from
the appropriate authority of the State concerned.

0283

<u>RE Paragraph 9 (a)</u>

The right to a prompt and speedy trial by the courts of the Republic of Korea shall include public trial by an impartial tribunal composed exclusively of judges who have completed their probationary period. A member of the United States armed forces, or civilian component, or a dependent, shall not be tried by a military tribunal of the Republic of Korea.

<u>RE Paragraph 9 (b)</u>

A member of the United States armed forces or civilian component, or a dependent, shall not be arrested or detained by the authorities of the Republic of Korea without adequate cause, and he shall be entitled to an immediate hearing at which such cause must be shown in open court in his presence and the presence of his counsel. His immediate release shall be ordered if adequate cause is not shown. Immediately upon arrest or detention he shall be informed of the charges against him in a language which he understands.

He shall also be informed a reasonable time prior to trial of the nature of the evidence that is to be used against him. Counsel for the accused shall upon request, be afforded the opportunity before trial to examine and copy the statements of witnesses obtained by authorities of the Republic of Korea which are included in the file forwarded to the court of the Republic of Korea scheduled to try the case.

0284

RE Paragraph 9 (c) and (d)

A member of the United States armed forces or civilian component, or a dependent who is prosecuted by the authorities of the Republic of Korea shall have the right to be present throughout the testimony of all witnesses, for and against him, in all judicial examinations, pretrial hearings, the trial itself, and subsequent proceedings, and shall be permitted full opportunity to examine the witnesses.

RE Paragraph 9 (c)

The right to legal representation shall exist from the moment of arrest or detention and shall include the right to have counsel present, and to consult confidentially with such counsel, at all preliminary investigations, examinations, pretrial hearings, the trial itself, and subsequent proceedings, at which the accused is present.

RE Paragraph 9 (f)

The right to have the services of a competent interpreter shall exist from the moment of arrest or detention.

RE Paragraph 9 (g)

The right to communicate with a representative of the Government of the United States shall exist from the moment of arrest or detention, and no statement of the accused taken in the absence of such a representative shall be admissible as evidence in support of the guilt of the accused. Such representative shall be entitled to be present at all preliminary investigations, examinations, pretrial hearings, the trial itself, and subsequent proceedings, at which the accused is present.

0285

A member of the United States armed forces or civilian component,
or a dependent, tried by the authorities of the Republic of Korea
shall be accorded every procedural and substantive right granted by
law to the citizens of the Republic of Korea. If it should appear
that an accused has been or is likely to be, denied any procedural or
substantive right granted by law to the citizens of the Republic of
Korea, representatives of the two Governments shall consult in the
Joint Committee on the measures necessary to prevent or cure such
denial of rights.

In addition to the rights enumerated in items (a) through (g) of
paragraph 9 of this Article, a member of the United States armed
forces or civilian component, or a dependent, who is prosecuted by the
authorities of the Republic of Korea:

(a) shall have the right to appeal a conviction or sentence;

(b) shall have credited to any sentence of confinement his
period of pretrial confinement in a United States or ~~Korean~~ confinement
facility;

(c) shall not be held guilty of a criminal offense on account
of any act or omission which did not constitute a criminal offense
under the law of the Republic of Korea at the time it was committed;

(d) shall not be subject to a heavier penalty than the one that
was applicable at the time the alleged criminal offense was committed
or was adjudged by the court of first instance as the original sentence;

(e) shall not be held guilty of an offense on the basis of rules of evidence or requirements of proof which have been altered to his prejudice since the date of the commission of the offense;

(f) shall not be compelled to testify against or otherwise incriminate himself;

(g) shall not be subject to cruel or unusual punishment;

(h) shall not be subject to prosecution or punishment by legislative or executive act;

(i) shall not be prosecuted or punished more than once for the same offense;

(j) shall not be required to stand trial if he is physically or mentally unfit to stand trial and participate in his defense;

(k) shall not be subjected to trial except under conditions consonant with the dignity of the United States armed forces, including appearing in appropriate military or civilian attire and unmanacled.

No confession, admission or other statement, obtained by torture, violence, threat, deceit, or after prolonged arrest, or detention, or which has been made involuntarily, and no real evidence which has been obtained by torture, violence, threat, deceit, or as a result of an unreasonable search and seizure without a warrant, will be considered by the courts of the Republic of Korea as evidence in support of the guilt of the accused under this Article.

In any case prosecuted by the authorities of the Republic of Korea under this Article no appeal will be taken by the prosecution from a

0287

judgment of not guilty or an acquittal nor will an appeal be taken by
the prosecution from any judgment which the accused does not appeal,
except upon grounds of errors of law.

The military authorities of the United States shall have the
right to inspect any ~~Korean~~ *of the Republic of Korea* confinement facility in which a member of
the United States armed forces, *the* civilian component, or *a* dependent is
confined, or in which it is proposed to confine such an individual.

In the event of hostilities, the Republic of Korea will take all
possible measures to safeguard members of the United States armed
forces, members of the civilian component, and their dependents who
are confined in ~~Korean~~ *of the Republic of Korea* confinement facilities, whether awaiting trial
or serving a sentence imposed by the courts of the Republic of Korea.
The Republic of Korea shall give sympathetic consideration to requests
for release of these persons to the custody of responsible ~~United~~
~~States~~ *of the United States.* military authorities. Necessary implementing provisions shall
be agreed upon between the two Governments through the Joint Committee.

Facilities utilized for the execution of a sentence to death or a
period of confinement, imprisonment, or penal servitude, or for the
detention of members of the United States armed forces or *the* civilian
component or dependents, will meet minimum standards as agreed by the
Joint Committee. The ~~United States~~ *of the United States* military authorities shall have
the right upon request to have access at any time to members of the

0288

United States armed forces, the civilian component, or their dependents who are confined or detained by the authorities of the Republic of Korea. During the visit of these persons at ~~Korean~~ confinement facilities of the Republic of Korea, the United States military authorities of the United States shall be authorized to provide supplementary care and provisions for such persons, such as clothing, food, bedding, and medical and dental treatment.

RE Paragraph 10 (a) and 10 (b)

1. ~~The United States~~ the military authorities of the United States will normally make all arrests within facilities and areas in use by the United States armed forces.

This shall not preclude the authorities of the Republic of Korea from making arrests within facilities and areas in cases where the competent ~~authorities~~ authorities of the United States armed forces have given consent, or in cases of pursuit of a flagrant offender who has committed a serious crime.

Where persons whose arrest is desired by the authorities of the Republic of Korea, and who are not members of the United States armed forces or the civilian component or dependents, are within facilities and areas in use by the United States armed forces, the ~~United States~~ military authorities of the United States will undertake, upon request, to arrest such persons. Any person arrested by or the United States the military authorities who is not a member of the United States armed forces or a civilian component or a dependent, shall immediately be turned over to the authorities of the Republic of Korea.

한·미국 간의 상호방위조약 제4조에 의한 시설과 구역 및 한국에서의 미국군대의 지위에 관한 협정(SOFA)
전59권. 1966.7.9 서울에서 서명 : 1967.2.9 발효(조약 232호) (V.48 의제 및 초안)

The United States military authorities may arrest or detain in the vicinity of a facility or area any person in the commission or attempted commission of an offense against the security of that facility or area. Any such person who is not a member of the United States armed forces or civilian component or a dependent shall immediately be turned over to the authorities of the Republic of Korea.

2. The authorities of the Republic of Korea will normally not exercise the right of search, seizure, or inspection with respect to any person or property within facilities and areas in use by the military authorities of the United States or with respect to property of the United States wherever situated, except in cases where the competent military authorities of the United States consent to such search, seizure, or inspection by the authorities of the Republic of Korea of such persons or property.

Where search, seizure, or inspection with respect to persons or property within facilities and areas in use by the United States armed forces or with respect to property of the United States in Korea is desired by the authorities of the Republic of Korea military authorities of the Republic of Korea, the United States military authorities will undertake, upon request, to make such search, seizure, or inspection. In the event of a judgment concerning such property, except property owned or utilized by the United States Government or its instrumentalities, the United States will in accordance with its laws turn over such property of the Republic of Korea to the authorities for disposition in accordance with the judgment.

ARTICLE XXIII

Claims

1. Each Party waives all its claims against the other Party for damage to any property owned by it and used by its armed forces, if such damage—

(a) was caused by a member or an employee of the armed forces of the other Party, in performance of his official duties; or

(b) arose from the use of any vehicle, vessel or aircraft owned by the other Party and used by its armed services, provided either that the vehicle, vessel or aircraft causing the damage was being used for official purposes or that the damage was caused to property being so used.

Claims for maritime salvage by one Party against the other Party shall be waived, provided that the vessel or cargo salved was owned by the other Party and being used by its armed services for official purposes.

2. (a) In the case of damage caused or arising as stated in paragraph 1 to other property owned by either Party, the issue of liability of the other Party shall be determined and the amount of damage shall be assessed, unless the two Governments agree otherwise, by a sole arbitrator selected in accordance with Subparagraph (b) of this paragraph. The arbitrator shall also decide any counterclaims arising out of the same incident.

0291

(b) The arbitrator referred to in Subparagraph (a) above shall be selected by agreement between the two Governments from amongst the nationals of the Republic of Korea who hold or have held high judicial office.

(c) Any decision taken by the arbitrator shall be binding and conclusive upon the Parties.

(d) The amount of any compensation awarded by the arbitrator shall be distributed in accordance with the provisions of paragraph 5(e)(i), (ii) and (iii) of this Article.

(e) The compensation of the arbitrator shall be fixed by agreement between the two Governments and shall, together with the necessary expenses incidental to the performance of his duties, be defrayed in equal proportions by them.

(f) Each party waives its claim in any such case up to the amount of 1,400 United States dollars or its equivalent in Korean currency of the Republic of Korea at the rate of exchange provided for in the Agreed Minute to Article XVIII at the time the claim is filed.

3. For the purpose of paragraphs 1 and 2 of this Article the expression "owned by a Party" in the case of a vessel includes a vessel on bare boat charter to that Party or requisitioned by it on bare boat terms or seized by it in prize (except to the extent that the risk of loss or liability is borne by some person other than such Party).

0292

4.    Each Party waives all its claims against the other Party for injury or death suffered by any member of its armed forces while such member was engaged in the performance of his official duties.

5.    Claims (other than contractual claims and those to which paragraph 6 or 7 of this Article apply) arising out of acts or omissions of members or employees of the United States armed forces, including those employees who are nationals of or ordinarily resident in the Republic of Korea, done in the performance of official duty, or out of any other act, omission or occurrence for which the United States armed forces are legally responsible, and causing damage in the Republic of Korea to third parties, other than the Government of the Republic of Korea, shall be dealt with by the Republic of Korea in accordance with the following provisions:

(a)    Claims shall be filed, considered and settled or adjudicated in accordance with the laws and regulations of the Republic of Korea with respect to the claims arising from the activities of its own armed forces.

(b)    The Republic of Korea may settle any such claims, and payment of the amount agreed upon or determined by adjudication shall be made by the Republic of Korea in won.

(c)    Such payment, whether made pursuant to a settlement or to adjudication of the case by a competent tribunal of the Republic of Korea, or the final adjudication by such a tribunal denying payment, shall be binding and conclusive upon the Parties.

0293

(d)  Every claim paid by the Republic of Korea shall be communicated to the appropriate United States authorities together with full particulars and a proposed distribution in conformity with Subparagraph (e)(i) and (ii) below.

In default of a reply within two months, the proposed distribution shall be regarded as accepted.

(e)  The cost incurred in satisfying claims pursuant to the preceding Subparagraph and paragraph 2 of this Article shall be distributed between the Parties as follows:

(i)  Where the United States alone is responsible, the amount awarded or adjudged shall be distributed in the proportion of 25 percent chargeable to the Republic of Korea and 75 percent chargeable to the United States.

(ii) Where the Republic of Korea and the United States are responsible for the damage, the amount awarded or adjudged shall be distributed equally between them.  Where the damage was caused by the armed forces of the Republic of Korea or of the United States and it is not possible to attribute it specifically to one or both of those armed forces, the amount awarded or adjudged shall be distributed equally between the Republic of Korea and the United States.

(iii)Every half year, a statement of the sums paid by the Republic of Korea in the course of the half-yearly period in respect of every case regarding which the liability, amount, and proposed distribution on a percentage basis has been approved by

0291

both Governments shall be sent to the appropriate authorities of the United States, together with a request for reimbursement. Such reimbursement shall be made in won within the shortest possible time. The approval by both Governments as referred to in this Subparagraph shall not prejudice any decision taken by the arbitrator or adjudication by a competent tribunal of the Republic of Korea as set forth in paragraphs 2(a) and 5(e) respectively.

(f) Members or employees of the United States armed forces, including those employees who are nationals of or ordinarily resident in the Republic of Korea, shall not be subject to any proceedings for the enforcement of any judgment given against them in the Republic of Korea in a matter arising from the performance of their official duties.

(g) Except insofar as Subparagraph (e) of this paragraph applies to claims covered by paragraph 2 of this Article, the provisions of this paragraph shall not apply to any claim arising out of or in connection with the navigation or operation of a ship or the loading, carriage, or discharge of a cargo, other than claims for death or personal injury to which paragraph 4 of this Article does not apply.

6. Claims against members or employees of the United States armed forces (except employees who are nationals of or ordinarily resident in the Republic of Korea) arising out of tortious acts or omissions in the Republic of Korea not done in the performance of official duty shall be dealt with in the following manner:

(a)  The authorities of the Republic of Korea shall consider the claim and assess compensation to the claimant in a fair and just manner, taking into account all the circumstances of the case, including the conduct of the injured person, and shall prepare a report on the matter.

(b)  The report shall be delivered to the appropriate United States authorities who shall then decide without delay whether they will offer an ex gratia payment, and if so, of what amount.

(c)  If an offer of ex gratia payment is made, and accepted by the claimant in full satisfaction of his claim, the United States authorities shall make the payment themselves and inform the authorities of the Republic of Korea of their decision and of the sum paid.

(d)  Nothing in this paragraph shall affect the jurisdiction of the courts of the Republic of Korea to entertain an action against a member or employee of the United States armed forces unless and until there has been payment in full satisfaction of the claim.

7.  Claims arising out of the unauthorized use of any vehicle of the United States armed forces shall be dealt with in accordance with paragraph 6 of this Article, except insofar as the United States armed forces are legally responsible.

0296

8.  If a dispute arises as to whether a tortious act or omission of a member or an employee of the United States armed forces was done in the performance of official duty or as to whether the use of any vehicle of the United States armed forces was unauthorized, the question shall be submitted to an arbitrator appointed in accordance with paragraph 2(b) of this Article, whose decision on this point shall be final and conclusive.

9.  (a) The United States shall not claim immunity from the jurisdiction of the courts of the Republic of Korea for members or employees of the United States armed forces in respect of the civil jurisdiction of the courts of the Republic of Korea except in respect of proceedings for the enforcement of any judgment given against them in the Republic of Korea in a matter arising from the performance of their official duties or except after payment in full satisfaction of a claim.

    (b) In the case of any private movable property, excluding that in use by the United States armed forces, which is subject to compulsory execution under the law of the Republic of Korea, and is within the facilities and areas in use by the United States armed forces, the authorities of the United States shall, upon the request of the courts of the Republic of Korea, render all assistance within their power to see that such property is turned over to the authorities of the Republic of Korea.

(c) The authorities of the United States and the Republic of Korea shall cooperate in the procurement of evidence for a fair disposition of claims under this Article.

10. Disputes arising out of contracts concerning the procurement of materials, supplies, equipment or services by or for the United States armed forces, which are not resolved by the Parties to the contract concerned, may be submitted to the Joint Committee for conciliation, provided that the provisions of this Paragraph shall not prejudice any right, which Parties to the contract may have, to file a civil suit.

11. Paragraphs 2 and 5 of this Article shall apply only to claims arising incident to non-combat activities.

12. For the purposes of this Article, members of the Korean Augmentation to the United States Army (KATUSA) shall be considered as members of the United States armed forces.

13. The provisions of this Article shall not apply to any claims which arose before the entry into force of this Agreement. Such claims shall be processed and settled by the authorities of the United States.

## Agreed Minutes

1. Unless otherwise provided,

(a) The provisions of Paragraphs 5, 6, 7 and 8 of this Article will become effective six months from the date of entry into force of this Agreement as to claims arising from incidents in the Seoul Special City area.

0298

(b) The provisions of paragraphs 5, 6, 7 and 8 will be progressively extended to other areas of the Republic of Korea, as soon as practicable as determined by the Joint Committee.

2. Until such time as the provisions of paragraphs 5, 6, 7 and 8 become effective in any given area,

(a) The United States shall process and settle claims (other than contractual claims) arising out of the acts or omissions of members or employees of the United States armed forces done in the performance of official duty or out of any other act, omission or occurrence for which the United States armed forces are legally responsible, which cause damage in the Republic of Korea to parties other than the two Governments;

(b) The United States shall entertain other non-contractual claims against members or employees of the armed forces and may offer an ex gratia payment in such cases and in such amounts as is determined by the appropriate United States authorities; and

(c) Each party shall have the right to determine whether a member or employee of its armed forces was engaged in the performance of official duties and whether property owned by it was being used by its armed forces for official purposes.

3. For the purposes of Subparagraph 2(d), Subparagraph 5(e) shall be effective throughout the Republic of Korea from the date of entry into force of this Agreement.

0289

# ARTICLE XXIV

## Vehicle and Drivers Licenses

1.    The Republic of Korea shall accept as valid, without a driving test or fee, the driving permit or license or military driving permit issued by the United States, or political subdivision thereof, to a member of the United States armed forces, the civilian component, and their dependents.

2.    Official vehicles of the United States armed forces and the civilian component shall carry distinctive numbered plates or individual markings which will readily identify them.

3.    The Government of the Republic of Korea will license and register those vehicles privately owned by members of the United States armed forces, the civilian component, or dependents. The names of the owners of such vehicles and such other pertinent information as is required by ~~Korean~~ law to effect the licensing and registration of such vehicles shall be furnished to the Government of the Republic of Korea by officials of the Government of the United States through the Joint Committee. Except for the actual cost of the issuance of license plates, members of the United States armed forces, the civilian component,

and their dependents shall be exempt from the payment of
all fees and charges relating to the licensing, registration,
or operation of vehicles in the Republic of Korea and, in
accordance with the provisions of Article XIV, from the
payment of all taxes relating thereto.

0301

## ARTICLE XXV
### Security Measures

The United States and the Republic of Korea will
cooperate in taking such steps as may from time to time
be necessary to ensure the security of the United States
armed forces, the members thereof, the civilian component,
the persons who are present in the Republic of Korea
pursuant to Article XV, their dependents and their property.
The Government of the Republic of Korea agrees to seek
such legislation and to take such other action as may be
necessary to ensure the adequate security and protection
within its territory of installations, equipment, property,
records, and official information of the United States and,
consistent with Article XXII (Criminal Jurisdiction), to
ensure the punishment of offenders under the applicable
laws of the Republic of Korea.

0302

# ARTICLE XXVI

## Health and Sanitation

Consistent with the right of the United States to furnish medical support for its armed forces, civilian component and their dependents, matters of mutual concern pertaining to the control and prevention of diseases and the coordination of other public health, medical, sanitation, and veterinary services shall be resolved by the authorities of the two Governments in the Joint Committee established under Article XXVIII.

0303

## ARTICLE XXVII

### Enrollment and Training of Reservists

The United States may enroll in its reserve forces and train, in the Republic of Korea, eligible United States citizens who are in the Republic of Korea.

0301

# ARTICLE XXVIII
## Joint Committee

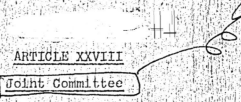

1.   A Joint Committee shall be established as the means for consultation between the Government of the United States and the Government of the Republic of Korea on all matters requiring mutual consultation regarding the implementation of this Agreement, except where otherwise provided. In particular, the Joint Committee shall serve as the means for consultation in determining the facilities and areas in the Republic of Korea which are required for the use of the United States in carrying out the purposes of this Agreement.

2.   The Joint Committee shall be composed of a representative of the Government of the United States and a representative of the Government of the Republic of Korea, each of whom shall have one or more deputies and a staff. The Joint Committee shall determine its own procedures, and arrange for such auxiliary organs and administrative services as may be required. The Joint Committee shall be so organized that it may meet immediately at any time at the request of the representative of either the Government of the United States or the Government of the Republic of Korea.

3.   If the Joint Committee is unable to resolve any matter it shall refer that matter to the respective Governments for further consideration through appropriate channels.

0305

## Agreed Minute

The exception provided for in the first sentence of Paragraph 1 is relevant only to Paragraph 2, Subparagraphs (b) and (c) of Article III.

0306

ARTICLE XXIX

Entry Into Force

1. This Agreement shall enter into force three months after the date of a written notification from the Government of the Republic of Korea to the Government of the United States that it has approved the Agreement in accordance with its legal procedures.

2. The Government of the Republic of Korea shall undertake to seek from its legislature all legislative and budgetary action necessary to give effect to its provisions of this Agreement.

3. Subject to the provisions of Article XXII, Paragraph 12, this Agreement shall, upon its entry into force, supersede and replace the agreement between the Government of the United States and the Government of the Republic of Korea on jurisdictional matters, effected by an exchange of notes at Taejon on July 12, 1950.

4. Within the scope of this Agreement, Paragraph 13 of Article III of the Agreement on Economic Coordination between the Republic of Korea and the Unified Command of May 24, 1952, shall not apply to members of the United States armed forces, civilian component, invited contractors, or dependents thereof.

0307

## ARTICLE XXX

### Revision of Agreement

Either Government may at any time request the revision of any Article of this Agreement, in which case the two Governments shall enter into negotiations through appropriate channels.

0308

## ARTICLE XXXI

### Duration of Agreement

This Agreement, and agreed revisions thereof, shall remain in force while the Mutual Defense Treaty between the United States and the Republic of Korea remains in force unless terminated earlier by agreement between the two Governments.

Done in duplicate, in the English and Korean languages. Both texts shall have equal authenticity but in case of divergence, the English text shall prevail.

Done at Seoul this          day of July, 1965.

0309

**외교문서 비밀해제: 주한미군지위협정(SOFA) 18**
**주한미군지위협정(SOFA) 서명 및 발효 18**

초판인쇄 2024년 03월 15일
초판발행 2024년 03월 15일

지은이 한국학술정보(주)
펴낸이 채종준
펴낸곳 한국학술정보(주)
주 소 경기도 파주시 회동길 230(문발동)
전 화 031-908-3181(대표)
팩 스 031-908-3189
홈페이지 http://ebook.kstudy.com
E-mail 출판사업부 publish@kstudy.com
등 록 제일산-115호(2000. 6. 19)

ISBN 979-11-7217-029-5 94340
     979-11-7217-011-0 94340 (set)